Books by Peter Gay

Style in History (1974)
(*with R. K. Webb*) Modern Europe (1973)
The Bridge of Criticism: Dialogues on the Enlightenment (1970)
The Enlightenment: An Interpretation, volume 2, The Science
of Freedom (1969)
Weimar Culture: The Outsider as Insider (1968)
A Loss of Mastery: Puritan Historians in Colonial America (1966)
The Enlightenment: An Interpretation, volume 1, The Rise
of Modern Paganism (1966)
The Party of Humanity: Essays in the French Enlightenment
(1964)
Voltaire's Politics: The Poet as Realist (1959)
The Dilemma of Democratic Socialism: Eduard Bernstein's
Challenge to Marx (1952)

TRANSLATIONS WITH INTRODUCTIONS

Voltaire: Candide (1963)
Voltaire: Philosophical Dictionary, two volumes (1962)
Ernst Cassirer: The Question of Jean Jacques Rousseau (1954)

ANTHOLOGIES AND COLLECTIVE WORKS

The Enlightenment: A Comprehensive Anthology (1973)
Eighteenth Century Studies Presented to
Arthur M. Wilson (1972)
(*with John A. Garraty*) The Columbia History of the World
(1972)
(*with Gerald J. Cavanaugh and Victor G. Wexler*) Historians
at Work, two volumes (1972)
Deism: An Anthology (1968)
John Locke on Education (1964)

Style in History

STYLE
IN
HISTORY

Peter Gay

BASIC BOOKS, INC.

PUBLISHERS   New York

Library of Congress Catalog Card Number: 73–91076
SBN: 465–08304–8
Manufactured in the United States of America
DESIGNED BY VINCENT TORRE
74 75 76 77 78   10 9 8 7 6 5 4 3 2 1

TO Bob Webb
Friend, Collaborator, Stylist

"It is most true, *stylus virum arguit,*
our style bewrays us."

—ROBERT BURTON,
Anatomy of Melancholy

PREFACE

THIS book, though short, has had a long history. During the years, I have often crossed the intellectual terrain it claims and mapped it from many perspectives. And my concern with style is much older than my decision to become a historian; I have been interested in it as long as I can remember. Also, I have been singularly fortunate in my readers. When I began to do my first serious writing in the early 1950s, I had perceptive critics who were also intimate friends—Richard Hofstadter and Henry Roberts. My first editor, Christopher Herold, while I knew him less well, taught me as much as they did; all three were candid, discriminating, and, at the same time, encouraging. In thinking of them with affection and with pain—for they are all dead—I have often thought, as I completed this book, of Sir Ronald Syme's closing sentence in his *Tacitus*: "Men and dynasties pass, but style abides." It is little comfort; the loss of a friend is irreparable. But I like to think that some of my friends' style has left its mark on the pages that follow.

The labor that style exacts from even its most graceful practitioners was borne in on me in the summer of 1954, when I shared a house with the Hofstadters and watched Dick composing the Introduction to his *The Age of Reform* and revising the whole manuscript for the publisher. It was in the same summer that I first read Erich Auerbach's *Mimesis*. It was a revelation, and for years I sought an opportunity to apply to historical writings the lessons of this inspired masterpiece, at once philology and sociology. That opportunity came in the early 1960s, when for several years I offered the course on historiography to incoming graduate students at Columbia University. Some of the ideas I develop in this book in detail I first adumbrated in that course in a much different and, I think, rather more primitive form. In those years, the inquiry into historical style was essentially an inquiry into the limitations that class and nation impose on the historian. Relativists, directly indebted to Karl Marx and Karl Mannheim or indirectly indebted to them by their reading of Charles Beard, held the field. It was an age of suspicion. Then, gradually, historiographical analysis grew more sophisticated and, in some measure, more optimistic. In my own lectures, I began to develop a kind of perspectival realism, suggesting that the objects of historical study are really that—objects—to be studied and understood, and that objectivity, though difficult, is possible. Perhaps the most rewarding reading I did on historiography in the late 1960s was not directly in that field at all, but in philosophy; I owe a particular debt to the logical and epistemological writings of Carl Hempel and Ernest Nagel and to the witty iconoclastic lectures of J. L. Austin. During the academic year 1970–1971, I summed up my sense of historical style in a series of three lectures, amid the fostering, hospitable surroundings of the Universities of St. Andrews and of Utrecht. These lectures, which I have much rewritten and greatly expanded, form the nucleus of this book. I have incorporated several passages from an Overseas Fellow's Lecture, which I delivered in the Spring of 1971 at Churchill College, Cambridge, into the Conclusion.

As with my other work in the past, now once again I consider myself lucky in my critics. I owe particular debts to Quentin Skinner, R. K. Webb, and my wife, Ruth, for their intense and repeated readings, which compelled me to revise and refine my general argument and to sharpen many lesser points. I am also grateful to Henry Turner for his thoughtful comments on the whole manuscript, to John Clive for his helpful criticism of the chapter on Macaulay, and to Henry Gibbons for a productive discussion of general strategy. I want to thank Betty Paine and Heather Anderson, amateur paleographers, for their ability to decipher my much-revised manuscripts. My editor, Paul D. Neuthaler, bears a heavy responsibility for there being a book at all. I hope it is not a complacent thought on my part to suspect, cheerfully, that a writer has the readers he deserves.

Peter Gay

1974

Since this is, after all, a book on style, I have quoted copiously from the original texts. In the two essays on historians whose language is German, I have placed excerpts from their work, short and long, directly into the text, in italics. When the passage is not enclosed in quotation marks, this means that the English sentences just preceding it are a close paraphrase but not a precise translation. The reader who has no knowledge of German and is compelled to skip the italicized passages will miss nothing more than whatever linguistic refinements I was unable to rescue into the English.

CONTENTS

[xiii]

Introduction

*Style—From Manner
to Matter*

STYLE is a centaur, joining what nature, it would seem, has decreed must be kept apart. It is form and content, woven into the texture of every art and every craft—including history. Apart from a few mechanical tricks of rhetoric, manner is indissolubly linked to matter; style shapes, and in turn is shaped by, substance. I have written these essays to anatomize this familiar yet really strange being, style the centaur; the book may be read as an extended critical commentary on Buffon's famous saying that the style is the man.

Buffon's epigram has a beautiful simplicity that makes it both possibly profound and certainly suspect. It seems frivolous, almost inappropriate, to be stylish about style, for it is necessary, and difficult, to disentangle the multiplicity of meanings and the thicket of metaphors that have accrued to the word in the course of centuries. Style, we are told, is the dress of thought and its sinews, its crowning glory and its expressive voice. There appear to be almost as many uses for style as there are users. The critic and the scholar, the lyric poet and the political publicist, each employs style in his own way and for his own purposes: to appreciate elegance and depreciate clumsiness, to decipher obscure passages, to exploit verbal ambiguities, to drive home a partisan point. The historian, who does all of these things—though one wishes that he would keep his lyricism in check and discard his politics when he writes history—encounters style in these and other dimensions. He is a professional writer and a professional reader. As a writer, he is under pressure to become a stylist while remaining a scientist; he must give pleasure without compromising truth. His style may be a conventional tool, an involuntary confession, or a striking illumination. As a reader, he prizes literary excellence, absorbs facts and interpretations, and explores the words before him for truths working beneath their surface; style may be, for him, an object of gratification, a vehicle of knowledge, or an instrument of diagnosis.

Yet this profusion is an opportunity as much as a problem. As I will show, it is desirable, for the sake of clarity, to discriminate among the varied meanings of style, but it is impossible, for the sake of understanding, to keep them permanently segregated. The use of a single word for many functions need not be a symptom of linguistic poverty; it can be a sign that these functions are related to one another. That the word *style* should enter diverse combinations—style of thought, style of life, and others—without strain reinforces the impression that the several kinds of style, and style and substance, have much to do with, and to say about, one another. Style is like Ranke's Venetian ambassadors: widely traveled, highly adaptable, superbly informed, and, if adroitly interrogated, splendidly indiscreet. For the historian, therefore, the evidential value of style—both in getting and in giving evidence—is enormous.

[4]

Style—From Manner to Matter

I have said that this book may be read as an extended critical commentary on Buffon's *Le style est l'homme même*. The commentary must be extended, for, though an important observation, the epigram is so laconic that we must, as the philosophers say, unpack it. And the commentary must be critical, for Buffon at once says too much and too little. In its day, his *bon mot* was an energetic, almost unprecedented demand that style not be taken lightly as mere decoration, but seen as reaching into the very foundations of the writer's work.[1] Yet style is not always the man, certainly not the whole man. If manner and matter are joined in a Catholic marriage, irrevocably, this does not mean that they can never be apart from each other. Much talk about style centers on the search for literary felicities, and for the traditional, if surprisingly elusive, virtue of clarity.

Moreover, it is a historical fact (which the historian may privately deplore but must professionally investigate like any other) that style has not always been profoundly anchored. There have been those—in advertising, in journalism, in politics, even in publishing—who treat it as an afterthought, as the Gothic facade irrelevantly plastered onto modern concrete walls. Middleton Murry once called this practice "the heresy of the man in the street" and thought it "the most popular of all delusions about style."[2] He anatomized this delusion half a century ago, but the heresy had been popular

---

[1] A rare early supporter of this modern view was Robert Burton; see his comment, "our style bewrays us," which is the epigraph of this book. The view I defend here was well put by Marcel Proust in an interview of 1913: "Style," Proust said, "is in no way a decoration as some people believe; it is not even a matter of technique; it is—as color is with painters—a quality of vision. . . ." I should note that in what follows, *style* is applied to writers only; obviously, composers, painters, architects confront stylistic problems in precisely the same way. See below, p. 189.

[2] *The Problem of Style* (edn. 1960), p. 10.

long before and remains as popular as it was when he wrote in 1922. Makers of verbal artifacts for mass consumption still find it convenient to ask researchers to do research, writers to write it up, and stylists to add the fine touches. Such Balkanization, I need hardly say, fatally divides what needs to be united; the products that such procedures throw on the market are, as we all know, persuasively packaged merchandise, decorated with obsessive puns, exhausted superlatives, and unauthentic anecdotes. Style here is a by-product of commercial enterprise; it is by no means the man but the system.

This vast, vulgar subliterature is a valuable reminder to the historian that the word *style* is not only a term of praise—"that novelist has style"—but also a neutral description—"that novelist works in the Naturalist style." He must remember that the very idea of style is infected with a central ambiguity: it must give information as well as pleasure. It opens windows on both truth and beauty—a bewildering double vista. Aesthetically indifferent or aesthetically offensive procedures, as long as they have a certain consistency and characteristic form, partake of style. Second-rate poets, painters—and historians—have a style. So do gangsters perpetrating gangland killings, songwriters manufacturing popular hits, priests performing religious ceremonies in standardized ways. The study of style has diagnostic value in all these instances; to the historian they are all valid clues to the past, though not to the same historical experiences. If style gives information not about the stylist but about his culture, the historian has no reason to be disappointed. When it comes to subject matter and to evidence, the historian is—or should be—a democrat.

Buffon, of course, was not a democrat, in his view of style or of anything else. He was speaking of the literary style of the accomplished writer. And what he meant to say about the writer, I think, was this: the cultivated manner of the writer instructively expresses his personal past as well as the culture's ways of thinking, feeling, believing, and working. The symptomatic value of style is therefore far greater than that of providing insights into literary habits.[3] Style is the pattern in the carpet—the unambiguous indication, to the informed collector, of place and time of origin. It is also the marking on the wings of the butterfly—the unmistakable signature, to the alert lepidopterist of its species. And it is the involuntary gesture of the witness in the dock—the infallible sign, to the observant lawyer, of concealed evidence. To unriddle the style, therefore, is to unriddle the man.

This exegesis makes a beginning, but it remains too elliptical to be conclusive. Both halves of Buffon's epigram, both *style* and *man*, require further explication. The most prominent and, for these essays, most productive kind of style is style in its narrow sense, literary style: the management of sentences, the use of rhetorical devices, the rhythm of narration. Gibbon's way of pairing phrases, Ranke's resort to dramatic techniques, Macaulay's reiteration of antitheses, Burckhardt's informal diction, taken by themselves, as single instances, mean what they say on the page. They describe a battle, analyze a political artifice, chronicle a painter's career. But once characteristic and habitual—that is, recognizable elements in the historian's mode of expression, of his style— they become signposts to larger, deeper matters. Partly idiosyncratic and partly conventional, partly selected and partly

---

[3] I should add that the four historians I have chosen do not in any way exhaust the possibilities of stylistic analysis; in principle, and in practice, the analysis of inferior historians should yield results that would be quite as interesting, if not quite so pleasing.

imposed by unconscious, professional, or political pressures, the devices of literary style are equally instructive, not always for the conclusive answers they supply but for the fertile questions they raise about the historian's central intentions and overriding interpretations, the state of his art, the essential beliefs of his culture—and, perhaps, about his insights into his subject.

While I have taken style in its strict sense as my principal witness, my materials have compelled me to reach out to other related forms of expression, to styles in looser senses of the word. Among the most revealing of these is what I want to call the historian's emotional style, his tone of voice as it emerges in the tension or repose of his phrases, his favorite adjectives, his selection of illustrative anecdotes, his emphases and epigrams. In a tightly regulated stylistic system like neo-classicism, in which expressive means are severely circumscribed, emotional style has potent diagnostic possibilities, for while accepted canons of rhetoric, say, proscribe "low" epithets for highly placed personages, the range of permissible expressions remains large enough to give room for instructive choices. Gibbon characterizing the Emperor Augustus as "artful" only tells us that Augustus was—or, rather, that Gibbon thought him—artful. But scattered liberally across the pages of *The Decline and Fall of the Roman Empire*, the word *artful* begins to trail clouds of meaning behind it and becomes an emblem for Gibbon's cynical appraisal of the Empire, a clue not merely to what he saw but what he, as an individual historian, was best equipped to see. In the freer, more loose-jointed writing of the nineteenth century, emotional style retains its capacity to yield dividends to the interpreter: Burckhardt's chilling stories about Renaissance despots point to perceptions more general than those the stories are designed to illuminate. They help to outline the contours of Burckhardt's historical vision. In our examination of a historian's emotional style, we come very close to the man indeed.

Instructive as the historian's selection of expressive techniques and unconscious coloring of narrative may be, his habit of doing research and offering proof—his *professional* style—provides additional and significant clues. It invites inferences subtler and more far-reaching than judgments of his competence or his diligence. Ranke assiduously visited all accessible archives; Macaulay preferred to spend his time poring over broadsides and printed collections of popular verses; Gibbon mastered the history of ancient Rome from modern compilations; Burckhardt studied the Renaissance from contemporary accounts. To know this is to know something about the sheer validity of each historian's conclusions, but it also delineates his attitude toward his material. Ranke's obsessive, almost religious conscientiousness, which left its distinctive signature on all his work, reflects his sense of history as a grand, dramatic, divinely guided contest, and his sense of the historian as a man of God in the world. Gibbon's occasional credulousness, which contrasts so sharply with his pronounced, often malicious skepticism, suggests, not professional laxity, but a will to believe—especially in the wickedness of priests and the lasciviousness of emperors. Like the other styles I have mentioned, professional style, too, points beyond itself.

The reality all these styles point to, the fish that the analyst of style hopes to catch, is, as I have suggested, nothing less than the historian's total perception of the past, the constraints within which he works and the truths he is uniquely capable of grasping. Yet this exalted region—the ultimate destination of stylistics—where matter seems to hold a complete monopoly, is invaded by manner also. I am speaking of the historian's style of thinking, a convenient and telling phrase that relates style to content in more than a mere metaphorical sense. For a historian's most fundamental and therefore least examined assumptions about the nature of the world, its ontological makeup, also have their expressive aspect which may leave its traces in his literary, emotional, or professional style. Yet styles of thought may also find other, more subterranean, channels of communication: a historian need not write, or feel, or work like another, and yet think like him and learn from him. Gibbon was deeply indebted to Tacitus' disenchantment, but Gibbon structured his sentences, chose his adjectives, and pursued his research in ways markedly different from the ways of Tacitus. Burckhardt had a pronounced affinity for Hegel's vision of cultural wholes, but it is—fortunately—impossible to mistake a passage, any passage, of the *Kultur der Renaissance in Italien* for a passage, any passage, of Hegel's lectures on history.

In general, though, intellectual affinities scatter more clues than they did in Gibbon and Burckhardt. The styles I have discussed do not normally lie side by side as strangers, without touching. It is significant that many stylistic qualities are hard to place: does Gibbon's irony or Macaulay's rhetoric form part of their literary or their emotional style? Do Burckhardt's stories serve to disclose his view of the world, his private pessimism, his wish to keep his readers interested, or all three? These questions suggest their answer: styles are a network of clues to one another, and, together, to the man—to the historian at work.

This brings me to the second half of Buffon's epigram. Man lives in several worlds at once, most notably in his private sphere, in the comparatively intimate realm of his craft, and in the wide public domain of his culture.[4] Like the various dimensions of style, these worlds intersect and continuously impinge upon one another: the private person internalizes the standards of craft and the commands of culture; craft by and large serves culture and obediently expresses its overriding ideals. A mature literary style is a synthesis of all these elements, variously combined; it is, therefore, at once individual and social, private and public, a combination of inherited ways, borrowed elements, and unique qualities. That is why the student of style can treat this synthesis analytically and sort out the threads of which the stylistic tapestry is composed. If, as some Romantics were inclined to think, style were simply the outward garb of inner states, the spontaneous overflowing of the springs of creativity, it would yield information about a writer's psyche, nothing more. But these Romantics were wrong. To begin with, literary style—and this is the style on which I shall concentrate—can be learned. Writers are not born stylists; they fashion their style through an unceasing effort to overcome dependence and find their own voice.[5] Normally, the apprentice writer—and here, as elsewhere, the historian acts like other writers—discovers the style appropriate to him by first following and then discarding admired models; imitation seems to be an essential phase in

[4] I intend to explore these worlds, and their meaning for the analysis of historical causation, in a forthcoming book, *Three Variations on the Theme of Cause: Manet, Gropius, Mondrian.*

[5] See Burckhardt's comment to his friend Friedrich von Tschudi: "My way is, through dependence to independence." See below, p. 161.

the process of self-discovery. Not even in the beginning, then, does writing come wholly from the heart; it comes, for the most part, straight out of other books. The higher naïveté comes later, the fruit of labor that conceals labor.

To say that style can be learned is therefore not precise enough. It is more accurate to say, rather, that style must be learned. It is only in part a gift of talent; beyond that it is an act of will and an exercise of intelligence. It is the tribute that expressiveness pays to discipline. Style is an instrument of the practical reason. Words, of course, do many things: they convey information, they disclose affection, they utter warnings; they are, often, the unedited transcription of emotions into verbal form. But style is the application of means to an end; though, as we well know, it too has its passional side and its involuntary revelations.

That is why styles have histories, even in individual writers. Gibbon is perhaps an exception: while even he found it necessary to experiment, he cast all his writings, early and late, into the same unmistakable mold. But, then, Gibbon was never young.[6] For nearly all other writers, style has been, in addition to being an endowment, a conquest; the study of style chronicles and analyzes that conquest. "Style," wrote Gibbon, "is the image of character."[7] Here is the first indication of the uses that stylistics may have for the historian: it gives him access to a writer's private, psychological world.

This is not the only world that the study of style serves to discover. Writing is an activity pursued within the texture of

---

[6] " I am tempted to enter a protest against the trite and lavish praise of the happiness of our boyish years, which is echoed with so much affectation in the world. That happiness I have never known, that time I have never regretted." *The Autobiography of Edward Gibbon*, ed. Dero A. Saunders (1961), p. 68.

[7] *Autobiography*, p. 27.

a literary tradition. Apart from a handful of innovators, most writers, even the greatest, speak in a language that others have made familiar. Even those, like the Dadaist poets, who aim at incomprehensibility find their vocabulary within the context of a society, no matter how select; their incomprehensibility is their way of communicating—comprehensibly—with the others in their circle. A writer's attitude to his tradition may be compliant, ambivalent, or rebellious. He may write as he does because others have written his way before, or because others have *not* written his way before. Whatever his attitude, he cannot be indifferent to the atmosphere that his choice of profession compels him to breathe.

Just as individual styles have a history, style itself has a history. In every epoch, writers have had specified expressive modes available to them. They have always been subject to rules laying down permissible language, to conventions channeling their private preferences, to hierarchies appropriate to any theme. Until modern times—which, in this context, means the 1890s—there have been some things historians must say and others that they would have found it unthinkable to say.

The boundaries within which historians have been compelled to maneuver are of peculiar importance for the history of history. That history is the history of the emancipation of a craft from powerful, normally overpowering, masters. Through long centuries, historians have lived in many houses, borrowing their speech and convictions from their hosts: the theatre in Greece, the law courts in Rome, the monastery in the Middle Ages, the salon in the Enlightenment. Ancient, medieval, and early modern historians proffered their works as pieces of rhetoric; they had to satisfy moral demands and employ accepted literary devices. The tradition of eloquence, reinforced and distorted in the early modern era by memories of antique oratory, pervaded historical writings down to the sixteenth and even the seventeenth century, when historians added to this antique rhetorical tradition the eloquence of the pulpit. The philosophe-historians' dependence on polite society in the eighteenth century was actually a giant step toward independence: history became a respectable literary genre among other respectable literary genres.

Then, in the nineteenth century, historians moved into their own house, the university—not, I might add, without some losses. But, whatever the losses, the modern autonomy of the historian has markedly increased the range of his stylistic options. As more aspects of the past have become accessible to inquiry, more ways of speaking about the past have become permissible. The relation of the historian to his work has changed; the craftsman has become a professional. Yet in principle, the debt that the individual historian owes to his craft—its dominant traditions, its current debates, its exploratory techniques—has neither increased nor diminished. The study of historians' style, therefore, whether of ancient, medieval, or modern practitioners, gives access to the world of their craft.

But it also gives access, finally, to culture itself, of which craftsmanship is only a specialized, and sometimes recalcitrant, representative. This is what Macaulay had in mind when he said of Herodotus that he "wrote as it is natural that he should write. He wrote for a nation susceptible, curious, lively, insatiably desirous of novelty and excitement."[8] Reading Herodotus tells us much about the Greece of his day, just as reading Mommsen or Namier tells us much about the Ger-

---

[8] Thomas Babington Macaulay, "History," *The Works of Lord Macaulay*, 2nd edn., ed. Lady Trevelyan, 8 vols. (1871), 5:124.

many or England of their day. Conversely, it also tells us much about their perception of their culture: we cannot read Mommsen's *Römische Geschichte*, with its stunning anachronisms, its Junkers in togas, without sensing within Mommsen, the objective scholar, another Mommsen, the passionate and frustrated political animal. We cannot read Namier's *Structure of Politics at the Accession of George III*, with its resolute anti-intellectualism, its affectionate portrayal of the political microcosm of mid-eighteenth-century England, without detecting in Namier, the minute researcher, a hidden Namier, the lover of English civility so infatuated that he must be a foreigner.

The social information that style provides is by no means infallible; if past words were addressed to the chosen few, and if we have lost the key that will unlock their message, the intentions of the writer, and with them the full bearing of his utterance, will remain opaque. It has long been a commonplace that men often use words to conceal their meaning behind veils of indirection, difficulty, and ambiguity.[9] In such circumstances, we must first solve the style before we can, with its aid, solve other puzzles: there are times when politics is as much a clue to style as style is a clue to politics. Fortunately this is not a logical but an existential circularity, a symptom of the mutual dependence of style and life and, hence, of the possibility that they may reciprocally illuminate each other.

While one school of intellectual historians, Leo Strauss and his disciples, has made a cottage industry of reading between the lines, reading the lines themselves remains, for the historian, a rewarding enterprise. Erich Auerbach, in his

---

[9] On words as concealment, see below, p. 26.

Mimesis, has shown the path that may take the historian from philology to sociology. It is easy to demonstrate, as he does, that the barbarous Latin of a Merovingian chronicle mirrors, with its impoverished vocabulary, the desperate decay of antique culture. But with his analysis of Tacitus' world view, Auerbach shows that stylistics may trap more elusive game: social perceptions. In describing a mutiny, he notes, Tacitus puts elevated words in the mouth of one of the mutineers, sprinkles his report with ethical adjectives, and employs the rhetorical devices current among cultivated orators in the Rome of his day.[10] Auerbach deduces from such linguistic habits Tacitus' blindness to the social and economic pressures bubbling beneath the surface of events. He sees this failure as more than the political bias of an aristocrat confronting the demands of famished soldiers; he sees it, rather, as characteristic for a Roman who does not, and cannot, *see* the lower social orders as full human beings. In sum, the study of style provides a diagnostic instrument as much for the historian's social and cultural as for his psychological and professional worlds, a decisive clue to their meanings, their limitations—and their insights.

I must add a final word. Style, I said earlier, is sometimes less than the man; often it is more than the man. In examining the styles of four great historians, I am in no way committing myself to the fashionable relativist implications that have usually been drawn from Buffon's epigram. Historians have

---

[10] Erich Auerbach, *Mimesis: The Representation of Reality in Western Literature* (1946; trans. Willard R. Trask, 1953), pp. 33–40. I shall return to this passage; see below, pp. 30–31.

long been engaged in a great, or at least persistent, debate over the essential nature of their craft, and Buffon has been taken as supporting the view that history cannot be a science, but must be an art—a subjective encounter between a literary man and the past, which he reshapes through his private vision and reports in that idiosyncratic manner we call his style. But a personal report may be an objective report. It is even possible that while style reflects the man, the man it reflects is a scientist. I do not want to decide this matter now and will return to it in the Conclusion. But on this much I want to insist here: there is no reason why style must be the undistorted reflection of the historian's private neurosis, social location, or historical epoch. If he has any professional conscience and competence at all, he is bound to say far more about the time of which he writes than the time in which he lives.[11] Individual stylists develop in rebellion against their past, their environment, even against themselves, and the results are not always predictable. While in all its aspects style is instructive, not all styles are instructive to the same degree: like other writers, a historian usually has two styles, formal and informal, and both are an intermixture of self-expression and self-control. There is no rule book, no prepared recipe, setting down in advance just what the study of style may disclose. All I claim is that it discloses much, and that it will contribute some light to the heated debate over the nature of history.

11 I shall examine this point at greater detail in the Conclusion; meanwhile, it should be obvious that I reject E. H. Carr's popular simplistic relativism: "When we take up a work of history, our first concern should be not with the facts which it contains but with the historian who wrote it. . . . Before you study the history, study the historian." *What Is History?* (1962), pp. 24, 54. While elsewhere in his book, Carr retreats from this extreme position, it is these formulations that have gained wide currency and undeserved acceptance.

1

Gibbon

A Modern Cynic among Ancient Politicians

The Scholar

THE architecture is familiar, its structure classical. The guide is Gibbon, surveying the ruins of the Roman Republic:

Every barrier of the Roman constitution had been levelled by the vast ambition of the dictator; every fence had been extirpated by the cruel hand of the Triumvir. After the victory of Actium, the fate of the Roman world depended on the will of Octavianus, surnamed Caesar, by his uncle's adoption, and afterwards Augustus, by the flattery of the senate. The conqueror was at the head of forty-four veteran legions, conscious of their own strength, and of the weakness of the constitution, habituated, during twenty years' civil war, to every act of blood and violence, and passionately devoted to the house of Caesar, from whence alone they had received, and expected, the most lavish rewards. The provinces, long oppressed by the ministers of the republic, sighed for the government of a single person, who would be the master, not the accomplice, of those petty tyrants. The people of Rome, viewing, with a secret pleasure, the humiliation of the aristocracy, demanded only bread and public shows; and were supplied with both by the liberal hand of Augustus. The rich and polite Italians, who had almost universally embraced the philosophy of Epicurus, enjoyed the present blessings of ease and tranquillity, and suffered not the pleasing dream to be interrupted by the memory of their old tumultuous freedom. With its power, the senate had lost its dignity; many of the most noble families were extinct. The republicans of spirit and ability had perished in the field of battle, or in the proscription.[1]

With its measured, almost military tread ("Every barrier . . . ; every fence"), this passage is vintage Gibbon. Its antique *gravitas* is singularly appropriate to its grand and tragic theme: the transition of a great power from one form of government to another. While Gibbon finds room for his unconquerable cynicism, dwelling with evident relish on the "secret pleasure" with which "the people of Rome" view "the humiliation of the aristocracy," he tactfully refrains from the kind of derisive joke that marks so much of his narrative. His survey, though rapid, is stately; it is striking how much political and military history it conveys to the reader, with its skillfully introduced glances at the past ("*After* the victory of Actium. . . ." "The provinces, *long* oppressed. . . .") and its informative parenthetical clauses ("The rich and polite Italians, *who had almost universally embraced the philosophy of Epicurus. . . .*"). Stateliness need not—and Gibbon takes care that it does not—entail tedium. Gibbon is essentially drawing up a list of structural changes that characterized the situation of Rome at the moment of Augustus' accession, but he takes the curse off his enumeration by the tense, if implicit, antitheses of his parallel clauses ("by his uncle's adoption . . . , by the flattery of the senate") and the music of his rhythmic repetitions ("vast ambition . . . , cruel hand"). His sentences are long—Gibbon's melodic line is rarely terse

---

[1] Edward Gibbon, *The History of the Decline and Fall of the Roman Empire*, ed. J. B. Bury, 7 vols. (1896–1902), [Chapter iii], 1:59–60.

—but he varies their apparent pace by introducing, at proper moments, the dramatic caesura of the semicolon. Yet, while this passage unmistakably belongs to Gibbon, he has here dressed himself in borrowed plumage. The passage is a close paraphrase, slightly rearranged and slightly rewritten, of a chapter in Tacitus' *Annals*:

When after the destruction of Brutus and Cassius there was no longer any army of the Commonwealth, when Pompeius was crushed in Sicily, and when, with Lepidus pushed aside and Antonius slain, even the Julian faction had only Caesar left to lead it, then, dropping the title of triumvir, and giving out that he was a Consul, and was satisfied with a tribune's authority for the protection of the people, Augustus won over the soldiers with gifts, the populace with cheap corn, and all men with the sweets of repose, and so grew greater by degrees, while he concentrated in himself the functions of the Senate, the magistrates, and the laws. He was wholly unopposed, for the boldest spirits had fallen in battle, or in the proscription, while the remaining nobles, the readier they were to be slaves, were raised the higher by wealth and promotion, so that, aggrandised by revolution, they preferred the safety of the present to the dangerous past. Nor did the provinces dislike that condition of affairs, for they distrusted the government of the Senate and the people, because of the rivalries between the leading men and the rapacity of the officials, while the protection of the laws was unavailing, as they were continually deranged by violence, intrigue, and finally by corruption.[2]

Reading these two paragraphs in tandem, we can see why Suzanne Curchot, the only girl whom Gibbon had briefly professed to love, and who knew her classics as well as she knew her Gibbon, should note that Tacitus was the "model

---

[2] Tacitus, *Annals*, trans. Alfred John Church and William Jackson Brodribb (1876, and often reprinted), Book I, chap. 2.

and perhaps the source"[3] of much that went into the *Decline and Fall.*

Gibbon, of course, was not plagiarizing; he was engaging in a favorite and wholly respectable eighteenth-century practice, although in his own way: he was writing an imitation. In his time, when the civilized orders still had much Latin, if less Greek, free allusion to the classics was a popular literary and artistic device. It placed the author in a mutually congratulatory relationship with his readers, whom he thus complimented for not forgetting what had been drilled into them in their youth. The parallels, and, even more, the subtle contrasts which these imitations could mobilize, invited the liberal play of wit, permitted daring yet restrained criticism of contemporary affairs and, with their resonances of well-beloved and half-remembered texts, gave the intimate shock of recognition. Alexander Pope's and Samuel Johnson's imitations employed ancient forms to write modern satire; they poured new acid into old bottles. Gibbon's imitation was closer than theirs, its echoes were louder; he was employing ancient substance to write ancient history. But his deliberate and, to the educated, obvious dependence on an ancient model was designed to make a point that a freer paraphrase would have dissipated.

But what point? And why Tacitus? He was, of course, a copious and eloquent reporter on events in the early Roman Empire. Yet some of Gibbon's contemporaries, notably Voltaire, from whom Gibbon learned a great deal, refused to credit Tacitus' somber reportage. They thought it too pessi-

---

[3] Quoted in G. M. Young, *Gibbon* (1932), p. 133. For an analysis of Gibbon's dependence on Tacitus, see Peter Gay, *The Enlightenment: An Interpretation*, vol. 1, *The Rise of Modern Paganism* (1966), pp. 117, 156–159.

mistic about human nature, too chilling in its account of human actions. Yet it was, I suggest, precisely Tacitus' coldness that made him so appealing and so useful to Gibbon. It is idle to speculate which of the two, model or imitator, was the colder; it is important to recognize that the sources of their mental temperature differed. Tacitus was an outraged moralist, Gibbon an erudite cynic. Like all human beings, both historians had something to hide: Tacitus, a tormented politician's guilt; Gibbon, a professional bachelor's conflicts. If Tacitus appears like a glacier concealing a volcano, Gibbon is the glacier concealing an iceberg.

But their affinity, their shared coldness, is more than a matter of temperament and of psychological mechanisms. It is a matter of method and of essential world view. Both historians concentrate on a purely human scene. Their causal baggage conspicuously omits supernatural intervention, divine providence, abstract forces; the principal, practically the sole, subject matter of their histories is man and his passions. Both therefore thought it the supreme task of the historian to probe historical actors to their depths. David Hume, himself one of the leading historians in the Age of the Enlightenment, appreciatively called Tacitus a "penetrating genius,"[4] and it was Tacitus' penetration that attracted Gibbon to him. "*Proprium humani ingenii est odisse quem laeseris*"[5]—this was the kind of disenchanted psychologist's epigram that a

---

[4] David Hume, *Enquiry Concerning Human Understanding*, in *The Philosophical Works of David Hume*, ed. T. H. Green and T. H. Grose, 4 vols. (1882), 4:100.

[5] "It is characteristic of human nature to hate the man whom you have injured." *Agricola*, 42. It was this classical remark that Macaulay remembered in his *History of England*, when he spoke of the petty persecution to which the Anglican parson subjected the dissenters: "He too often hated them for the wrong which he had done them." *The Works of Lord Macaulay*, 2nd edn., ed. Lady Trevelyan, 8 vols. (1871), 1:261.

Tacitus could formulate and a Gibbon relish if scarcely repeat, for, unlike his master, he was not given to the laconic dictum. But as there are several styles of coldness, there are several methods of penetration; Gibbon's affinity with Tacitus was fundamental rather than superficial, his stylistic debt less to the forms of Tacitus' style than to its substance.

I do not want to suggest that penetration and coldness are distinct qualities; they are but two aspects of a single capacity —the gift of analysis. For it takes a cool head and a clear mind to strike through the masks that men put on to disguise their thoughts and their actions. Now as then, despite carbon dating and family reconstitution, words are historians' most significant raw material, are as deceptive as they are indispensable. "The true use of speech," wrote Oliver Goldsmith, Gibbon's acquaintance and himself something of a historian, "is not so much to express our wants as to conceal them,"[6] a truth, almost a truism, about the human animal which, as Tacitus had said, finds it natural to hate the person he has injured. The chief use of the historian's penetration, therefore, was to dig beneath appearance to reality.

Secularists are of course not alone in arguing that appearance and reality are distinct and often in conflict: medieval philosophers saw the natural world of human experience as a mere screen. But for the Christian the reality concealed by appearance was a higher world of religious fulfillment, while the secularist treats this hidden reality as the mundane world of secret reasons. Tacitus saw Caesar Augustus as dominating men while, and *by*, proclaiming that he is obeying them. The private motives of the ruled were significant for him too; while they are less accessible, they are threads in the fabric

---

[6] Oliver Goldsmith, "On the Use of Language," Essay V, in *The Works of Oliver Goldsmith*, ed. Peter Cunningham, 4 vols. (1854), 3:159.

Edward Gibbon

After the portrait by Sir Joshua Reynolds

of reality—soldiers want bonuses, civilians want cheap food, politicians want power, and everyone wants peace.

It is easy to see why Voltaire, a philanthropist masquerading as a cynic, should wince at Tacitus' savage portraits. But to depreciate Tacitus as a sour debunker is to miss the subtlety, the sheer virtuosity, of his psychological insight. His Augustus is a gigantic fraud, but not simply a fraud; he deceives men not solely for his own profit, but largely for theirs. The social process pursues its devious course behind the arcana that a shrewd government has set up; political speeches must be read with care to disclose the gulf that yawns between profession and practice. But appearance and reality are not always cleanly separable; they are also, and often, subtly intertwined. Tacitus' curt antitheses—"*Solitudinem faciunt, pacem appellant*"[7]—intimate that rhetoric serves at once to disguise and, for the perceptive reader, to underscore, the terrors of politics and of war.

Such disillusioned perception of complexity requires a large measure of critical distance. As long as there are areas decently veiled from criticism, this perception is blunted. Gibbon, like his intellectual allies, the philosophes, insisted that inquirers must be at liberty to employ their critical faculties everywhere, including, and especially, in the two sacred regions of politics and religion. Recalling, in his *Autobiography*, the miserable slavery of his schooling, Gibbon sonorously announced that "Freedom is the first wish of our heart; freedom is the first blessing of our Nature."[8] And in the *Decline and Fall* he made it plain that freedom was also the indispensable instrument of the scholar. Every pious averting of eyes, every

---

[7] "They make a desert and call it peace." *Agricola*, 30.
[8] *The Autobiography of Edward Gibbon*, ed. Dero A. Saunders (1961), p. 69.

compulsory panegyric, cripples the pursuit of historical truth. Moreover, to be real and effective, freedom must be internal as well as external; it must embrace, not merely immunity from harassment and guarantees against starvation, but freedom from constricting prejudgments and from unquestioning acceptance of authority. Whatever his ultimate merits, Tacitus' way of writing and, even more, his way of thinking provided Gibbon with a model for this kind of double freedom. Gibbon's Tacitean remark, "Augustus was sensible that mankind is governed by names,"[9] reads like a delicate acknowledgment of his debt.

In our self-conscious, self-analytical age, ridden as we are with the suspicion that our several loyalties impose strict limits on our vision, we are apt to doubt that the demand for this kind of inner freedom can be at all realistic. It seems like just another, in fact the worst kind of, self-deception. Surely it is true that total detachment implies a dispassionateness not granted to human beings; the historian without presuppositions is like Aristotle's man without a city, either a beast or a god. Yet it is all too easy to underestimate the pressures toward objectivity that craftsmanship can apply. Tacitus was an aristocrat, an accomplice in the terrible reign of Domitian, a Roman of his day. He was not an atheist, and he was deeply attached to Rome's traditional values, values at a discount in his lifetime. And, as Auerbach has shown, Tacitus' historical work is the product of a specific world view that entailed a specific set of social perceptions.[10] Yet none of this compromises his masterly anatomies; they are something better than subtle apologies for himself or

[9] Gibbon, *Decline and Fall* [iii], 1:71.
[10] Erich Auerbach, *Mimesis: The Representation of Reality in Western Literature* (1946; trans. Willard R. Trask, 1953), pp. 33–40.

for his order. One need not be a metaphysical skeptic to be a methodological skeptic; one need not be a cynic to claim the right to question everything. Gibbon's skepticism, even more than Tacitus' skepticism earlier, was a method, not a conclusion. To the extent that it *was* a conclusion, it did not follow inescapably from his method.

What Gibbon learned from Tacitus, then, was a kind of discriminating disenchantment. He was persuaded that it was a kind of lesson that Christian historians could not teach; the critical temper was available only to pagans, ancient and modern. It was this temper that Gibbon glimpsed in Tacitus when he singled him out as perhaps the only ancient who could truly be called a "philosophical historian."[11] To Gibbon, as to Hume, Voltaire, and the other philosophes, the philosopher is a man who has conquered prejudices and given the critical spirit free play. And to Gibbon, Tacitus was such a man.[12] In the company of Seneca, the Plinys, Epictetus, and a few others, he had "purified" his mind with "Philosophy," leaving behind the "prejudices" of "popular superstition," and improving his "excellent" understanding through study and the pursuit of truth.[13] It was plain—at least to Gibbon— that in the centuries when Christianity had shaped men's minds, history, like philosophy, had obediently served as handmaiden to a glittering superstition. But now, in the eighteenth century, civilized men were living once again in what Gibbon liked to call an "age of light and liberty,"[14] an

---

[11] *Essai sur l'étude de la littérature*, in *Miscellaneous Works of Edward Gibbon, Esq.* . . . , 2nd edn., ed. John Lord Sheffield, 5 vols. (1814), 4:66. To Gibbon, Tacitus was "the first of historians who applied the science of philosophy to the study of facts." *Decline and Fall* [ix], 1:213.

[12] See Gay, *Enlightenment*, vol. 1, chapter 3, "The Climate of Criticism."

[13] Gibbon, *Decline and Fall* [xv], 2:68. See Harold L. Bond, *The Literary Art of Edward Gibbon* (1960), pp. 9–13, 125.

[14] *Autobiography*, p. 175. See below, p. 39.

age, therefore, supremely adapted to the writing of truthful history.

From this perspective, Gibbon's choice of Tacitus as his antique model (rather than, say, Livy or Caesar) acquires considerable diagnostic significance. It amounts to a decisive rejection of the Christian view of the world, a view that continued to pervade the writing of history in Gibbon's own century. Much as the philosophes liked to think so—or, rather, to say so—Christian history was by no means synonymous with mendacious or superstitious history. In the seventeenth and early eighteenth centuries, an impressive band of devout *érudits* found it possible to reconcile the most scrupulous scholarship with the most unimpeachable piety, and to serve their God by refining the methods of historical research. While most of these scholars found it reasonable, in fact obligatory, to assert the supremacy of God in history as its ultimate causal agent, they made room for the mundane analysis of historical causation by recognizing that God often worked through "secondary causes": the passions and the reason of men, the practice of statecraft, the application of intelligence in military affairs. At the same time, many popular and influential histories, like Bossuet's *Discours sur l'histoire universelle* of 1681, continued to present Scriptures as an infallible historical document, use events decisive for the ancient Hebrews or the early Church to determine historical periodization, and take the course of history as God's way of rewarding the faithful and punishing the heretic. As late as the 1750s, when Gibbon was meditating his future vocation, the most popular histories of the ancient world were the volumes of the French Jansenist Charles Rollin, who had published an expansive *Ancient History* and an equally expansive *Roman History* in the 1730s, and whose historical views were, if anything, more subservient to religious imperatives than Bossuet's. David Hume rightly thought Rollin's histories loaded down with "puerilities," yet he noted at the same time that his work "is so well wrote with respect to style, that with superficial people it passes for sufficient."[15]

The history that in the 1750s passed with superficial people for sufficient wholly neglected recent scholarship whether pious or impious, quoted Seneca, Livy, and the Old Testament with indiscriminate credulity, and treated secular history as a set of demonstrations for the veracity of Scriptures. While "profane history," Rollin wrote, "treats only of nations who had imbibed all the absurdities of a superstitious worship," it nevertheless "proclaims universally the greatness of the Almighty, his power, his justice, and above all the admirable wisdom with which his providence governs the universe." Nearly every page of history displays "the precious footsteps and shining proofs of this great truth, namely that God disposes all events as supreme Lord and Sovereign; that he alone determines the fate of kings and the duration of empires; and that he transfers the government of kingdoms from one nation to another, because of the unrighteous dealings and wickedness committed therein." History properly begins with "the dispersion of the posterity of Noah," and all history is simply the working out of a divine mysterious plan, of which only part has been revealed, in Scriptures.[16] History, in short, is principally a proving ground for theology, an edifying tale calculated to keep the reader safe in the bosom of

---

[15] Hume to William Robertson, February 8, 1759, in *The Letters of David Hume*, ed. J. Y. T. Greig, 2 vols. (1932), 1:297; Hume to Robertson, (Summer 1759), *Letters*, 1:315.

[16] Charles Rollin, *Ancient History*, "Preface," in an anonymously translated two-volume eighteenth-century edition, published by George Virtue (n.d.), 1:i–ii.

the Faith. The measure of the aid that an ancient writer like Tacitus could give Gibbon with his liberation emerges most forcefully when we read the popular puerilities of Gibbon's rivals.

Yet Gibbon's use of antiquity had its predicaments for him. He was compelled to maneuver in a convoluted maze of intellectual forces. In taking Tacitus (as Suzanne Curchot had perceptively noted) not only for a model but also for a source, Gibbon was distancing himself from the most advanced scholarship of his day, a scholarship that Gibbon was equipped to appreciate better than any other philosophe. While erudite historians were beginning to discriminate with the most sure-fingered delicacy among the sources on which they had to rely, Gibbon was almost credulous in accepting the word of writers he admired.[17] Gibbon was a philosophe; his world view—his secularism, his hostility to "superstition," his commitment to criticism, his love of freedom—was that of Hume, of Voltaire, of Diderot. Yet as a historian, Gibbon identified himself, consciously and bravely, with the *érudits*, the scholars whom graceful stylists like Voltaire found tedious beyond the call of duty. While the "learning and language of Greece and Rome," he later remembered, were "neglected by a philosophic age," Gibbon followed the *érudits*, who neglected neither, and amassed an impressive range of eru-

---

[17] See Arnaldo D. Momigliano, "Gibbon's Contribution to Historical Method" (1954), in Momigliano, *Studies in Historiography* (1966), pp. 40–55, passim. At the same time, as a look at his scholarly notes reveals, it will not do to minimize Gibbon's scholarship. See, especially, *The English Essays of Edward Gibbon*, ed. Patricia B. Craddock (1972).

dition.[18] He studied ancient coins and inscriptions, mastered the geography of the Roman Empire, digested masses of specialized scholarship. He was beholden not merely to congenial skeptics like Bayle, but also to Benedictines like Mabillon and Montfaucon, Jansenists like Tillemont, Huguenots like Beausobre. He devoured their learning: he accepted their settling of disputed dates, their reading of uncertain texts, their collections of elusive documents. And he was duly grateful, in his characteristic feline way that made his acknowledgments often sound like an insult. Reaching the year 519 in his *Decline and Fall*, and, with that date, the end of his use for Tillemont's great ecclesiastical history, Gibbon bids his mentor farewell in one of his typical footnotes: "And here I must take leave forever of that incomparable guide—whose bigotry is overbalanced by the merits of erudition, diligence, veracity, and scrupulous minuteness."[19]

The tone of this valedictory reveals more than a failure of generosity; it throws light on the paradox of Gibbon's scholarship. Just as he could not accept the cavalier literary contempt for "pedants" characteristic of his intellectual allies, the philosophes, he could not accept the pronounced piety of his professional allies, the *érudits*. While he populated the pages of his *Autobiography* and the footnotes of his *Decline and Fall* with references to his seventeenth- and early eighteenth-century authorities, he was all too vividly aware that nearly all of them had worked not to blacken the name, but to sustain the glory, of the Christian religion. At once dependent and independent, Gibbon the philosophical historian had to

[18] *Autobiography*, p. 123. Gibbon for his part, I think, rather overstates the philosophes' contempt for learning; they detested pedantry far more than erudition.
[19] Gibbon, *Decline and Fall* [xlvii], 5:132n.

take a leap that Gibbon the scrupulous scholar found it hard even to contemplate. Yet he took it. Studying Beausobre's critical history of Manicheanism with care, he found that the book "discusses many deep questions of Pagan and Christian theology: and from this rich treasury of facts and opinions I deduced my own consequences, beyond the holy circle of the author."[20] Tacitus, preeminent among others, helped him to step out of the holy circle.

Tacitus was, of course, far from being Gibbon's only antique inspiration. While much Enlightenment history concentrated on the recent past, on Charles XII of Sweden or Louis XIV of France, classical antiquity exercised a continuing fascination on the eighteenth-century mind. Today, when classical learning is dying and has fled to privileged sanctuaries in the university, it takes historical imagination to reconstruct how much of a living force it was only two centuries ago. Gibbon's *Autobiography* amply testifies to its vitality; the writings of his contemporaries—Diderot or Hume, Adam Smith or Samuel Johnson, Lessing or Jefferson—confirm that Gibbon was not unique in feeling its power but typical, though it is fair to add that Gibbon experienced the lure of antiquity as particularly irresistible. "Rome," he wrote, "is familiar to the schoolboy and the statesman,"[21] but to no one so familiar as to him. His famous discovery of Rome in October 1764 was a rediscovery. Calm as he normally was, his Italian diary shows him feverish with excitement; arriving in the city on October 2, he walked about in a *"songe d'antiquité"*[22]—he was in a very real sense coming home. He later recalled in his *Autobiography*:

---

[20] *Autobiography*, pp. 135–136.
[21] *Autobiography*, p. 175.
[22] October 2, 1764. *Gibbon's Journey from Geneva to Rome: His Journal from 20 April to 2 October 1764*, ed. Georges A. Bonnard (1961), p. 235. Evidently the metaphor pleased him; on October 9, 1764, he wrote to his

Gibbon: *A Cynic among Ancient Politicians*

My temper is not very susceptible of enthusiasm, and the enthusiasm which I do not feel I have ever scorned to affect. But at the distance of twenty-five years I can neither forget nor express the strong emotions which agitated my mind as I first approached and entered the *Eternal City*. After a sleepless night I trod, with a lofty step, the ruins of the Forum; each memorable spot where Romulus stood, or Tully spoke, or Caesar fell, was at once present to my eye, and several days of intoxication were lost or enjoyed before I could descend to a cool and minute investigation.[23]

It is tempting to discount the passage; it is so familiar and its diction so elevated: Gibbon does not walk, he treads, and with a lofty step at that. And the pairs of verbs ("neither forget nor express," "several days . . . were lost or enjoyed") are in the rhythm of his formal speech, his set pieces. Yet this is not a set piece; it is, in its own way, an outpouring of emotion, recollected in genuine excitement. Gibbon knew Rome better than most Romans he saw about him. Behind modern and Renaissance Rome, the Rome of Caesar and of Cicero was vividly and accurately present to his schooled mind's eye.

He was indeed the best-prepared traveler ever to enter the "*Eternal City.*" He had been over the ground before, many times, poring over maps, imagining historic moments, hearing the immortal orations. In general, his reading, a voracious affair, had been continuously—I am tempted to say gluttonously—classical. When he was compelled to forego the ancients during his service with the militia, he regretted it and remembered it as a time of starvation: "After this long

---

father from Rome that he had "found such a fund of entertainment for a mind somewhat prepared for it by an acquaintance with the Romans, that I am really almost in a dream." *The Letters of Edward Gibbon*, ed. J. E. Norton, 3 vols. (1956), 1:184.

[23] *Autobiography*, p. 152.

fast, the longest which I have ever known, I once more tasted at Dover the pleasures of reading and thinking, and the hungry appetite with which I opened a volume of Tully's philosophical works is still present to my memory."[24]

The foundations of this passion for Cicero as for the others had been laid long before. As a young scholar in Lausanne, he read Cicero through, and

after finishing this great author, a library of eloquence and reason, I formed a more extensive plan of reviewing the Latin classics under the four divisions of (1) historians, (2) poets, (3) orators, and (4) philosophers, in a chronological series from the days of Plautus and Sallust to the decline of the language and Empire of Rome; and this plan, in the last twenty-seven months of my residence at Lausanne . . . I *nearly* accomplished.

Nor was this review, however rapid, either hasty or superficial. I indulged myself in a second and even third perusal of Terence, Virgil, Horace, Tacitus, etc., and studied to imbibe the sense and spirit most congenial to my own.[25]

We can always rely on Gibbon to supply the telling phrase. The ancients were men of a "sense and spirit most congenial to his own." They were congenial, first, because they furnished a continuously interesting subject of study. I need not insist that Gibbon's work, which took him perhaps twenty years to write, is *about* antiquity; nor need I insist that other eighteenth-century writers thought and wrote much about the ancient world. And for all of them, antiquity had been ideal as well as theme. Gibbon did not need to teach his readers to love antiquity—that they did without him. He filled out the outlines of their love with his gripping gift for narrative, his

---

[24] *Autobiography*, p. 135.
[25] *Autobiography*, pp. 99–100.

blessed specificity. Suzanne Curchot, who remained Gibbon's friend long after she had become Mme. Necker, thanked him with her usual perceptiveness for "filling an immense gap in history, and throwing over the chaos this bridge joining the ancient to the modern world."[26] After all, the two most famous—or notorious—chapters of the *Decline and Fall* are the fifteenth and sixteenth, the chapters on Christianity. They cost Gibbon immense effort and brought him more controversy than anything else he ever wrote. They are Gibbon's natural history of Christianity, the historian's counterpart to Hume's *Natural History of Religion*. He had flattered himself, Gibbon wrote, "that an age of light and liberty would receive, without scandal, an inquiry into the *human* causes of the progress and establishment of Christianity."[27] These scandalous chapters on Christianity belong within a larger frame. They come after Gibbon has extolled the greatness of Roman statesmen, the dignity of Roman ethics, and the decency of Roman toleration. Such praise was not wholly disinterested. With an artist as conscious as Gibbon we are entitled to assume that the very placement of his chapters has a purpose and reveals an intention. Gibbon intones his hymn to Roman greatness at the beginning, in the first three chapters. These are more than perfunctory stage settings; they are strategically placed. They establish a norm against which the Christian millennium appears as a dismal falling off. To be sure, even under the Antonines Rome is not perfect: Gibbon is recounting a tragedy, and Rome, his protagonist, has its tragic flaw. In some

---

[26] Quoted in Young, *Gibbon*, p. 134. See Mme. Necker's long and brilliant appraisal of the first volume of the *Decline and Fall*, in her letter to Gibbon of September 30, 1776, reprinted in Gibbon, *Miscellaneous Works*, 2:176–180.

[27] *Autobiography*, p. 175.

memorable phrases, Gibbon describes the sense of unease, the emptiness amidst prosperity, the drift in political life, the fatal seeping away of cultural vitality: "A cloud of critics, of compilers, of commentators, darkened the face of learning, and the decline of genius was soon followed by the corruption of taste."[28] Yet these flaws of ancient civilization only made it human. Gibbon presents his Rome facing the insidious subversion of Christianity as a believable hero pitted against a believable villain. His scholarship made his protagonists seem believable; his style made his version of their combat seem just—in fact, inescapable.

The Ironist

IT was at Rome," so runs the famous recollection, worth recording once again, "on the fifteenth of October 1764, as I sat musing amid the ruins of the Capitol, while the barefooted friars were singing vespers in the temple of Jupiter, that the idea of writing the decline and fall of the city first started to my mind."[29] Gibbon thus first glimpsed his life work, the bold enterprise of narrating in exhaustive detail and with scholarly precision the tragedy of the greatest of all historic empires, in the guise of an ironic confrontation. We know—Gibbon himself tells us—that he enlarged his canvas as he began to reflect on the task he was imposing on himself. And we may note, as he labors on his successive volumes, an

[28] Gibbon, *Decline and Fall* [ii], 1:58.
[29] *Autobiography*, p. 154.

increasing complexity of causal judgment. But the stance he took at the beginning of his great work long preceded it and did not change as it progressed: it was the sight of a noble monument of his beloved antiquity in ruins, and of superstitious intruders desecrating, with their noisy piety, the ancient pagan temple, that gave his diffuse ambition the concentration he had so long sought. It was only afterwards that his choice of subject and his mode of treatment assumed the massive shape of inevitability.

Gibbon insinuates his ironic perception into the very first paragraph of his masterpiece. In introducing his hero, Rome, he resorts to a device he rarely uses—short sentences: "In the second century of the Christian Æra, the empire of Rome comprehended the fairest part of the earth, and the most civilized portion of mankind." From the outset, then, Gibbon establishes the grandeur of his protagonist. The empire appears secure: "The frontiers of that extensive monarchy were guarded by ancient renown and disciplined valour. The gentle, but powerful, influence of laws and manners had gradually cemented the union of the provinces." Rome's "peaceful inhabitants"—and here the irony emerges, the first cuckoo in the imperial nest—"*enjoyed and abused* the advantages of wealth and luxury." And, just as these peaceful inhabitants challenged jealous fate by squandering, instead of husbanding, their unprecedented prosperity, their polity rested on a supreme sham: "The *image* of a free constitution was *preserved with decent reverence.* The Roman senate *appeared to* possess the sovereign authority, and devolved on the emperors all the executive powers of government."[30] The Roman people saw only the image, the appearance, of political reality; fiction

[30] Gibbon, *Decline and Fall* [i], 1:1. Italics mine.

and fact were at war, though politicians prudently kept the warfare below the surface.

Deceit, in fact, lay at the very heart of Rome's happiness. While Gibbon is willing to dwell on that fragile happiness, this is mainly to provide brilliant contrasts for his chiaroscuro; it is the deceit that really engages his attention and occupies the center of the stage he is setting. The most obvious, and most important, forum for that deceit is the temple: "The various modes of worship which prevailed in the Roman world, were all considered by the people, as equally true; by the philosopher, as equally false; and by the magistrate, as equally useful." And, Gibbon points out, they *were* useful: "Toleration produced not only mutual indulgence, but even religious concord."[31] Roman toleration was not a liberal passivity; it was an active manipulation of popular sentiment, a subject on which Gibbon expatiates with the greedy pleasure of a gourmet of duplicity: "Notwithstanding the fashionable irreligion which prevailed in the age of the Antonines, both the interests of the priests and the credulity of the people were sufficiently respected." Here, as so often, Gibbon's highly wrought parallels ("the interests of the priests . . . the credulity of the people") serve his two favorite masters, euphony and irony, at the same time.

In their writings and conversation, the philosophers of antiquity asserted the independent dignity of reason; but they resigned their actions to the commands of law and of custom. Viewing, with a smile of pity and indulgence, the various errors of the vulgar, they diligently practised the ceremonies of their fathers, devoutly frequented the temples of the gods; and sometimes condescending to act a part on the theatre of superstition, they concealed the

---

[31] Gibbon, *Decline and Fall* [ii], 1:28.

sentiments of an Atheist under the sacerdotal robes. Reasoners of such a temper were scarcely inclined to wrangle about their respective modes of faith, or of worship. It was indifferent to them what shape the folly of the multitude might choose to assume; and they approached, with the same inward contempt, and the same external reverence, the altars of the Libyan, the Olympian, or the Capitoline Jupiter.[32]

The self-serving but politically useful hypocrisy of the intellectuals was matched and exploited by the shrewdness of their governors:

Imperial government . . . may be defined an absolute monarchy disguised by the forms of a commonwealth. The masters of the Roman world surrounded their throne with darkness, concealed their irresistible strength, and humbly professed themselves the accountable ministers of the senate, whose supreme decrees they dictated and obeyed.[33]

These passages are worth pondering for a moment. Their analytical insights are by no means unique to Gibbon. The ancients—Cicero, Ovid, Juvenal among others—had already exposed the political utility of a public worship in which the rulers do not believe. Gibbon's favorite modern master, Montesquieu, had devoted an essay to the "religious politics" of antique Roman statesmen: "They made a religion for the state while others had made the state for religion."[34] And David Hume had anticipated Gibbon's description of the studied piety that Rome's most admirable writers and thinkers did not scruple to practice as a kind of patriotic service:

---

[32] Gibbon, *Decline and Fall* [ii], 1:30.
[33] Gibbon, *Decline and Fall* [ii], 1:68.
[34] *Sur la politique des Romains dans la religion*, in *Œuvres complètes*, ed. André Masson, 3 vols. (1950–1955).

If there ever was a nation or a time in which the public religion lost all authority over mankind, we might expect, that infidelity in Rome, during the Ciceronian age, would openly have erected its throne, and that Cicero himself, in every speech and action, would have been its most declared abettor. But it appears, that, whatever sceptical liberties the great man might take, in his writings or his philosophical conversation, he yet avoided, in the common conduct of life, the imputation of deism and profaneness. Even in his own family, and to his wife Terentia, whom he highly trusted, he was willing to appear a devout religionist.[35]

There is thus nothing new in the substance of Gibbon's religious (which is really political) sociology. What is new is Gibbon's ironic treatment. He has adopted the smile of pity and indulgence that he imagined on the faces of Roman philosophers, to expose, in his history, the needy irrationality of mankind; but with him, it has become a smile of derision.

Yet that smile, though persistent, does not become monotonous, for Gibbon knows how to vary it; if, as Gibbon said, it is the mark of style to express the writer's mind, it is, as he knew, the task of style to hold the writer's audience. At times, Gibbon compresses the ironic tension between public lies and private convictions into a simple contiguous antithesis ("with the same inward contempt, and the same external reverence," the "masters of the Roman world" humbly professed themselves "the ministers of the senate," whose decrees they "dictated and obeyed"). At other times, the antithesis is less direct ("viewing, with a smile . . . , they diligently practiced"; ancient philosophers "asserted the independent dignity of reason; but they resigned their actions . . ."). And there are times when Gibbon puts aside his in-

[35] David Hume, *The Natural History of Religion*, in *Works*, 4:347. On this question, see Gay, *Enlightenment*, 1:145–155.

direction and his sly polarities: "Imperial government . . . may be defined an absolute monarchy disguised by the forms of a commonwealth." However much Gibbon indulges himself, he never forgets his obligations to his readers.

Gibbon's irony informs his large themes: the incongruity of rhetoric and reality in Roman politics, of potential and practice in Roman culture, of pious humility and impious pride in the Christian Fathers. But it penetrates, as we have had some occasion to observe, his very choice of words and structuring of clauses. One instance of his pervasive irony is the strategic frequency with which he uses the word *artful*. It fits Gibbon's wily Augustus to perfection, but he applies it to others as well. It is a good word for an ironist, capable of carrying heavy loads of meaning on both shoulders; it suggests both skill and concealment, *craft* in both senses of the word—it is the opposite of "natural," both in the sense of straightforward and of crude. Using it as he does, Gibbon implies that he has seen through his subject and is sharing his discovery with his readers. In Chapter 3 of the *Decline and Fall*, the words "artful," "artfully," "arts," and "artificial," always in the ironic sense, occur at least six times. In addition, Gibbon varies the word with a rich array of synonyms: "fictitious," "subtle," "studied," "crafty," among the adjectives; "represented," "professed," "disguised," "affected," "deceived," "dissembled," "seemed," among the verbs; "comedy" and "illusion," among the nouns. The whole chapter, in fact, abounds with phrases designed to secure the same effect. The balance of the sentences does more than describe, it *embodies* the dignified political charade of the early empire. Gibbon writes that Augustus was "compelled to accept" a large grant of power from the senate; the "tender respect of Augustus for a free constitution which he had destroyed" is explained by the character of "that subtle tyrant." In these phrases, and many others like them, Gibbon imprisons the conflict between thought and action, word and deed, constitutional rhetoric and despotic fact, pious profession and vicious character, into the narrowest space; he crowds them to achieve the greatest possible explosive effect. What the late J. Robert Oppenheimer said of the intimate hostility between the United States and the Soviet Union in the years of the cold war aptly applies to Gibbon's taut antitheses: they are two scorpions in a bottle.

The adjective *artful* drew its force from its patent sincerity. Other adjectives in Gibbon draw their force from their patent insincerity—or, at least, from their studied ambiguity. Gibbon's chapters on the rise of the Christian religion were so irritating to believers and so enjoyable to unbelievers in part because they contain such two-edged words in profusion. Christianity, Gibbon writes, was a *"pure* and *humble"* religion that *"gently* insinuated itself" into men's minds; the materials on which the "candid but rational" ecclesiastical historian must base his inquiries are *"scanty* and *suspicious"*; the remarkable victory of the Christian faith under such untoward circumstances was assisted, in part, by the *"inflexible,* and if we may use the expression, the *intolerant* zeal" of the Christians; the professors of the new religion were distinguished by an *"exclusive* zeal for the truth of religion"—[36] unexceptionable adjectives all, if read in one way; highly offensive, if read in another. Gibbon here exercises his irony in behalf of one part of his readership against another part. Dividing, he conquered.

---

[36] Gibbon, *Decline and Fall* [xv], 2:1–2. Italics mine. Gibbon's phrase "candid but rational" is worth noting—his passion for antithesis is apparently so powerful that he cannot resist constructing one even when there is no opposition requiring the "but."

Uniting, he conquered as well; the ironic polarities, which I have already noted, catch the mood of his style—tension rather than repose—to perfection. Emperor Constantius embraced a "generous but artful system of policy"; Julian was moved to resist his proclamation as emperor by "prudence as well as loyalty"; Clovis' wife, a Catholic, found it to "her interest, as well as her duty, to achieve the conversion of a Pagan husband, and Clovis insensibly listened to the voice of love and religion"; Mohammed rested the truth of his mission on the truth of the Koran "in the spirit of enthusiasm or vanity."[37] There are countless instances of this technique, each invariably following the same formula. I cannot exaggerate its importance for Gibbon and for the understanding of his mind: Gibbon closely couples a higher and a lower motive and implies that the former is the ostensible reason while the latter is the actual moving force. And because he only implies this, he compels the reader to become his accomplice and to draw the unpleasant, generally cynical, inference for himself. Gibbon's irony, a splendid instrument for unmasking others, was at the same time an equally splendid screen for protecting his own privacy.

In a well-deserved tribute, Byron pictures Gibbon as studious, meditative, and learned, shaping

> his weapon with an edge severe,
> Sapping a solemn creed with solemn sneer;
> The lord of irony.

Yet, though "lord of irony" was an appropriate title for Gibbon, irony was far from being his only stylistic resource, just

[37] Gibbon, *Decline and Fall* [xix], 2:263, 402, 4:106, 5:343. It is clear from Gibbon's letters that this way of thinking was perfectly natural to him. Writing to his father about Commodore Acton, whom he had met in Italy, he refers to his religious conversion as springing "either from motives of interest or devotion." October 9, 1764, *Letters*, 1:184.

as the discovery of Rome had been far from his only shaping experience. Gibbon himself celebrates two events in his adult life—his service with the militia between 1760 and 1762, and his stint in the House of Commons between 1774 and 1780—as serviceable to his historian's vocation. "The captain of the Hampshire grenadiers . . ." he wrote of the first, "has not been useless to the historian of the Roman empire," because it gave him "a clearer notion of the phalanx and the legions" of ancient Rome.[38] "The eight sessions that I sat in Parliament," he wrote of the second, "were a school of civil prudence, the first and most essential virtue of an historian."[39] We may doubt that his far from onerous military interlude or his silent "senatorial life"[40] did much more than to amplify what he had already experienced through his books. But they widened his angle of vision on the outside world and gave his descriptions in the *Decline and Fall* a sure sense of intimacy. They permitted him to *see*. Exotic landscapes and great cities rouse Gibbon to word painting in which he subdues his sarcasm and slows the pace of his narrative to obtain, and convey, a view, at once comprehensive and concrete, of novel scenes. In contrast, battles or moments of intense political combat induce him to speed up his narrative step and to enlist each detail in the service of the whole. Thomas Mann once said that only the exhaustive is truly interesting, a dictum that Mann himself did less to justify than Gibbon.

Gibbon, of course, was more than a painter, a narrator, and a courtly jester. He thought of himself as a philosophical historian in the tradition of Tacitus. Accordingly he amply

[38] *Autobiography*, p. 134. The passage from Byron is in Book III of *Childe Harold's Pilgrimage.*
[39] *Autobiography*, p. 174.
[40] *Autobiography*, p. 184.

supplies his *Decline and Fall* with observations about human nature, about politics, warfare, and religion. These are neither funny nor colorful; they are witty but didactic: "The public favour . . . seldom accompanies old age";[41] and "Civil governments, in their first institution, are voluntary associations for mutual defense";[42] and again, "Bigotry and national aversion are powerful magnifiers of every object of dispute."[43] It is as a philosophical historian that Gibbon establishes his presence in every sentence of his history; he rarely steps out on stage to speak a line in the first person, but his firm management of the pace, his value-charged epithets, his psychological and sociological pronouncements alert the reader to the philosopher's mind behind the narrative surface. He is always weighing, comparing, judging. And it is as a philosophical historian that, in Chapter 38, having reached the critical year 476, Gibbon stops the historical narration to deliver from his high vantage point some "General Observations on the Fall of the Roman Empire in the West." As a secular historian, he has insisted throughout on the human and geographic causes of historical events, but he has nowhere listed them; now, looking back, he makes explicit the causal nexus of the awful spectacle he has been recounting. "The rise of a city, which swelled into an empire," he notes, "may deserve, as a singular prodigy, the reflection of a philosophic mind." The fall of a city, he intimates, deserves such reflection quite as much; now, with the first—and, it will turn out, the better —half of his majestic recitation complete, he thinks out loud about the ironies with which the history of Rome abounds: the cancer of decay in the vitals of prosperity, the victor's adoption of his captives' vices, the conversion of the

[41] Gibbon, *Decline and Fall* [xviii], 2:207.
[42] Gibbon, *Decline and Fall* [ix], 1:224.
[43] Gibbon, *Decline and Fall* [lx], 6:368.

army from the protector for imperial security into its nemesis. Finally, as a philosopher—and philosophe—Gibbon can at this moment step back from history altogether, to speculate whether the fall of Rome implies the fall of modern civilization. As always, Gibbon's philosophic stance is firmly within the cosmopolitan and rational ambiance of the Enlightenment: "It is the duty of a patriot to prefer and promote the exclusive interest and glory of his native country; but a philosopher may be permitted to enlarge his views, and to consider Europe as one great republic, whose various inhabitants have attained almost the same level of politeness and cultivation." It is to this great republic that Gibbon has been addressing his history, and is now addressing his reassurances concerning "the probable causes of our actual security." Because civilization has been steadily diffused, men may "acquiesce in the pleasing conclusion that every age of the world has increased, and still increases, the real wealth, the happiness, the knowledge, and perhaps the virtue, of the human race." Yet Gibbon shares not only the Enlightenment's optimism, he shares its pessimism in the same measure and for the same reason; like d'Alembert, like Hume, like Wieland, Gibbon guards his castle of hope with the moat of caution. In the company of the philosophes, Gibbon holds to a law of compensation: every advance must be paid for in some way. And so Gibbon modifies his hopeful conclusion with a footnote in which he reflects that "the merit of discovery has too often been stained with avarice, cruelty, and fanaticism; and the intercourse of nations has produced the communication of disease and prejudice."[44] In the midst of his paean to progress, the ironist is as alert as ever.

[44] Gibbon, *Decline and Fall* [xxxviii], 4:161, 163, 164, 169, 169n. As will appear later, Macaulay shared this philosophic view; see below, p. 131.

as tempting as it is perilous to discover in the *Decline*
ll Gibbon's whole past—a past that we have pieced
:r from other sources. Yet that whole past went into
king of his history. It draws on that immense and
: scholarship he acquired, in spite of his dreary days
dalen College, Oxford, during his diligent years at
:e; it draws, too, on that impressive library he assem-
th such greedy appetite. It embodies the polemical
ess and urbane self-possession he had perfected in
roversies with lesser scholars like Warburton and
ersations with equals like Burke. And in the most in-
'ay it incorporates his ironic perception of life; the
n of an observer as penetrating as he is self-protective,
ian whose highest ideal is accuracy but whose vision
tter calculated to see blemishes than virtues, decep-
her than sincerity. His famous abortive infatuation
anne Curchot, and the equally famous sentence with
: records his renunciation of a brilliant and charming
m his father would not permit him to marry, suggest
whose robustness was rhetorical, and whose virility
ely borrowed. "I sighed as a lover; I obeyed as a son."[45]
dience, one senses, came readily; the sigh was a sigh

e, for Gibbon, then, gravity and levity coexisted
: strain, and while both together define his historical
it is with levity that Gibbon was most at home. He
not to keep from weeping but because so much of

tobiography, p. 109. The words are justly famous; less familiar is
r comment, "A matrimonial alliance has ever been the object of
or rather than that of my wishes." *Autobiography*, p. 157. In his
f farewell to Suzanne Curchot, Gibbon placed his familiar antitheses
nporal sequence, thus for once giving an impression of courtesy rather
nicism: "Mademoiselle. Je ne puis commencer! Cependant il le faut.
nds la plume, je la quitte, je la reprends." October 24, 1758,
, 1:106.

history is laughable. What Byron called his "solemn sn
is never far from the surface of Gibbon's consciousness.
history of Rome's decline and fall, though a serious e
inciting the philosophical historian to his most philosopl
reflections, also has many moments of high, and of l
comedy. Gibbon's irony reflects his awareness of this
mixture in the human past; his sarcastic wit fastens on
sheer humor that, to his mind, the human spectacle so fr
scatters across the pages of history. Again and again, Gibl
the genial author seems to be leering companionably at
reader: in the early twelfth century, when a troop of Manic
ans desert the standard of Alexius Comnenus, the empe
"dissembled till the moment of revenge; invited the chiefs
a friendly conference; and punished the innocent and gu
by imprisonment, confiscation, and baptism."[46] It is relig
—especially, of course, the Christian religion—that activa
Gibbon's most sneering humor. "His reflections," the form
able eighteenth-century classicist Richard Porson tartly, l
fairly, complained, "are often just and profound; he ple
eloquently for the rights of mankind, and the duty of tol
tion; nor does his humanity ever slumber, unless when wom
are ravished, or the Christians persecuted."[47] Gibbon lil
to crowd his footnotes not merely with erudite citatic
and shrewd appraisals, but also with jokes. About the depc
tion of an antipope at the Council of Constance, he writ
"Of the three popes, John the twenty-third was the first v
tim: he fled and was brought back a prisoner: the most sca
dalous charges were suppressed; the vicar of Christ was or
accused of piracy, murder, rape, sodomy, and incest."[48] l

[46] Gibbon, *Decline and Fall* [liv], 6:122.
[47] Quoted in Michael Joyce, *Edward Gibbon* (1953), p. 137.
[48] Gibbon, *Decline and Fall* [lxx], 7:289.

quotes David Hume on the fate of the chapter of Seez, which had presumed to elect a bishop without authorization: Geoffrey had all the clerics castrated and their testicles brought to him in a platter. Gibbon cannot refrain from adding his gloss: "Of the pain and danger they might justly complain, yet, since they had vowed chastity, he deprived them of a superfluous treasure."[49] Speaking of controversies among Arab scholars, Gibbon notes: "Among the Arabian philosophers, Averroes has been accused of despising the religion of the Jews, the Christians and the Mahometans. . . . Each of these sects would agree that in two instances out of three his contempt was reasonable."[50] But it is needless to go on quoting; each reader can gather his own bouquet, admiring the wit or deploring the malice, in accord with his own taste and convictions.

Seriously as Gibbon's humor deserves to be taken, it must not obstruct our view of his craftsman's virtues—the magnificence of his design, the polish of his performance, the precision of his scholarship, the judiciousness of his opinions, however extravagantly expressed. Brilliantly parading political, military, and religious history, Gibbon presided over the arranged but happy marriage of erudition and philosophy. Coercing potentially incompatible qualities into a peaceful kingdom enabled Gibbon to build a monument of historical literature. His summary of the fall of Rome, "the triumph of barbarism and religion," does less than justice to his judg-

---

[49] Gibbon, *Decline and Fall* [lxix], 7:216n.

[50] Gibbon, *Decline and Fall* [lii], 6:33n. The jokes get into the text as well. Speaking of the younger Gordian, Gibbon writes, "Twenty-two acknowledged concubines, and a library of sixty-two thousand volumes, attested the variety of his inclinations; and from the productions which he left behind him, it appears that both the one and the other were designed for use rather than for ostentation." *Decline and Fall* [vii], 1:176.

ment. Gibbon actually included among the causes of the fall the long peace, which engendered effeminacy and intellectual sterility; economic exploitation, which made most Romans unwilling to defend what did not really belong to them; the lack of freedom, which deprived institutions of all flexibility; the very size of the empire, which made it hard to defend. Not even the widespread charge that his lack of sympathy with the religious temper incapacitated him for religious history is wholly just; with all his marked, at times ferocious, animosity, his professional probity and his sheer curiosity raised him above his rancor to nuanced appraisals —at least some of the time. For Gibbon, take him all in all, the simplicities of irony—indeed, all simplicities—were simply not enough.

Yet Gibbon's irony remains highly visible and raises a final, ironic, question. His modern reader, accustomed to leaner fare, is inclined to wonder whether with Gibbon style adapted itself to matter, or matter yielded to style. He certainly worked hard at submitting his style to his will. He lost his "literary maidenhead"[51] in 1761 in French, with an *Essai sur l'Etude de la littérature,* but then returned, with a first and short draft of the *Decline and Fall,* to his native English— "conscious," as he recalled later, "that my style, above prose and below poetry, degenerated into a verbose and turgid declamation."[52] He continued to experiment with his history.

At the outset all was dark and doubtful, even the title of the work, the true era of the decline and fall of the empire, the limits of the introduction, the division of the chapters, and the order of the narrative. . . . Many experiments were made before

[51] *Autobiography,* p. 127.
[52] *Autobiography,* p. 159.

I could hit the middle tone between a dull chronicle and a rhetorical declamation. Three times did I compose the first chapter, and twice the second and third, before I was tolerably satisfied with their effect.

Yet, though he testifies that he was "tempted to cast away the labor of seven years,"[53] he also testifies that writing his great history gave him great pleasure. He describes himself as a happy man and attributed much of that felicity to his work; let gloomy sages like Solomon, or the Spanish caliph Abdalrahman, count their happy days few and lament the vanity of this world: "Their expectations are commonly immoderate, their estimates are seldom impartial. If I may speak of myself (the only person for whom I can speak with certainty), *my* happy hours have far exceeded, and far exceed, the scanty number"—fourteen days—"of the caliph of Spain; and I shall not scruple to add that many of them are due to the pleasing labour of the present composition."[54] We have little reason to quarrel with this self-appraisal, for Gibbon so clearly succeeded in doing what he set out to do. His repressions were deep, his symptoms few, his sublimations splendid. "The style of an author," he wrote, "should be the image of his mind,"[55] and he forged his style into exactly that. Yet that style, interposing its highly wrought screen between the writer and the reader, revealed, precisely in the measure that it mirrored his mind, more than he wished it to reveal. His wit, his humor, his irony—scalpels that he wielded with the deftness of the trained surgeon—suggest that his vision, though panoramic in scope, was telescopic in depth. He lacked that oceanic feeling for unmixed motives.

[53] *Autobiography*, p. 173.
[54] Gibbon, *Decline and Fall* [lii], 6:26n.
[55] *Autobiography*, p. 173.

Is it right to conclude, then, that while for this learned gnome, there was much in the past that he saw better than anyone, there was also much in the past that he had no way of seeing? That the question should arise at all is the final irony of Gibbon's history.

2

Ranke

The Respectful Critic

The Dramatist

LATE in Book VII of his *Französische Geschichte*, Ranke approaches a critical moment in French history: the assassination of Henri IV. For scores of pages, Henri IV, one of Ranke's favorite world-historical figures, has dominated his account; now, in 1610, the king is bursting with imaginative plans for France and for the European balance of power. Yet Ranke now stops—*jedoch ich halte inne*: "It is all too easy," he writes,

pondering possibilities, to find oneself in the realm of the improbable; suffice it to say that this prince was filled with great ideas. He fancied that he still saw his star hovering over him, destined to do something marvelous—*Wie leicht ist es, Möglichkeiten erwägend, in das Reich des Unwahrscheinlichen zu geraten! Genug, dass dieser Fürst von grossen Gedanken voll war. Er meinte noch seinen Stern über sich zu sehen und bestimmt zu sein, etwas Wundervolles auszurichten.*[1]

But one of Henri's nightmares was about to come true; a hideous destiny—*ein grässliches Geschick*—emerging from

---

[1] Leopold von Ranke, *Französische Geschichte*, vol. 2, in *Sämmtliche Werke* (1868), 9:107.

dark underground regions, awaited him. Ranke reports the unfolding of that destiny; he characterizes the assassin with a few derisive epithets as a wild uneducated fellow—*ein wilder Mensch ohne Erziehung*—and then speculates about Ravaillac's motives. He opts for religious mania. But he immediately adds that the assassination, though the act of a madman, happened to be a windfall for Henri's mortal enemies, for the Jesuits, the Spaniards, and for dissident French grandees. Having raised this point, Ranke seems to retreat from it; he offers no comment, expresses no opinion. Instead, he tells three stories. The first is about a nun in faraway Normandy who, they say, proclaimed Henri's death at the very hour, but who insisted that she had heard it from the birds in the air. The second reports that Pope Paul V saw the thrust of Ravaillac's knife as a divine chastisement for the king's worldly loves and ambitions. The third sets out the sentiments of the Spaniards in the words of the Cardinal of Toledo, telling the assembled Council of State: "If God is with us, who can be against us?—*Wenn Gott für uns ist, wer ist wider uns?*"[2]

With this complacent, even triumphant, rhetorical question, Ranke brings Book VII of his *History of France* to a close. He sets the next book, "The Regency of the Queen, Maria Medici," into motion with a stark, one-sentence paragraph: "There was one man less in the world—*Ein Mann weniger war in der Welt.*"

The effect is stunning. Ranke has staged a memorable scene in a few tautly written paragraphs; he has individualized the main actors with a handful of choice adjectives; he has aroused grave suspicions about a major power and an august institution with three pointed anecdotes. By ringing down the

[2] Ranke, *Französische Geschichte*, vol. 2, in *Werke*, 9:108–110.

curtain, not with the victim but with the suspected villains, and by ushering in the next act with a tight-lipped, ostentatiously understated reference to the actor who has just left the world stage forever, Ranke has secured for Henri IV the most monumental stature. Just as Hamlet, dead, dominates the closing moments of his play, so Henri, dead, dominates his country as Louis XIII begins his nominal reign.

The stage metaphors I have used in my analysis of this passage are anything but fortuitous. I intend them to underline the point I wish to make. Ranke's modern reputation is rent by conflicting appraisals. The most casual student of historiography knows Ranke as the founder of scientific history. Even those, like some of his English critics, who have thought him bereft of ideas and too much enamored of facts, have drawn the familiar portrait of a cool scientist, only distorting it, slightly, into caricature.[3] Ranke's American admirers, though more inclined to extol his achievement than to read his books, hailed him as the great emancipator who had disentangled history from metaphysics and theology; Herbert Baxter Adams, one of the founders of American graduate training, characteristically called Ranke the "father of scientific history."[4] Popular introductions to the historical discipline have hardened this stereotype: to the reader of history who wants "systematized erudition, inexorable logic, a scientific attention to the arrangement of facts in neat categories," Allan Nevins recommends Ranke.[5] But other currents of opinion have long crisscrossed the map of Ranke's repute: for some historians, Ranke, far from holding ideas at a discount, spoiled his realism with his theology; for others,

---

[3] See Herbert Butterfield, *Man on His Past: The Study of The History of Historical Scholarship* (1955), p. 100.

[4] Georg G. Iggers, *The German Conception of History: The National Tradition of Historical Thought from Herder To the Present* (1968), p. 63.

[5] Allan Nevins, *The Gateway to History* (rev. edn., 1962), p. 42.

he was, precisely as an Idealist, "one of the summits of human achievement";[6] for still others, and their number is increasing, he was an apologist for power, especially German power. It is hard to imagine how Ranke could have been scientist, dramatist, and theologian all at once without ruining the coherence of his work, but this is just what I wish to argue.

The passage with which I began is characteristic of Ranke's style. In more than sixty years of indefatigable scribbling and in more than sixty works, Ranke displayed the gifts we normally associate with storytellers or playwrights: speed, color, variety, freshness of diction, and superb control. He cunningly uses absences; he takes care never to spoil climaxes with elaborate explanations; he establishes his characters with the precision of a novelist. Ranke is an active storyteller in the nineteenth-century German vein; as we hear the author's voice in the tales of Wilhelm Raabe or Gottfried Keller, so we see Ranke unrolling his narrative and arranging his scenery. As Ranke's diaries suggest, these metaphors accurately represent his own sense of his craft; repeatedly, and from his early years on, he returns to the imperative need for form. Nature itself, he notes, strives to produce form, and the works of the mind must strive in the same direction; form alone raises them above the commonplace and the traditional—*Nur durch die Form erheben sie sich über die Menge des Hervorgebrachten.*[7] Form alone, eternal, pure—*die ewige, reine*—grants immortality to the tendencies and conversations making up daily life.[8] Like Goethe, Ranke insists that self-imposed discipline alone brings excellence to all art, to the shaping of all

---

[6] Friedrich Meinecke, "Leopold von Ranke: Gedächtnisrede," January 23, 1936, in Meinecke, *Die Entstehung des Historismus* (edn., 1959), p. 585.
[7] Ranke, *Tagebücher*, ed. Walther Peter Fuchs (1964), p. 158; from the 1830s.
[8] Ranke, *Tagebücher*, p. 180; from the end of the 1830s.

noble writing—*Alle Vortrefflichkeit in der Kunst, alle Bildung eines edlen Stoffs in angemessener Form geht aus der Beschränkung hervor, die sich der Geist selbst setzt.*[9] Significantly, Ranke thinks of the drama as the genre peculiarly qualified to penetrate into the inner man; equally significantly, he wonders whether poetry will outlive prose—*Lebt wohl Poesie länger als Prosa?*[10] In Ranke, the shaping hand of the literary artist is never far from the constructive effort of the historian.

Any of his histories may serve to illustrate Ranke's techniques, for, certainly by the 1830s, his techniques were fully matured. His treatment of Martin Luther in his *Deutsche Geschichte im Zeitalter der Reformation* is particularly instructive, for Luther is one of Ranke's, and one of Protestant Germans', greatest heroes. While Luther is the giant in the tale, his rebellion makes sense to Ranke only against the background of the German Reich around 1500, a realm rent by political, social, and religious disturbances. In Book I, Ranke's *Reformation* is silent on Luther; he looms over its pages like a brooding presence—or, rather, absence—as Ranke concentrates on the politics of the Reich and gradually builds up to a climactic scene of harrowing disorganization. Then Luther steps onto center stage, but not into action, not yet. Luther is so important, his character expands to such vast dimensions, that Ranke feels compelled to devote scores of pages to Luther's early years. There is never anything mechanical about Ranke's allocation of space. It reflects his assessment of the dramatic potential that his material contains.

His *Reformation* gives evidence of another decision, dictated like his allocation of space by dramatic considerations.

[9] Ranke, *Tagebücher*, p. 169; from 1814.
[10] Ranke, *Tagebücher*, p. 180; from the end of the 1830s.

Ranke likes to plant early information he will use later. Long before he recounts the famous proclamation that puts Luther outside the protection of the laws, he analyzes the declining power of the legal device of outlawry; long before he reaches the epoch-making day in October 1517, when Luther nails his theses to the church door at Wittenberg, Ranke analyzes the dubious proliferation of sacraments and the shabby profiteering in indulgences. Then, when he comes to the historic moments themselves, Ranke is free to devote all his space to narration, undistracted by explanation. It is the same tactical reason that made Ranke use certain historical personages less on their own account than as prefigurations. Erasmus plays John the Baptist to Luther, the savior: in Ranke's detailed discussion of Erasmus and of Erasmus' quarrel with the Church, he is rehearsing for a greater figure and an even greater quarrel. Erasmus' noble failure prepares the reader for Luther's still nobler success, and it is Ranke who has so thoughtfully prepared him.

No doubt, Ranke's free employment of dramatic devices places him in the camp of those historians who treat their craft as a branch of the storytelling art. By no means all stories derive their power from suspense; epic and tragedy alike depend on the unfolding of tales whose end is known, while the classic detective story, the murder mystery, usually begins with the end—the murder. But, however accepted the technique, a well-told tale raises problems for all storytellers, including the historian, whose stories must meet the unique requirement of having to be true. We know, after all, that in the imperial election of 1519 it was Charles V of Burgundy who was elected emperor over his competitor Francis I of France. Ranke's account of that election shows the dramatist at work; he enlists the very foreknowledge of his readers to heighten the tension. Ranke refuses to trick them into for-

Leopold von Ranke

getting for a single moment that Charles was victorious; that would have been a cheap and probably ineffective device. Instead, he demonstrates how nearly the outcome might have been different. The counterfactual alternative, Charles' losing the election, is held before the reader's eyes and keeps him interested until Charles' election is a certainty.

Ranke produces his effects not merely by manipulating space and sequences. He achieves them, also, by choosing his words with care and feeling; Ranke's self-effacing ideal of *Selbstauslöschung* certainly does not extend to his adjectives. He describes the Spanish Inquisition early in the sixteenth century as taking the "most terrible—*furchtbarsten*" form. He considers that the prayerbooks written at the height of Mariolatry were "peculiar—*sonderbare*" monuments to a "naïve" and "credulous—*wundergläubig*" devotion. He sees the Catholicism of the age as an odd mixture of "spiritual and worldly power, imagination and arid—*dürre*—scholasticism, tender devotion and coarse—*rohe*—violence, religion and superstition." And he wonders if a "manly . . . religion" could have flourished under such circumstances. Nor does he hesitate to find room for his patriotism in his history: he speaks appreciatively of German honesty—*deutsche Ehrlichkeit*.

The Scientist

To characterize Ranke as a dramatist raises the doubt whether he was a scientist as well. Of course, there is no law holding that a scientist must be unreadable; the giving of pleasure does not in itself compromise the telling of truth. It is worth noting, moreover, that Ranke chose to focus his historical research on the rise of the great powers, the three centuries between the emergence of Martin Luther and the death of Frederick the Great, times of outsize figures and stirring events that it would take some effort to make tedious. Yet Ranke resorts to the dramatic style so consistently that these explanations explain too little. His celebrated commitment to science remains in question.

Ranke's aspiration to become a scientist of the past arose early and, once acquired, never wavered. That aspiration is hard to disentangle from his mystical leanings, his Romantic tastes, his admiration for Fichte's philosophy, none of them calculated to strengthen the vein of empiricism in anyone. The origins of the eminently effective intellectual instrument that Ranke made of himself will occupy us in the rest of this essay. But it is clear that whatever its principal impulses, the methods and results of Ranke's way as a historian were aimed straight at science: the systematizing of research, the withdrawal of ego from presentation, the unremitting effort at objectivity, the submission of results to critical public scrutiny.[11] Ranke's two best-known aphorisms, which have been much quoted and much misunderstood, are in essence appeals to the scientific method. In the preface to his first book, the *Geschichten der Romanischen und Germanischen Völker von 1494 bis 1514*, he repudiated all pretensions to word-painting, and assigned himself a humbler task; he would write history "as it had really been—*wie es eigentlich gewesen.*" It was the modest pronouncement of a scientist intent on doing his work, and on concentrating on what could be reliably known; it was a programmatic declaration in the tradition initiated

[11] See Ranke, *Tagebücher*, p. 233, and related aphorisms of the late 1810s.

by Bacon, exemplified in Newton's famous assertion that he did not feign hypotheses, and transmitted by the Enlightenment—all ancestors, by the way, whom Ranke would have disclaimed. The second aphorism, which Ranke threw out in one of his lectures to King Maximilian of Bavaria, was the affirmation of a professional: the historian must give all ages, all individuals, their due, and see them in their own terms. This, as we will see, is a devout call for empathy, but it is at the same time a call for objectivity, for the separation of the inquirer from his inquiry: "Every epoch is immediate to God, and its value in no way depends on what it has produced, but in its existence itself, in its very self—*Ich aber behaupte, jede Epoche ist unmittelbar zu Gott, und ihr Wert beruht gar nicht auf dem, was aus ihr hervorgeht, sondern in ihrer Existenz selbst, in ihrem eigenen Selbst. . . .*" Ranke's career was an extended commentary on these two sayings, the patient, purposeful working out of a program conceived in his youth. Ranke's professional history is that greatest of rarities, a fully achieved life work.

The life of Ranke the dramatist was, in its externals, singularly undramatic. He was born in 1795 in a small Thuringian town, into a family that had traditionally entered the Lutheran ministry. His parents were deeply religious and were tied as closely to their soil as to their faith. It was an environment—familial, pious, and disciplinarian—against which Ranke never rebelled. Yet he did not enter the ministry, as his parents had wished: the classics, philology, and German literature burgeoning in the midst of the Napoleonic wars interested him more than dogma. He was sure of his religious faith, but it was diffused rather than concentrated. His vocation lay elsewhere. When he obtained his doctorate at the University of Leipzig in 1817, he wrote his dissertation on

Thucydides' political ideas, though this was not a dark hint of great things to come: it was classical philology, not history, that drew Ranke to his topic. His turn to history came later, during the seven years he spent teaching in a *Gymnasium* in Frankfurt an der Oder. Teaching the boys the ancients, Ranke decided that he must know them well: it was the first application of his cardinal principle that thorough knowledge of the sources is, if not everything, the indispensable precondition for everything else. His first book, on the Romanic and Germanic peoples between 1494 and 1514, was published late in 1824. It earned him the recognition he craved—not, perhaps, so much for himself as for his craft, which possessed him more and more. Early in 1825, he was appointed *Ausserordentlicher Professor* of History at the University of Berlin. Though the post did not carry tenure with it, it showed that the *Geschichten der Romanischen und Germanischen Völker* was recognized as an important work; it gave Ranke entrée to stimulating society and influential officials. It gave him, above all, access to the royal library, with its forty-eight volumes of documents crammed with tantalizing materials on the history of Italy, Spain, the papacy, barely touched by anyone. What he called his "archival curiosity"—*archivalische Neugier*[12] which we might just as well call "archival greed," or "archival obsession"—had been aroused earlier, in Frankfurt, only to be frustrated. In Berlin it was gratified, only to be whetted further. The result, his second book, on the Ottomans and the Spanish monarchy, induced the Prussian government to give Ranke extended leave to study the famous *relazioni* of the Venetian ambassadors. These secret reports, submitted to their government over three centuries by those brilliant

---

[12] To Ferdinand Ranke (August 31, 1839), in *Neue Briefe*, ed. Bernhard Hoeft and Hans Herzfeld (1949), p. 268.

accredited spies, politely called "ambassadors," were copious, candid, highly personal yet beautifully informed. I have called them famous, but it was Ranke who made them so—no historian had touched them before. The use he made of these documents constituted more than the exploitation of unfamiliar historical material; it was the application of an unfamiliar historical method.

Ranke went on his leave late in 1827. He remained abroad for over three years, hunting documents in Vienna, in Florence, in Rome, in Venice. He had good connections and he used them to good purpose, securing access to archives that had been kept locked before. He was patient, tenacious, diplomatic. His letters to his brothers and to Karl Freiherr vom Stein zum Altenstein, the Prussian minister of education, read like the diary of a discoverer; Ranke poured into them his tension, his pleasure, his pride at being the first to see what had so long been concealed or neglected. Aptly enough, he likened himself to Columbus,[13] but his triumphs were as much the fruit of a pedant's diligence as of a conquistador's boldness. Up early, he would spend the best hours of the day in the archives, showing copyists the documents he wanted, and moving on, reading, finding new treasures, day after day.

His long searches in Italy set the pattern for later leaves of absence; he punctuated his teaching with research trips to London, to Paris, to Brussels, to The Hague, often lasting many months. For a short time after his return to Prussia, he toyed with politics: late in 1831, he became editor of a semiofficial—which is to say, moderately conservative—political journal, the *Historisch-Politische Zeitschrift*. In the four years

---

[13] See Theodore von Laue, *Leopold Ranke: The Formative Years* (1950), p. 34.

of its tenuous existence, Ranke supplied it with most of its copy, including his instructive essay on the great powers. But, fascinating—and useful—as he found present politics, it was past politics that would give shape to his long life. When he was appointed *Ordentlicher Professor* at the University of Berlin in 1834, his course was set, and he followed it without deviations for over half a century. Even after his retirement in 1871, he continued to exert his influence and widen his fame. Once settled in a post of high prestige and good pay, his ties to the Prussian state became closer, his ties to his brothers remained close, and his ties to other men relaxed, as he wrote and traveled and taught his celebrated seminars. He did not marry until 1843, when he was forty-eight, and though he was an attentive husband and affectionate father, his family life appears as a pleasing restful interlude that helped him to replenish his seemingly inexhaustible energies. He lived on until 1886, past his ninetieth year, his intellectual powers near their peak to the end, a lifelong monk in the historical order—or, perhaps more to my point, a lifelong technician in its laboratory.

The uniform, almost monotonous curve of Ranke's external existence documents his devotion to the science of history. That his greatest works should now be dated is a tribute to the exacting vocation he helped to transform. Ranke recognized that history is a progressive discipline. He claimed, after all, that his own work was superior to that of his predecessors; it was hardly strange that the unearthing of new documents, or the application of auxiliary techniques which, as it were, create new documents, should allow lesser practitioners, fortunate to be born after him, to write histories superior to his. It is a familiar fact, he noted in the 1840s, that history is always being rewritten. The only way to reduce this persistent need for revision is to return to the most pristine sources—*Rückkehr zu der ursprünglichsten Mitteilung*, and thus rise to pure perception—*sich zu reiner Anschauung zu erheben*.[14] Ranke was often amazed to find and pleased to record how much of their past other countries and other craftsmen allowed him to discover; how many documents he was the first to read; how many events he was the first to interpret, or, at least, the first to interpret on any sound factual foundation. Ranke, who did so much to set the heavy train of history into motion, would have been neither surprised nor displeased to see it disappear beyond his horizon. But had someone told him that it would use other locomotives than his, he would not have believed him. Ranke could never have imagined that there were ways of reading documents not dreamt of in his philosophy of history.

Ranke's contribution to historical science, then, lay in his exalted view of documents. This was less a matter of technical innovation than of personal style. He applied, consistently and on a large scale, what earlier scholars had confined to specialized subjects, and used for narrowly defined purposes. Probably it is the French Benedictine Jean Mabillon who has the best claim to be the father of the scientific study of documents; his *De re diplomatica* of 1681 has never been superseded. In Germany, a distinguished group of eighteenth-century scholars, centered at the University of Göttingen, applied the most minute attention to the authentication of past records; in 1788, one of the group found it possible to

[14] Ranke, *Tagebücher*, p. 241; from the 1840s. The idea of *Anschauung* will recur in Burckhardt—very prominently; see below, pp. 176–179.

be rather patronizing to Gibbon for his relative naïveté about the sources.[15] And in Ranke's own day, Barthold Georg Niebuhr wielded source criticism to penetrate the veil of legend behind which the history of the early Roman Republic moved in barely recognizable form. Ranke, who greatly admired Niebuhr, generalized these practices into a principle. That principle was the unique, privileged status of the contemporary document; it alone held the key to historical truth. The time will come, he prophesied in the preface to his *Reformation*, when historians will no longer write modern history from derivative treatments or even from contemporary historians—except insofar as these had direct knowledge—but will depend wholly on the reports of eyewitnesses, and on the most authentic, most immediate sources—*Ich sehe die Zeit kommen, wo wir die neuere Geschichte nicht mehr auf die Berichte, selbst nicht der gleichzeitigen Historiker, ausser insoweit ihnen eine originale Kenntnis beiwohnte, geschweige denn auf die weiter abgeleiteten Bearbeitungen zu gründen haben, sondern aus den Relationen der Augenzeugen und den echtesten, unmittelbarsten Urkunden aufbauen werden.*[16] Ranke shaped his prefaces into the record of his documentary researches; they are enthusiastic travel reports by a traveler who visited, not city after city, but library after library. In his second book, on Ottoman-Spanish relations in the sixteenth and seventeenth centuries, published in 1827, he notes with evident pride that, had he been compelled to depend on history books, even on those that were relatively well documented—*urkundlicheren*—he would not have written his ac-

---

[15] See Arnaldo D. Momigliano, "Gibbon's Contribution to Historical Method," (1954), in Momigliano, *Studies in Historiography* (1966), pp. 40–55.

[16] Leopold von Ranke, *Deutsche Geschichte im Zeitalter der Reformation*, vol. 1, in *Werke* (1873), 1:ix–x.

count. Fortunately, he had found other aids, often extremely valuable yet still unknown—*Hilfsmittel, oft von ausgezeichnetem Wert und doch noch unbekannt*—the Venetian *relazioni*.[17] Collected together with other despatches and letters and placed into the Venetian state archives, these reports had later come a little mysteriously on the international market; some of them had ended up in the royal library at Berlin, others in the ducal library at Gotha. Ranke had examined them all, delighting in their informativeness and mourning their incompleteness: *Wären nur niemals Lücken darin!* In the midst of wealth, Ranke felt poor—*mitten in dem Reichtum fühlen wir uns arm*—yet still rich enough to travel confidently among events now three centuries in the past.[18]

It was from this perspective—the sole authority of the immediate—that Ranke launched, at the very beginning of his career, into an aggressive critique of those among his predecessors who had written histories out of other histories, crediting partial and passionate chroniclers like Guicciardini with a historian's detachment, and falsely assigning their writings the status of a document. Ranke certainly would have taken Tacitus not as an authority to be followed but as a witness to be interrogated. In the light of the later charge that he was an ideologist for Germany—a charge to which I will return—it is instructive to note that his first and most consistent German critics were the so-called "political" historians, nationalistic and partisan scholars who wanted to propel the historical profession into an active part in the

---

[17] Leopold von Ranke, *Fürsten und Völker von Südeuropa* (fourth, enlarged edition of *Die Osmanen und die Spanische Monarchie im 16. und 17. Jahrhundert*, 1877), in *Werke*, 35:v–vi. See above, pp. 70–71.
[18] Ranke, *Fürsten und Völker*, in *Werke*, 35:xii.

unification of Germany and the glorification of her stature. To these enthusiasts—Droysen, Sybel, Treitschke, and others —Ranke's famous objectivity was excessive, downright irresponsible. However we judge the indictments brought by his critics, however we appraise his objectivity, it is certain that Ranke at least took science seriously. He did not become the accomplished writer he became to compromise, or merely to decorate, that science. If he was indeed a formidable dramatist, the sources of his commitment to style cannot be literary alone; they go to the heart of his vocation as a historian.

The Believer

RECOUNTING the bloody massacre of French Huguenots in August 1572, Ranke places the responsibility for the crime directly at the door of Catherine de Medici. She acceded to the scheme of the ruling clique to ruin the Protestant party; she did her utmost to lure as many Huguenots to Paris as possible; she was aware that however many would come, the fanatical, easily roused and well-organized Parisian populace would be superior to them; she awakened in her miserable son, Charles IX, all the fanaticism slumbering within him; she spoke the word that called the people to arms; she insisted that she had wanted only six persons killed, and would take only their deaths on her conscience, but actually some 50,000 were slaughtered—*Katharina hat gesagt, sie habe nur sechs Menschen umzubringen gewünscht; nur deren Tod nehme sie auf ihr Gewissen;—es sind bei 50,000 umgebracht worden.*[19] The cadences have the efficient rhythm of sober reportage; Ranke keeps his sentences short or breaks up his longer sentences with emphatic semicolons. The events themselves, it would seem, are extraordinary enough to pronounce judgment on the perpetrators of the St. Bartholomew's Day massacre. But then Ranke's tone changes. The plot seemed to have fulfilled its purpose: the Huguenot leadership had been decimated, while Catholic princes, lay and ecclesiastical, sent their congratulations to the triumphant Catherine and to her puppet, her son. And yet, Ranke muses, can such murderous actions ever truly succeed? Do they not contradict the deepest mystery of human affairs, the incomprehensible, innermost, inviolable principle of the eternal world order? Men can deceive themselves; they cannot shake the laws of the spiritual world order on which their existence rests. That order, which rules the course of the stars, governs all existence —*Können aber wohl Attentate von so blutiger Natur jemals gelingen? Widerstreiten sie nicht dem tieferen Geheimnis der menschlichen Dinge, den unbegriffenen, in dem Innern wirksamen, unverletzlichen Prinzipien der ewigen Weltordnung? Die Menschen können sich verblenden; das Gesetz der geistigen Weltordnung, auf dem ihr Dasein beruht, können sie nicht erschüttern. Mit der Notwendigkeit beherrscht es sie, die den Gang der Gestirne regelt.*[20] Without missing a step, without uttering a false note, Ranke the historian has become Ranke the believer.

The work from which I have been quoting was published

---

[19] Leopold von Ranke, *Die Römischen Päpste in den letzen vier Jahrhunderten*, vol. 2, in *Werke* (1878), 38:44–45.

[20] Ranke, *Die Römischen Päpste*, vol. 2, in *Werke*, 38:45. See Ranke, *Tagebücher*, pp. 119–120; from the late 1830s.

between 1834 and 1836; from the long vista of Ranke's productive life, it was a relatively young man's book. It was also one of his most widely read works, and its style doubtless contributed to its popularity. Macaulay, greeting a fine English translation of the *Päpste* in 1840, noted that Ranke's original version was "known and esteemed wherever German literature is studied."[21] While in Ranke's greatest works— the histories of the German Reformation, of France and of England, which occupied him from the late 1830s to the late 1860s—the pious asides are rarer than they are in the *Päpste*, the emotional religious substratum is the same. Ranke lacks the fervor of the preacher, whether it is the patriotic exaltation of a Treitschke or the prophetic anxiety of a Burckhardt. The music of Ranke's style is lyrical; he strives for breadth and for smoothness. Even the one-sentence paragraph, one of his trademarks, with which he likes to punctuate his more expansive exposition, serves not to interrupt but to speed his narrative. Like Gibbon, Ranke maintains distance from his materials, but unlike Gibbon, Ranke uses few tense antitheses, little if any biting humor; his distance is not that of the ironist but that of the Olympian. He writes dramas of action, yet their surfaces are unruffled. However baroque the events he is chronicling, Ranke's impulse is classicizing. He liked to reflect on man's calm dwelling in the higher elements—*ruhiges Dasein in dem höhern Elemente, in dem wir sind*—on the golden middle way akin to Horace's *aurea mediocritas*—*ein idealer Schwung der Mehrzahl, der Mittelmässigkeit.*[22] In the same review in which Macaulay remarks

---

[21] Thomas Babington Macaulay, "Ranke's History of the Popes," *The Works of Lord Macaulay*, 2nd edn., ed. Lady Trevelyan, 8 vols. (1871), 6:454.
[22] Ranke, *Tagebücher*, p. 159; from the late 1830s.

upon the prominence of Ranke's *Päpste* in German literature, he also notes its "admirable spirit, equally remote from levity and bigotry; serious and earnest, yet tolerant and impartial."[23] Ranke's religiosity, in a word, like his style, is serene. He has his moments of exaltation, though he reserves these for his letters, normally to his most intimate confidant, his brother Heinrich. Yet even that exaltation has something rather complacent about it.

The relevance of Ranke's religion to Ranke's history is not a new discovery; his readers have observed it for a century. Yet its workings deserve still closer definition. Ranke's religiosity was at once cultural and personal. Ranke was, in many ways, a characteristic product of his time and place. As a good German Protestant, he saw no conflict between science and religion; if anything, for him science had religious grounding. To speak of Ranke as a pious scientist is, therefore, to speak not metaphorically but literally. But the precise quality of his religion was very much his own. It was, as I have already said, a matter of experience, not theological so much as, in the highest sense of the word, vocational. God has composed an eternal poem, and it is the historian's task to read and to translate it.[24] Ranke had no use for the "lazy" separation of knowledge and belief; belief is a lower form of knowledge, and knowledge leads to belief; scholarship thus has religious justification.[25] Ignorance, he noted in the late 1830s, is original sin; insight alone is blessedness—*Ich denke noch immer: Unwissenheit ist auch Erbsünde. . . . Seligkeit bestünde in der Fülle der Einsicht.*[26] Because God is in man, and man in

---

[23] Macaulay, "Ranke's History of the Popes," *Works*, 6:454.
[24] Ranke, *Tagebücher*, p. 105; from 1818–1824; for parallel ways of thinking, see Burckhardt, below, p. 181.
[25] Ranke, *Tagebücher*, p. 111; from 1816–1817.
[26] Ranke, *Tagebücher*, p. 127; from after 1836.

God, the knowledge that man carries in his heart speaks to us of God's life within us—*Was sagt denn das Wissen im Herzen? Es redet von dem Leben Gottes in uns.*[27] It is not surprising, then, that Ranke can dispense with traditional Christian doctrines; man's life on this earth is in itself a religious event. He explicitly notes that he would prize the divine *Logos* even more highly if there were no miracles—*er wäre mir noch lieber ohne die Wunder.*[28]

In these reflections, Ranke commits the blasphemy of seeing the historian himself as divine. God alone truly rules—*nur Gott regiert*; but, Ranke adds, the writer, the teacher, reigns too, as long as the world accepts his views; it will reject them if they are not truthful, or arbitrary, not founded in God, in the divine on earth—*Es ist der Schriftsteller, der Lehrer nur insofern mächtig, als er die Wahrheit sagt. Er regiert ebenfalls, insofern die Welt seine Meinungen annimmt. Aber sie wird dieselben nicht annehmen, wenn sie sich erst der Wahrheit enthalten, wenn sie willkürlich sind, nicht in Gott, d.h. dem Göttlichen auf Erden gegründet.*[29] This is not the defiance of a young rebel, but the rumination of a mature scholar; the entry is dated December 21, 1850, when Ranke was fifty-five.

In fact, Ranke's sense of his craft bears a striking resemblance to the position that literary critics from Matthew Arnold to Oscar Wilde were developing in these years, almost, if not quite, seriously: criticism outranks creation. Just as the painter paints and the novelist writes so that the critic has something on which to exercise his discrimination, so a Cromwell or a Napoleon changes the world so that a Ranke can discover *wie es eigentlich gewesen*. It was this self-esteem that

---

[27] Ranke, *Tagebücher*, p. 154; from 1817.
[28] Ranke, *Tagebücher*, p. 122; from the 1830s.
[29] Ranke, *Tagebücher*, pp. 132–133.

enabled the aged Ranke to say, with a perfectly straight face, that Prince Metternich had won for himself immortal merit by following Gentz's advice and giving him—Ranke—access to the archives—*Fürst Metternich hat ein unsterbliches Verdienst erworben, dass er mir auf den Rat des geistvollen Gentz die Erlaubnis zur Benutzung des Archives gab.*[30] In Ranke, at once historian and believer, humility and pride are happily combined; like others who have thought themselves the lowly instrument of a higher being, Ranke did not fail to borrow some of the prestige from the divinity whose servant he professed himself to be.

At the heart of Ranke's conception of his work, then, is the idea of service. Whatever the unconscious impulses behind it, its consequences are unremitting labor and, at least in the early stages, its dark companion, solitude. Ranke speaks of his loneliness in touching letters to his brothers, into which he pours his thirst for intimacy. "I live," he told his brother Heinrich in late 1820 from Frankfurt an der Oder, "not especially well, not especially badly, without happiness or misery, without love and friendship, without failure, without success; like an intermundane god of Epicurus' and like a Stoic soul." He confesses that he is one of those whose "whole passion is study." Then, for a moment, doubt clouds his self-assurance: is his consuming desire to make something excellent or, at the very least, to aim at excellence, a truly religious impulse? "Is that worldly? you ask, Is there really anything worldly in this world, anything Godless?"[31] Later, in Berlin

---

[30] Autobiographical dictation of November 1885, in *Werke* (1890), 53–54:63; see von Laue, *Ranke*, p. 35n.

[31] November 1820, in *Das Briefwerk*, ed. Walther Peter Fuchs (1949), p. 24. Ranke's diary jottings, especially those of his early years, reveal a persistent, nagging concern with "selfishness" and a prayerful wish to wipe out *Selbstsucht* through the practice of historical scholarship. See, for one instance, Ranke, *Tagebücher*, p. 59; from 1816–1817.

salons, and in his intimacy with his students in whom he took paternal pride, the loneliness receded. But the labor went on, and his social connections increasingly reflected the requirements of his craft. His intimates were men in high office, not men of letters; men who in some way might help him. This was not self-seeking on his part; he was, after all, not serving himself. "We must adjust ourselves," he wrote with sublime naïveté to his brother Heinrich in 1824, "to conditions prevailing even in the scholarly world."[32] The "Instrument of History" needed instruments of his own.

His devotion to service sounds an unvarying refrain in his letters. In March 1820 he tells his brother Heinrich that to grasp historical events superficially is to make men miserable, their life flat, their thinking rigid: "God dwells, lives, is manifest in all history. Every act gives witness of him, every moment preaches his name, but most of all, I think, in the great connections of history. There he stands, like a holy hieroglyphic."[33] What good servant can rest while the divine script remains undeciphered? Normally, the motto a man chooses reflects a genealogist's ingenuity; the motto that Ranke adopted, *labor ipse voluptas*, was literally true. The *voluptas* that his labor brought him was only rarely infected with self-questioning. In 1824, he confessed to Heinrich that he thought his first book woefully incomplete: "One thing is certain, I was born for study, and I am no good for anything else in the world; on the other hand, it is not certain whether I was born for the study of history." But he immediately shakes it off: "I have chosen it, and live in it, and it makes

[32] February 18, 1824, in *Briefwerk*, p. 54.
[33] End of March 1820, in *Briefwerk*, p. 18. This letter is justly famous; Pieter Geyl quotes, "Ranke in the Light of the Catastrophe," in Geyl, *Debates with Historians* (1955), p. 7; see also von Laue, *Ranke*, p. 42.

my soul feel blissful, contented, and gay."[34] For Ranke, doubt is passing and bliss lasting, for the joys of history are endless.

And, I repeat, they are in essence religious: Ranke did not presume to understand God and history directly—"No," he told Heinrich late in 1820, "not to understand God, but in sensing him to understand the rest." And in the same letter, in a beautiful metaphor, he translated Plato's theory of knowledge into Christian vocabulary: man's most persistent complaint, really his sole complaint, is that he forgets, that he knows nothing of his former life. "All teaching is but remembering, a legend of God from the present and the past—*Das Lehren all ist ein Erinnern, eine Legende Gottes aus der Gegenwart und der Zeit.*"[35] Persistently he claimed that he had not sought to be that teacher; as Ranke told his brother Heinrich in 1832, it was a compelling duty to which he was not equal but which he could not shirk—*Pflicht ist Pflicht. Müssen: müssen. Was will man da lange machen?* He could live blissfully doing history, this hard but splendid profession —*diesem so schweren, aber so grossem Berufe.* "It is a higher calling," he repeated, "We do not seek it out, it comes to us—*Es ist ein höherer Beruf. Man sucht es nicht, es kommt uns.*"[36]

Worldly success therefore counts only as it promotes the divine plan for the individual: pinched for money, short of time, and far from influence, the young Ranke still declared himself willing to remain without tenure forever, if only he could serve Clio. But he conceded that one could serve her better occupying a university chair. Writing to his favorite

[34] February 18, 1824, in *Briefwerk*, p. 53.
[35] (December 23, 1820), in *Neue Briefe*, pp. 17–18.
[36] (End of April 1832), in *Neue Briefe*, pp. 170–171.

brother in December 1833, Ranke announces the government's promise of promotion to a full professorship in Berlin, and a sizable increase in salary, and adds: "I have just sent the same news to our dear old parents and wept out loud as I fully visualized the gracious care of God for us all, and the merciful hand he has extended over us all. . . . All ambition falls away, like a discarded coat; I declare that I need nothing else on earth. . . ."[37] He needs nothing because now he is truly the instrument of providence. This, he told his brother Ferdinand from Paris in 1843, is not *hubris*: "What would providence be if it did not care for the individual too! That we are thought by an eternal thought, not transitory like the falling leaf of autumn, that we belong to the essence of things—that is the sum of all religion."[38] It was, in any event, the sum of Ranke's religion—sincerely felt, consistently heartening, and totally convenient.

In his formal prose, Ranke struck this note a little more softly, but, though subdued, it was there, and unmistakably the same. Ranke, the supreme embodiment of the Protestant ethic was not an uncomplicated Lutheran, but a philosophical mind who had been touched by the mystical hand of Neoplatonism. His religion was the precipitate of wide reading and vague thinking. But whatever its shortcomings as theology, it impelled him, in his historical work, to relentless labor.

For Ranke, religion was more than a motive for the historian, it was also a key to history. In large and in small, history

[37] *Neue Briefe*, p. 184.
[38] July 30 (1843), in *Neue Briefe*, p. 299.

exemplifies divine work. While Ranke saw the overarching processes of world history as the noblest expression of the divine intent, he thought, at the same time, that this symphonic whole was composed of an immense number of subsidiary themes. The particular is a mirror, a worthy miniature, of the universal. In the progression of his historical writings, Ranke exhibited his organic vision almost as if by design: he began with the study of single areas like the Ottomans in Spain, or the German Reformation; he continued with comprehensive histories of great states; he concluded his career with universal history. That last effort, the *Weltgeschichte*, was cut off in the Middle Ages, by his death. Its six volumes are his monument; in the preface, he reiterates what he had said so often before: world history is the capstone of national history. The divine scheme realizes itself by and large through nations or states, but in that great international conflict we call history, the universal element is always implicit: "Great nations and states," he wrote, "have a double vocation, national and world-historical."[39]

Because God works both through the universal and the particular, each epoch, each act has its own dignity. This is the religious source of what I have called Ranke's professional affirmation that "every epoch is immediate to God."[40] This dictum, which is the single most important pronouncement in the historicist school, consummates the nineteenth-century rebellion against the historiography of the Enlightenment. It is the final repudiation of the antique doctrine that all disciplines, including history, have an explicit ethical end. The

[39] Ranke, *Französische Geschichte*, vol. 1, in *Werke*, 8:v.
[40] See above, p. 69. For a searching, if excessively sympathetic, analysis of this famous remark of 1854, see Friedrich Meinecke, "Deutung eines Rankewortes," in *Aphorismen und Skizzen zur Geschichte*, 2nd edn. (n.d.), pp. 100–129.

historian does not praise or condemn; he seeks only to understand—to understand from within, by adopting standards of the period under study.[41] In religious terms, this is an invitation to give each epoch its chance of immortality; Meinecke called this a Christian demand. This injunction had far-reaching professional reverberations because it called upon all historians to cast aside private prejudices and to rise above their position in class and time. History, Ranke once noted, is present to the historian as he studies it; yet it is not the past as present, but the past as past that is his proper concern —*nicht auf diese gegenwärtige Vergangenheit, sondern auf die Vergangenheit als die vergangene ist es dem Menschen gemäss sich zu richten.*[42] Ranke wrote these words as a young man, in 1814, but his work was a lifelong assault on present-mindedness, in particular on the Whig view of history, in which liberals appear as good and conservatives as wicked, and religious men as either superstitious, or crafty, or stupid. If Ranke for his part did not quite succeed in overcoming the Tory interpretation of history, his religious ideal for the historian allowed the profession to do so.

Moreover, Ranke's theology of history demands the most scrupulous pursuit of the truth. I have already spoken of Ranke's obsession with archives. Historians must generalize—without that history is dry chronicle. But they must base their generalizations on the most intimate knowledge of all possible detail. Again and again in Ranke's life we see the cheerful

---

[41] I have argued elsewhere that despite the charges of historicists against philosophes, the philosophic historians of the eighteenth-century Enlightenment recognized the need to see the past through its own eyes, even though the practice of Voltaire and Gibbon and Hume often left something to be desired in this regard. But then so did the practice of the historicists. See Peter Gay, *The Enlightenment: An Interpretation*, vol. 2, *The Science of Freedom* (1969), pp. 368–396.

[42] Ranke, *Tagebücher*, p. 109.

revisionist at work exposing ignorance and battling prejudice. There is Ranke in 1827 asking the publisher of his second book to return the final draft of his manuscript because he has found a document that requires him to revise a chapter.[43] There are his reports from Italy, ravenous with his desire to master everything and get everything right.[44] There is his willingness to be guided by his materials; in 1830 he writes that he has spent three months in Florence collecting "excellent material" on the Medicis, which might add up to a handsome half-volume.[45] There is, above all, the probity with which he visits *all* the archives, for he knows that diplomats lie to their masters as well as to their counterparts.[46]

While Ranke saw religion as being of critical importance for the historian and for history alike, the principal agent in world history is, in his view, political power. To be sure, Ranke the pious servant was no stranger to the advantages of worldly power; as he once put it, he found it a source of deep happiness to be able to work within a state he could respect. But whatever the place of power in Ranke's own situation, in history, he insisted, power did not have things all its own way. While history stood under its sign, it was shaped also, and significantly, by the ideal of service. Only in school or in literature, he writes, can we keep church history separate from political history; in life they are intertwined at every moment —*in dem lebendigen Dasein sind sie jeden Augenblick verbunden und durchdringen einander.*[47] The European state

---

[43] To Friedrich and Heinrich Brockhaus, January 17, 1827, in *Neue Briefe*, p. 94.

[44] To Heinrich Ritter (August 1, 1829), in *Neue Briefe*, pp. 125–126.

[45] To Friedrich Perthes (August 12, 1830), in *Neue Briefe*, p. 137.

[46] To Fürst zu Sayn-Wittgenstein and Johann Friedrich Ancillon, October 27, 1836, in *Neue Briefe*, p. 228.

[47] *Reformation*, vol. 1, in *Werke*, 1:3.

system has embodied this interpenetration for many centuries; the state of warriors and priests—*der kriegerisch-priestliche Staat*—first arose in the eighth century,[48] and world-shaking events like Martin Luther's rebellion stand as visible symbols of their intimacy and their tension.

In Ranke's scheme of things, the relation of power to religion is not merely one of coexistence or even of cooperation. There are times when it rises to identity. After all, power can happily claim the same exalted origins as service: God's will. The family demonstrates how power can be exercised within the matrix of divine justice. In some striking metaphors, Ranke projects his loyalty to the institution of the family, with its dominant and loving paterfamilias, onto society, organized into hierarchies of authorities and subjects, and onto the universe, governed by its all-powerful, all-creative, and all-loving God. The hierarchical family is Ranke's master image, sometimes explicit, often implicit. In the good state, as in the good family, the two poles of power and service coincide; service works to advance power and power exists to make service effective. Ranke saw all manifestations of power large and small as expressions of divine activity in the historical world. The creative statesman, the state, and the world-historical interplay of all forces, are so many sparks from the divine flint.

In this optimistic vision, all tragedy dissolves; for Ranke, power is rarely problematical. It is not simply that Ranke concentrates on the good that power can do and pushes the evil out of sight; more important, he actually sees the evil as an instrument of the good. The divinely created historical mechanism is in the long run self-regulating; crime and cruelty play the role that Goethe's Mephistopheles found

[48] *Reformation*, vol. 1, in *Werke*, 1:5.

himself compelled to play: wishing to do evil, he does good. War, mendacious diplomacy, ruthless politics all are God's experiments for solving the world's riddles; they are so many divine muscle exercises. Not even Ranke's own side, Protestantism and conservatism, ought to live exempt from battle; the good comes from the battle itself, as well as from its preordained outcome. In 1872, countering the pessimism of his conservative friends who saw the world they knew coming to an end in universal conflict, Ranke suggested that each needs his enemy, and bad intentions will find their correction within themselves—*die falschen Intentionen werden ein Korrektiv in sich selbst finden.*[49] Ranke does not glorify brutality, and he expects that wickedness, like the St. Bartholomew's Day massacre, will be punished. But above all, he treats such things as parts of a drama, and a drama, by its very nature, demands resolutions.

In his last years, Ranke saw such resolutions at hand everywhere. He was thoroughly aware that he was living through an age of revolutions; his persistent, even passionate preoccupation with the politics and diplomacy of his own time provided him with the kind of insight he found invaluable in his historical work. But while he thought struggle inevitable and in fact indispensable, he thought it far from endless. His very last undertaking, the world history, reflected his confidence in the ultimate triumph of the forces of order; without that, he said, he would not have undertaken so vast a project. Liberalism, he conceded, has its place in the general dialectical scheme: it goads statesmen, it calls their attention to wrongs needing correction. But its proper function was opposition; whatever its form—popular sovereignty, liberalism, or socialist radicalism—it was at heart negative, at worst destructive, and

[49] Ranke, *Tagebücher*, p. 413; from December 31, 1872.

did not deserve to rule. The two essential foundations of the best form of government, the monarchical state, Ranke reflected in 1871, are finances and the army. To subject these two to the caprices of a deliberative body would be to surrender the sound and tested principles of good government: "Everything we have achieved in the last few years has rested on these elements."[50]

Power, then, is the march of God through the world. This is one reason why most of Ranke's writings deal with critical moments in political history, and with the centuries when the modern state took its characteristic form. In France, England, Prussia, Ranke could trace the decisive clash between centralizing institutions and feudal privileges. The clash differed from state to state, a difference for which Ranke's individualizing perception had prepared him well. But the historical function of that clash was everywhere the same: to find a way of controlling territories large enough to command adequate natural and human resources, and a proper balance in a network of competing states. And this, too, is why Ranke concentrated his attention not merely on the state but on the *large* state. It was the age of the great powers, and Ranke wrote their history in the confident conviction that he was concentrating on the main theme. The important powers were important quite simply because they were important. Ranke's God was bored by losers.

In recent decades, the baneful consequences of such complacency have received intense study and hostile comment.

[50] To Edwin Freiherr von Manteuffel (before September 10, 1871); in *Neue Briefe*, 561.

Ranke: *The Respectful Critic*

After the Nazi catastrophe, it induced even so devout a Rankean as Friedrich Meinecke to declare Burckhardt's moral vision superior to the sunny acceptance that characterized the writings of his master. This much is undeniable: Ranke blandly affirmed the powers that be; he adroitly fitted treaty breaking, illegal invasions, economic warfare into God's scheme for man; he threw the mantle of spiritual respectability over terrible men and terrible deeds. Ranke's philosophy of history induced him to forgive the unforgivable.[51] But more damaging than his much-criticized refusal to judge was his less widely noticed readiness to judge. Behind the screen of scientific objectivity, Ranke made definite political choices. He preferred the power of the German monarchy to the power of the German Socialist movement. Thus he found his most earnest injunction to treat all historical forces with an even hand quite impossible to carry out: in Ranke's scheme, Bismarck was obviously more immediate to God than Bebel.

It would be a mistake to treat this set of biases as a mere accident or aberration. I would argue instead that Ranke's piety forced him in this direction, both by preventing him from gaining distance on his cherished political convictions through cool critical inspection, and by predisposing him to prefer the powerful to the powerless. In Ranke's religion, the first shall be first. Thus, ultimately, Ranke's deepest impulse,

---

[51] Foreign critics, especially after the Nazi tyranny, have made this charge often; Pieter Geyl's essay (*Debates With Historians*, pp. 1–18) is a splendid and fair-minded instance of such criticisms. But even Germans, reevaluating their past, have taken a new and critical look at Ranke. See especially Hans-Heinz Krill, *Die Ranke Renaissance: Max Lenz und Erich Marcks* (1962); while Krill concentrates his fire on two of Ranke's best-known disciples, many of his bullets hit the master quite directly. Even Friedrich Meinecke, Ranke's most enthusiastic supporter in the German historical guild, found the Nazi catastrophe shedding a new and somewhat harsher light on the historian he admired more than anyone else. See "Ranke und Burckhardt," in *Aphorismen und Skizzen zur Geschichte*, pp. 143–180.

which was the source of his greatest work, was the source also of his most crippling defect.

These are deep waters, I know. After all, all angles of vision are open to bias; precisely as an atheist, an atheist can write one-sided history just as much as a Christian. The history of history assumes the prevalence of perspectives, whether it is a German historian underestimating the merits of France, a bourgeois historian the maturity of the proletariat, a male historian the intelligence of women. But Ranke was peculiarly vulnerable. Early in the 1840s, he noted that the historian needs three cardinal qualities, common sense, courage, and honesty; the first, to grasp things at all; the second, not to become frightened at what he sees; the third, not to fall into self-deception; in short, the simplest moral qualities govern science as well—*Etwas zu machen, dazu gehört dreierlei: gesunder Menschenverstand, Mut und Redlichkeit. Der erste, um nur die Sache einzusehn, der zweite, um vor den Resultaten nicht zu erschrecken, der dritte, um sich nicht selber etwas vorzumachen. So dass die einfachsten moralischen Eigenschaften auch die Wissenschaft beherrschen.*[52] But precisely because Ranke knew he had science and tirelessly strove for objectivity, precisely because he had strong reasons to believe that he was not deceiving himself, he was particularly susceptible to self-deception. It is true that Ranke, publishing immensely, subjected himself to the public forum in which alone self-deception can be detected and corrected—the judgment of his professional peers. But the shape of the German historical profession was such that the criticism he got he could not use, and the criticism he could have used he did not get.

[52] Ranke, *Tagebücher*, p. 240; from the early 1840s.

Ranke has sometimes been charged with ignoring the social dimension of history, those realities of technology and economics, of mass politics and mass communications, that were transforming the world in Ranke's lifetime and that should, in retrospect, have deepened his analysis of the past. In a few scattered notebook jottings, Ranke in fact suggests the tantalizing prospect that he was playing with social history. He professes himself interested in population, classes, and games, and he hints that the task of history might well be to describe the rise of all elements—*Das wäre nun die Aufgabe einer Geschichte, das allmähliche Emporkommen aller Elemente zu schildern.*[53] But his practice was less comprehensive. Certainly, in view of the broadsides and popular songs that Macaulay was freely using in his *History of England,* the sexual mores and public festivals that Burckhardt thought suitable for cultural history, Ranke's conception of society was narrow. The cast of his characters was like a neoclassical tragedy, with the speaking parts almost exclusively reserved to the higher orders. But Ranke did not so much ignore the social world as distort it, by subjecting conflict to the pathos of reconciliation. Even the "social movement," which he saw all about him from the 1830s on, negative as it seemed to him, was destined in Ranke's mind to be assimilated into an ever-growing social order.[54] Ranke was nothing if not a consensus historian. His

---

[53] Ranke, *Tagebücher,* p. 323; from 1843. See also the important entry in the same work (pp. 239–40) from the 1830s. Rudolf Vierhaus has explored the question in detail in his *Ranke und die soziale Welt* (1957), which includes some hitherto unpublished notes from Ranke's *Nachlass.* Significantly, Burckhardt argued that the totality of perception that Ranke's writings seemed to offer at first glance was in fact an illusion—*die Totalität der Anschauung, die seine Schriften bei dem ersten Anblick zu geben scheinen, ist illusorisch.* Burckhardt to Heinrich Schreiber, October 2, 1842; *Briefe,* ed. Max Burckhardt, 7 vols. to date (1949–1969), 1:216.

[54] Ranke, *Tagebücher,* p. 167; from August 11, 1880.

wish for harmony led him to see in the Paris of 1843 not merely the rise of equality but also the disappearance of classes.[55]

Thus Ranke's serene dramatic conception governed his historical perceptions from beginning to end. He recognized that the mere piling up of documents and eyewitness relations, no matter how reliable, would only introduce a new kind of distortion into history, by presenting history as a spectacle of a casual, disorderly, ultimately meaningless accumulation of facts, in desperate need of the ordering hand. Drama, as long as it had a happy ending, was congenial to his temperament, but it also impressed him as the appropriate form for a history that God had conceived dramatically. Ranke's God was not the Deists' watchmaker God who, having created the world and all its laws, withdraws from his creation. He was much closer to Calvin's God, who has left man with intimations of his decrees. He gives continuous evidence of himself in history, and has called a few exceptional men to testify to it, truthfully. That is why the historian is so important: he is the critic who, after devout study, accepts God's work and sees that it is good. Ranke's God was the immortal dramatist who has written the play, designed the sets, supervised the production, and who continues to observe the actors speaking their lines. And, since God is never dull, it is the historian's highest duty not to be dull, either. Style, for Ranke, was a form of prayer.

[55] Ranke, *Tagebücher*, p. 320; from 1843.

3

Macaulay

Intellectual Voluptuary

The Acrobat

THE failings of Macaulay's style have been thoroughly explored; it is unlikely that the most unsympathetic reader will discover any new grounds for complaint. In Macaulay's lifetime, wits found its extravagances ample provocation for lampoons; after his death, serious students of literature raised the most far-reaching objections to his way of writing. A formidable array of essayists and historians— Thomas Carlyle and Walter Bagehot, Matthew Arnold and Lord Morley, Sir Leslie Stephen and Sir Charles Firth—condemned it as verbose, artificial, overemphatic: a virtuoso's instrument played not to interpret the music but to glorify the performer. Macaulay's most discriminating readers found his style wearisome and ultimately profoundly irritating, the style of an orator who smuggles onto the printed page tricks suitable to a debate in the House of Commons, if there. As a committed public speaker, he exaggerates his points, constructs false antitheses, grows heated beyond measure, expands immense ingenuity underlining the obvious and proving the self-evident. He argues all the time: he is always making a case, and sounds as sure of it as only a debater can. His airs and graces, his acrobatic pirouettes, far from concealing, only advertise the essential corruptness of his historical work: he is an advocate rather than a historian, and, to make things worse, a Whig advocate. He professes to detest—and, worse, he really detests—what he is too limited to grasp: the subtler points of philosophy, the mysteries of poetry, the sheer historical interest of personages or causes he does not find sympathetic. Matthew Arnold called Macaulay a philistine, in fact the "Prince of Philistines," a verdict with which Leslie Stephen, with all due caution, concurred; Gladstone called him vulgar—in Greek.[1] All his critics conceded Macaulay the quality of clarity, but he seemed to them clear with illegitimate means and for illegitimate purposes. With Macaulay, clarity somehow becomes a vice.

I do not intend to minimize the gravity of the case against Macaulay. His rhetorical self-indulgence and his Whiggish bias are too blatant to be denied. Some of his mannerisms are impossible to defend; his work is marked by a failure of restraint and of taste. And, as his detractors rightly observed, it is not only the tone that is in question; with Macaulay, as with the other historians I am considering in this book, the style is most, if not all, of the man. His way of writing raises uncomfortable doubts about his way of thinking as a historian. He rarely seeks simply to understand; he judges, dealing out marks like an imperious and far from impartial teacher. Lord Morley, reading in Macaulay's *History of England*, found it "full of cleverness, full of detailed knowledge, extraordinarily

---

[1] Matthew Arnold, "Joubert," in *Works*, 15 vols. (1903–1904), 3:333, and *Friendship's Garland*, letter 8, in *Works*, 6:307. Yet, when Macaulay died, Arnold wrote to his mother: "It is said he has left no more history ready, which is a national loss." December 31, 1859, in *Works*, 13:150. Leslie Stephen, "Macaulay," in *Hours in a Library*, 3 vols. (new edn., 1892), 2:355, 362. For Gladstone, see G. M. Young, "Macaulay," in Young, *Victorian Essays* (1962), p. 38.

graphic and interesting. But," he added, "I cannot make myself like the style. That is not the way in which things
happen."[2] This is a devastating indictment: it is, of course,
the historian's business to record the way in which things
happen.

Yet it seems to me that we have done to Macaulay what
he did to others. We have judged him from our perspectives
rather than his, and we have done this because we live in
an age to which the mentality of a Macaulay is unhappily a
stranger. Whigs, I think I can safely say, make the modern
temper uncomfortable; Tories, their sense of tragedy intact,
suit it far better. Macaulay, writes Pieter Geyl, speaking for
this temper, "rouses distrust and annoyance"; lacking all true
historical empathy, "vituperative" and "cocksure," his "writing
of history strikes us as decidedly old-fashioned."[3] There is
much truth in this. But Macaulay's style has other, more
attractive aspects. And, in addition, it has many more personal
and cultural resonances than are immediately apparent; its
surfaces hide a richly complex man, living in a richly complex
age.

We must, as the Scholastics would have said, distinguish.
I want to submit in evidence three samples of Macaulay's
prose. "Such a scene as the division of last Tuesday I never
saw, and never expect to see again." The time is March 1831,
the stage the House of Commons, the occasion the decisive
second reading of the Reform Bill, the recipient of this letter
Thomas Flower Ellis, Macaulay's best and, apart from his
sisters, only friend.

[2] Entry for May 9, 1905, in Lord Morley, *Recollections*, 2 vols. (1917),
2:133. In the same entry, Morley significantly quotes Lord Acton as being
"full of praise for the careful labour and good judgment of the *History*."
[3] Pieter Geyl, "Macaulay in his Essays," in Geyl, *Debates with Historians*
(1955), pp. 20–23.

If I should live fifty years the impression of it will be as fresh and sharp in my mind as if it had just taken place. It was like seeing Caesar stabbed in the Senate House, or seeing Oliver taking the mace from the table, a sight to be seen only once and never to be forgotten. The crowd overflowed the House in every part. When the strangers were cleared out and the doors locked we had six hundred and eight members present, more by fifty-five than ever were at a division before. The Ayes and Noes were like two vollies of cannon from opposite sides of a field of battle. When the opposition went out into the lobby—an operation by the bye which took up twenty minutes or more—we spread ourselves over the benches on both sides of the House. For there were many of us who had not been able to find a seat during the evening. When the doors were shut we began to speculate on our numbers. Every body was desponding. "We have lost it. We are only two hundred and eighty at most. I do not think we are two hundred and fifty. They are three hundred. Alderman Thompson has counted them. He says they are two hundred and ninety-nine." This was the talk on our benches. I wonder that men who have been long in parliament do not acquire a better coup d'oeil for numbers. The House when only the Ayes were in it looked to me a very fair house—much fuller than it generally is even on debates of considerable interest. I had no hope however of three hundred. As the tellers passed along our lowest row on the left hand side the interest was insupportable—two hundred and ninety-one—two hundred and ninety-two—we were all standing up and stretching forward, telling with the tellers. At three hundred there was a short cry of joy, at three hundred and two another—suppressed however in a moment. For we did not yet know what the hostile force might be. We knew however that we could not be severely beaten. The doors were thrown open and in they came. Each of them as he entered brought some different report of their numbers. It must have been impossible, as you may conceive, in the lobby, crowded as they must have been, to form any exact estimate. First we heard that they were three hundred and three—then the number rose to three hundred and ten, then went down to three hundred and seven. Alexander

Baring told me that he had counted and that they were three hundred and four. We were all breathless with anxiety, when Charles Wood who stood near the door jumped on a bench and cried out—"They are only three hundred and one." We set up a shout that you might have heard to Charing Cross—waving our hats—stamping against the floor and clapping our hands. The tellers scarcely got through the crowd: for the house was thronged up to the table, and all the floor was fluctuating with heads like the pit of a theatre. But you might have heard a pin drop as Duncannon read the numbers. Then again the shouts broke out— and many of us shed tears—I could scarcely refrain. And the jaw of Peel fell; and the face of Twiss was as the face of a damned soul; and Herries looked like Judas taking his neck-cloth off for the last operation. We shook hands and clapped each other on the back, and went out laughing, crying, and huzzaing into the lobby. And no sooner were the outer doors opened than another shout answered that within the house. All the passages and the stairs into the waiting rooms were thronged by people who had waited till four in the morning to know the issue. We passed through a narrow lane between two thick masses of them; and all the way down they were shouting and waving their hats; till we got into the open air. I called a cabriolet—and the first thing the driver asked was, "Is the Bill carried?" "Yes, by one." "Thank God for it, Sir." And away I rode to Grey's Inn—and so ended a scene which will probably never be equalled till the reformed Parliament wants reforming. . . .[4]

This fine victory was, as we know, only temporary; the Reform Bill did not receive the royal assent until more than a year later, in June 1832, after a prolonged and intense political crisis complete with elections, resignations, and threats to swamp a recalcitrant House of Lords. In these proceedings, Macaulay took a prominent part. He had entered

<hr>

[4] March 30, 1831. Quoted in Sir George Otto Trevelyan, *The Life and Letters of Lord Macaulay* (edn., 1908), pp. 146–147.

the House of Commons in 1830; he was just turning thirty, already widely appreciated as a lucid and forceful essayist. On March 2, 1831, just three weeks before the historic vote he reported to Ellis, Macaulay rose to speak in behalf of the bill that Lord John Russell had introduced the preceding day. It was one of his best performances, like the others memorized and memorable. The House sat silent, intently trying to catch his rapid delivery, for Macaulay was, though a great speech-writer, a bad speaker. "Turn where we may, within, around, the voice of great events is proclaiming to us, Reform, that you may preserve." This was his peroration:

Now, therefore, while every thing at home and abroad forebodes ruin to those who persist in a hopeless struggle against the spirit of the age, now, while the crash of the proudest throne of the continent is still resounding in our ears, now, while the roof of a British palace affords an ignominious shelter to the exiled heir of forty kings, now, while we see on every side ancient institutions subverted, and great societies dissolved, now, while the heart of England is still sound, now, while old feelings and old associations retain a power and a charm which may too soon pass away, now, in this your accepted time, now, in this your day of salvation, take counsel, not of prejudice, not of Party spirit, not of the ignominious pride of a fatal consistency, but of history, of reason, of the ages which are past, of the signs of this most portentous time. Pronounce in a manner worthy of the expectation with which this great debate has been anticipated, and of the long remembrance which it will leave behind. Renew the youth of the State. Save property, divided against itself. Save the multitude, endangered by its own ungovernable passions. Save the aristocracy, endangered by its own unpopular power. Save the greatest, and fairest, and most highly civilised community that ever existed, from calamities which may in a few days sweep away all the rich heritage of so many ages of wisdom and glory. The danger is terrible. The time is short. If this bill should be rejected, I pray

Thomas Babington Macaulay

to God that none of those who concur in rejecting it may ever remember their votes with unavailing remorse, amidst the wreck of laws, the confusion of ranks, the spoliation of property, and the dissolution of social order.[5]

Four years after this speech, in 1835, while he was in India as a legal member of the Supreme Council, he began pondering the historical work that would make him immortal;[6] four years after that, in 1839, he began to write it. Late in 1848, the first two volumes of his *History of England* finally appeared. The work has no wholly representative passages; like Gibbon, Macaulay had occasion to narrate battles and invasions, describe ways of living, depict character, and moralize over the course of events. Devoted craftsman that he was, he varied his manner to do his matter justice. But in any passage of sufficient length, he is sure to deploy most of his techniques.

If we would study with profit the history of our ancestors [this is from the beginning of his famous third chapter on social history] we must be constantly on our guard against that delusion which the well known names of families, places, and offices naturally produce, and must never forget that the country of which we read was a very different country from that in which we live. In every experimental science there is a tendency towards perfection. In every human being there is a wish to ameliorate his own condition. These two principles have often sufficed, even when counteracted by great public calamities and by bad institutions, to carry civilisation rapidly forward. No ordinary misfortunes, no ordinary misgovernment, will do so much to make a nation wretched, as the constant progress of physical knowledge and the constant effort of every man to better himself will do to

---

[5] Speech on Parliamentary Reform, in *The Works of Lord Macaulay*, 2nd edn., ed. Lady Trevelyan, 8 vols. (1871), 8:24–25.
[6] See John Clive, *Macaulay: The Shaping of the Historian* (1973), 476.

make a nation prosperous. It has often been found that profuse expenditure, heavy taxation, absurd commercial restrictions, corrupt tribunals, disastrous wars, seditions, persecutions, conflagrations, inundations, have not been able to destroy capital so fast as the exertions of private citizens have been able to create it. It can easily be proved that, in our own land, the national wealth has, during at least six centuries, been almost uninterruptedly increasing; that it was greater under the Tudors than under the Plantagenets; that it was greater under the Stuarts than under the Tudors; that, in spite of battles, sieges and confiscations, it was greater on the day of the Restoration than on the day when the Long Parliament met; that, in spite of maladministration, of extravagance, of public bankruptcy, of two costly and unsuccessful wars, of the pestilence and of the fire, it was greater on the day of the death of Charles the Second than on the day of his Restoration. This progress, having continued during many ages, became at length, about the middle of the eighteenth century, portentously rapid, and has proceeded, during the nineteenth, with accelerated velocity.[7]

The three passages I have just quoted are clearly the work of one mind. Yet they are far from identical in their techniques. The letter is intimate and spirited, the speech is hectoring and biblical, the passage from the *History*, though consistently rhetorical, is notably flexible. Macaulay's stylistic repertoire is larger than its dominant tone would indicate. It is as untrue to say that all his writings are disguised orations as it is to say that his orations are spoken essays. He has every string to his lyre except perhaps true simplicity, and there are moments when he rises even to that. His letter to Ellis, presumably a spontaneous performance, shows how rapidly he could compose a finished piece of reportage. Writing a

<hr/>

[7] Thomas Babington Macaulay, *History of England* [Chapter iii], in *Works*, 1:219–220.

week after the dramatic moment, Macaulay faces the problem that haunts every historical storyteller—his reader knows the end of the story: 302 to 301 for the bill. But Macaulay piques Ellis' interest by dwelling on the uncertainty of that ending ("'We have lost it.' . . . I had no hope however of three hundred. . . . First we heard . . . then the number rose"). Without evident compunction, Macaulay, pulling on his reader's lapel, emphatically characterizes the event as exciting ("the interest was insupportable . . . we were all breathless with anxiety"); but also, more subtly, he dramatizes the suspense ("two hundred and ninety-one—two hundred and ninety-two"). He lends his moment, visible as it is on its own, the stilts of the most extraordinary historical parallels ("like seeing Caesar stabbed . . . or seeing Oliver taking the mace from the table"). He makes his narrative brilliantly visual by making it wholly concrete ("we spread ourselves over the benches. . . . we were all standing up. . . . all the floor was fluctuating with heads like the pit of a theatre"). He does not disdain pathos ("many of us shed tears") or, writing as he is to a friend, the homely cliché ("you might have heard a pin drop"). And he completes his report by constructing a dialogue suitable for the stage, with laconic question and laconic response, neatly illustrating the popularity of the Whig program and the blessings of a deferential society ("the first thing the driver asked was, 'Is the Bill carried?' 'Yes, by one.' 'Thank God for it, Sir.' "). Yet, throughout all this agile narrative, Macaulay also sounds a deeper, more natural note, a pure boyish exuberance that will not be denied ("And the jaw of Peel fell . . . and Herries looked like Judas taking his neck-cloth off for the last operation"). Macaulay is not too starchy to admit that it had been sweet to fight, sweeter still to win.

[107]

When he ventures onto the public stage, Macaulay reso-
lutely suppresses all such levity. In the House of Commons,
he is grave, urgent, humorless. The emphatic music of his
sentences resounds like the rhythmic beating of a drum in
the jungle, designed less to inform than to arouse. That is
the point of Macaulay's insistent eightfold reiteration of
"now," a technique he borrowed from the rhetoric of the
Bible and intensified for his own secular assignment. That is
the point also of his equally insistent short sentences, either
beginning with the same word ("Save property. . . . Save the
multitude. . . . Save the aristocracy. . . . Save the greatest,
the fairest, the most highly civilised community")[8] or cast
in the same shape ("The danger is terrible. The time is
short.") Here is the demagogy of a connoisseur steeped in
the oratory of the ages, employed for the delectation of other
connoisseurs, Macaulay's fellow MPs. The Commons dearly
loved a rousing speech, and hankered after the good old days
of parliamentary oratory, the 1790s, when giants like Pitt and
Fox and Burke had harangued and swayed the House. While
Macaulay does not scruple on occasion to play on the widespread fear of violent upheaval, his is a demagogy less of
message than of tone, a half-instinctive, half-calculated appeal

---

[8] Macaulay's rage for anaphora is really relentless. Here is a sample from
his essays, which are not quoted in my text. Speaking of the practices for
which Lord Bacon was punished, he writes: "That these practices were
common, we admit. But they were common, just as all wickedness to
which there is strong temptation always was, and always will be common.
They were common just as theft, cheating, perjury, adultery, have always been common. They were common, not because people did not
know what was right, but because people liked to do what was wrong. They
were common, though prohibited by law. They were common, though
condemned by public opinion. They were common, because in that age law
and public opinion united had not sufficient force to restrain the greediness of
powerful and unprincipled magistrates. They were common, as every crime
will be common when the gain to which it leads is great, and the chance of
disgrace and punishment small. But though common, they were universally
allowed to be altogether odious. . . ." "Lord Bacon," in Works, 4:194–195.

to inarticulate, indeed unconscious, inner periodicities. Yet if this is demagogy, it is elevated; the concreteness of Macaulay's letter to Ellis has given way to circumlocutory grandiosity: "while the roof of a British palace affords an ignominious shelter to the exiled heir of forty kings," is a roundabout and rather precious way of alluding to France's former king, Charles X, dislodged by the Revolution of 1830, and living at Castle Lulworth in Dorset. Considering the five hundred bottles of Bordeaux that the royal family had remembered to bring along to sweeten the bread of exile, Macaulay's choice of adjective—"ignominious"—seems a little strained.[9] But Macaulay was interested in decorum and in the resounding effect, not in mundane details that might spoil them. His paraphrase of St. Paul's familiar *Epistle to the Romans* ("Now it is high time to awake out of sleep: for now is our salvation nearer than when we believed,")[10] underscores Macaulay's sense that he is addressing himself to the most solemn of occasions. His sober statesman's warning ("Reform, that you may preserve"), which carried reminders of the conservative authority of Burke and the populist threat of Cobbett, redoubles that solemnity.

The *History* is something rather different. It is ingratiating, like all Macaulay's work, but since with the *History* he is courting popularity with a new public, he adapts his devices to its tastes within the limits of his convictions. He is still making points ("we must be constantly on our guard . . . and must never forget"), but at a less feverish, less ominous temperature than in his speeches. He is still laying down obiter dicta ("In every experimental science. . . . In every human being. . . ."), but he now takes the time to prove, or

---

[9] For the bottles of Bordeaux, see David H. Pinkney, The *French Revolution of 1830* (1972), p. 179.
[10] *Epistle to the Romans*, 13:11.

at least elaborate, his assertions, and to press his argument in more leisurely fashion. He is still inescapably orotund, employing the single phrase, "that it was greater," four times in a single sentence to link his evidence into an iron chain. Yet he is sensitive to the perils of repetitiousness; what makes for power in speeches may make for boredom in books. Whether his sentences are monotonous or not depends on the taste of the reader.[11] But it is certain that he tried to avoid monotony. That long sentence beginning, "It has often been found" has the contours of a sleigh ride. Starting on level ground, it picks up momentum as it slides downhill with its list of two- and three-word phrases ("profuse expenditure, heavy taxation"), further accelerates with a rushing sequence of single words ("seditions, persecutions"), and then coasts gently to a stop with a neat antithesis ("not been able to destroy . . . able to create"). In general, though, Macaulay likes his sentences to be short and perspicuous: "But at the court Jeffreys was cordially welcomed." Macaulay is, of course, describing Lord Jeffreys, notorious for the Bloody Assizes.

He was a judge after his master's own heart. James had watched the circuit with interest and delight. In his drawing room and at his table he had frequently talked of the havoc which was making among his disaffected subjects with a glee at which the foreign ministers stood aghast. With his own hand he had penned accounts of what he facetiously called his Lord Chief Justice's campaign in the West. Some hundreds of rebels, His Majesty wrote to The Hague, had been condemned. Some of them had been hanged; more should be hanged; and the rest should be sent to the plantations.[12]

---

[11] "His sentences are monotonous and mechanical." Stephen, "Macaulay," p. 364.
[12] Macaulay, *History of England* [v], in *Works*, 1:515.

Macaulay's youthful affection for Ciceronian antithesis and Augustan balance did not diminish: "But the liberality of the nation had been made fruitless by the vices of the government"[13] is one of his summaries; "To bend and break the spirits of men gave him pleasure; and to part with his money gave him pain. What he had not the generosity to do at his own expense he determined to do at the expense of others"[14] is one of his characterizations, this one of King James II.

The profusion of parallel clauses in Macaulay's writings suggests that he perceived history as a succession of dilemmas, debates, and combats—between conscience and ambition, bravery and cowardice, Protestants and Catholics, Cavaliers and Roundheads, Whigs and Tories, passive obedience and manly rebelliousness. For Macaulay, history was a vast antithesis. His character sketches, which he scatters across his *History* with a liberal hand, simulate the complexity of human beings by wallowing in antithetical traits.[15] And those paired

---

[13] Macaulay, *History of England* [iii], in *Works*, 1:234.

[14] Macaulay, *History of England* [viii], in *Works*, 2:99.

[15] In his early essay on history, Macaulay made some observations he did not always remember himself; but even had he remembered them, the pairing of contrary traits would have made his sketches psychologically inadequate: "In every human character and transaction there is a mixture of good and evil: a little exaggeration, a little suppression, a judicious use of epithets, a watchful and searching scepticism with respect to the evidence of one side, a convenient credulity with respect to every report or tradition on the other, may easily make a saint of Laud, or a tyrant of Henry the Fourth. This species of misrepresentation abounds in the most valuable works of modern historians." "History," quoted in Sir Charles Firth, *A Commentary on Macaulay's History of England* (1938), p. 23. Macaulay's critics fastened on his inability to draw character: "There are no half tones, no subtle interblending of different currents of thought," writes Sir Leslie Stephen. "It is partly for this reason that his descriptions of character are often so unsatisfactory. He likes to represent a man as a bundle of contradictions, because it enables him to obtain startling contrasts. . . . To anyone given to analysis, these contrasts are actually painful." Stephen, "Macaulay," p. 365. And Lord Morley noted: "Macaulay, great though he was, did not find his way to the indwelling man of many of his figures." Morley, *Recollections*, 1:118.

lists he called the "declamatory disquisition,"[16] with which he sets out first the claim of one, then those of the other party, are simply antitheses writ large. The declamatory disquisition, a technique he had learned from ancient historians, illustrates collective aspirations or grievances not by quoting the words of historical individuals, but by constructing an embracing summary. Macaulay begins the great Chapter 9 of his *History*, which he will crowd with such historic action as the English expedition of William and the flight of James, with an extensive examination of the English conscience, divided to its depths between those who feel compelled to obey the king no matter what his crimes, and those who argue that under extreme circumstances rebellion is justified. Macaulay strews this debate with another favorite device, the rhetorical question that drags its answer behind: "What Christian really turned the left cheek to the ruffian who has smitten the right? . . . Was there any government in the world under which there were not to be found some discontented and factious men who would say, and perhaps think, that their grievances constituted an extreme case?"[17]

This narrative manner involves the reader, and is brilliantly calculated to keep his interest at a continuously high pitch. Macaulay's book is long, but he vigorously labors to make it seem short. In his essay on history, an early effort, Macaulay had lamented the decline of the narrative genre and praised "the art of interesting the affections and presenting pictures to the imagination." He practiced that art by moving the story along with apt quotations, changes of pace, and finely

[16] Macaulay noted in his diary that his declamatory disquisitions were a modern counterpart to the orations of the ancient historians. See Journal, December 10, 1850, in Trevelyan, *Macaulay*, p. 547.
[17] Macaulay, *History of England* [ix], in *Works*, 2:185–190, especially 187.

contrived opening sentences, which point forward like arrows: "The acquittal of the Bishops," thus begins Chapter 9, *"was not the only event* which makes the thirtieth of June 1688 a great epoch in history."[18] Much like Ranke, he likes to hint at what might have happened: recounting the trial of the seven bishops, which ended with their sensational acquittal, he observes, with disarming ingenuousness, "that they would be convicted it was scarcely possible to doubt." Stirred by the improbability of the actual outcome, the reader reads on.

Performing all these acrobatic rhetorical feats, Macaulay never forgets to be concrete. Following his own advice, he presents pictures to the imagination where later historians might have offered footnotes, charts, or tables. In 1685, "There was scarcely a rural grandee," he writes about the Tory opposition to a standing army,

who could not tell a story of wrongs and insults suffered by himself, or by his father, at the hands of the parliamentary soldiers. One old Cavalier had seen half of his manor house blown up. The hereditary elms of another had been hewn down. A third could never go into his parish church without being reminded by the defaced scutcheons and headless statues of his ancestry, that Oliver's redcoats had once stabled their horses there.[19]

His declamatory disquisitions are models of concreteness, and when Macaulay has a dramatic moment to relate, he nurses its details with an experienced storyteller's affection. "It was ten o'clock. The coach of the Lieutenant of the Tower was ready"[20]—so begins his celebrated account of the execution of Monmouth. "When William caught sight of the

---

[18] Macaulay, *History of England* [ix], in *Works*, 2:185. Italics mine.
[19] Macaulay, *History of England* [iii], in *Works*, 1:230.
[20] Macaulay, *History of England* [v], in *Works*, 1:486.

valley of the Boyne, he could not suppress an exclamation and gesture of delight"[21]—so begins his equally celebrated account of the battle of the Boyne. In fact, Macaulay imaginatively translates even the social history of Chapter 3 into pictures that can be comprehended without effort:

Of the old baronial keeps many had been shattered by the cannon of Fairfax and Cromwell, and lay in heaps of ruin, overgrown with ivy. Those which remained had lost their martial character, and were now rural palaces of the aristocracy. The moats were turned into preserves of carp and pike. The mounds were planted with fragrant shrubs, through which spiral walks ran up to the summer houses adorned with mirrors and paintings.[22]

Macaulay is here really analyzing the decline of the military nobility, but the one long word in the passage is the indispensable "aristocracy." Instead of bearing the burden of abstract concepts, the reader can, as it were, see the decline from the martial to the pastoral, with the ivy on the ruins, the carp in the moats, and the pictures on the walls. With the fragrant shrubs, he can even smell it.

The Son

To probe beneath these techniques to the feelings that underlie them is to encounter expansiveness and anxiety, the first candid, even aggressive, the second concealed and sublimated. Macaulay's versatility does not bespeak

[21] Macaulay, *History of England* [xvi], in *Works,* 3:287.
[22] Macaulay, *History of England* [iii], in *Works,* 1:227.

incoherence; his style expresses the unity of his intentions and, though more reluctantly, the strenuousness of his execution. Macaulay fervently wishes to please and to persuade, and to persuade by pleasing. This is continuously hard work; Macaulay wrote a great deal, but his apparent ease of execution does not preclude continuing travail—he just did not wrestle with himself in public. "What labour it is to make a tolerable book," he confided to his private notebook on February 6, 1854, "and how little readers know how much trouble the ordering of the parts has cost the writer!"[23] Whatever contrivance Macaulay chose to adopt, his writing emerges from an intense self-consciousness. He has wrought and polished every phrase; he grants his reader not a moment of the relief that stretches of plain writing would provide. Thomas Carlyle, himself scarcely a relaxed writer, saw this strenuousness plain. "Macaulay is well for a while," he said in the late 1830s, "but one wouldn't *live* under Niagara."[24] While, as I have suggested, Macaulay fits his style to his readers, he does not pay them the ultimate compliment of letting them make their own discoveries. Much like a provincial hotel keeper of the old days, he constantly reappears to ask if everything is satisfactory.

Of the two essential qualities that make up Macaulay's temper and inform Macaulay's style—expansiveness and anxiety—the first, being more public in its origins and its effects than the second, is also easier to comprehend. Macaulay was expansive in a quite literal sense. If he avoided repetitiousness in adjoining sentences or monotony within a single paragraph, he escaped neither vice in the longer

[23] See Trevelyan, *Macaulay*, p. 613.
[24] Extracts from Commonplace Book. See Sir T. Wemyss Reid, *The Life, Letters, and Friendships of Richard Monckton Milnes, First Lord Houghton*, 2 vols. (1890), 2:478.

stretches: he is never content to report only once an irony that amuses him, or an interpretation he is the first to offer. That James II owed his throne to the Anglican clerics whom he mistreated once he became king, that it was the seventeenth-century practice to blame the misconduct of rulers on evil counsellors, are observations that Macaulay presses upon his readers with the insistence of a nervous hostess. He was aware, regretfully, that the historian must select from the profusion of the past, and so he bravely made his choices.[25] But when he erred, he did not err on the side of economy.

Macaulay, indeed, lengthened his history by shortening its time span. In 1838, when he began to think about it seriously, he wanted it to reach from 1688 to 1832, beginning with the "Revolution which brought the Crown into harmony with the Parliament," and ending with the "Revolution which brought the Parliament into harmony with the nation."[26] When he published the first volumes of the *History* ten years later, this grand harmonious design still dominated his mind: "I propose to write the history of England," runs the opening sentence, "from the accession of King James the Second down to a time which is within the memory of men still living." These two volumes were already gluttonous in their consumption of space: apart from the two introductory chapters, which provide a glance backward, they covered only three years, the reign of James II. And Chapter 3, the most original and most famous chapter in these two volumes, did not advance chronology in any way; it provided an extensive survey

[25] "No picture . . . and no history, can present us with the whole truth: but those are the best pictures and the best histories which exhibit such parts of the truth as most nearly produce the effect of the whole." Macaulay in the *Edinburgh Review*, May 1828, quoted in Sir Charles Firth, *Commentary on Macaulay's History*, p. 19.
[26] Macaulay to Napier, July 20, 1838; quoted in Clive, *Macaulay*, p. 478.

of English society—population, cities, classes, popular taste—
in the year 1685. The chapter was intimately relevant, and
in a sense introductory, to the political drama that King James
was about to launch,[27] but it stands very much on its own,
as the partial fulfillment of Macaulay's commitment to treat,
as he said in an introductory passage, more than "battles and
sieges" or the "rise and fall of administrations." He proposed
to "relate the history of the people as well as the history of
the government, to trace the progress of useful and ornamental
arts, to describe the rise of religious sects and the changes of
literary taste, to portray the manners of successive generations
and not to pass by with neglect even the revolutions which
have taken place in dress, furniture, repasts, and public amuse-
ments."[28] In view of this ambitious commitment he made to
his reader, and from the perspective of modern social history
which, among all branches of history, has doubtless advanced
the most since Macaulay's day, Chapter 3 did not fulfill his
promise. He returns to its chief preoccupations only rarely—
it is like an overture whose themes make only sporadic ap-
pearances in the opera for which it was written—and in any
event, he did not live to balance it with a similar chapter
surveying England's society in more recent times. It is not
complete, and far from adequately analytical, though, looking
backward instead of forward, it is an immense leap beyond
the occasional forays that David Hume made into social history, and an advance beyond the brilliant intuitions that
Voltaire had offered. With all its failings, Chapter 3 permitted social history to become a serious discipline, and

[27] The political relevance of Macaulay's social history has been most
forcefully stressed in an interesting pamphlet by Mark A. Thomson, *Macaulay*
(1959).
[28] Macaulay, *History of England* [i], in *Works*, 1:2–3.

the measure of its success is the question it compelled later historians to raise—even about the chapter itself.

But whatever our final judgment, the point here is that this chapter did nothing to speed up the pace of Macaulay's *History* and served instead to slow it down. The great success of Chapter 3, and the enormous success of the two volumes with the history-reading public, induced Macaulay to revise his scheme, and to study, with even greater diligence than he had planned, the pamphlets and the battle sites of the reign of William III. He never got beyond his hero. The fifth volume of his *History* was published posthumously in 1861; it concluded with a fragmentary account of the last days and the death in 1702 of Dutch William. Incomplete as it was, the history retained Macaulay's celebrated specificity to the end. "When his remains were laid out, it was found that he wore next to his skin a small piece of black silk riband. The lords in waiting ordered it to be taken off. It contained a gold ring and a lock of the hair of Mary."[29] A history once designed to span a century and a half had contracted, by expanding, into a history covering every inch of seventeen years. This was the reward, and the penalty, of expansiveness.

Macaulay's expansiveness also set the tone of his *History*. Lord Melbourne is reported to have said that he wished he could be "as cocksure about anything as Macaulay is about everything," while Walter Bagehot complained that in Macaulay's writings "You rarely come across anything which is not decided. . . ." This, he added, making a charge that was rapidly becoming familiar, "is hardly the style for history."[30] Macaulay does seem to know everything—a posture that tempts skeptical readers to wonder how much he really knows. He describes the thoughts and feelings of his char-

[29] Macaulay, *History of England* [xxv], in *Works*, 4:556.
[30] Both quoted in Firth, *Commentary on Macaulay's History*, pp. 54–55.

acters as though he had been inside them: Sunderland in 1688 is haunted by "visions of an innumerable crowd covering Tower Hill and shouting with savage joy at the sight of the apostate, of a scaffold hung with black, of Burnet reading the prayer for the departing";[31] William of Orange, reflecting on the foreign policy of Louis XIV, "smiled inwardly at the misdirected energy of his foe."[32] Macaulay's sweeping, magisterial assertions tolerate no exceptions. When the public learns that James II's queen, Mary of Modena, is pregnant, "From the Prince and Princess of Denmark down to porters and laundresses nobody alluded to the promised birth without a sneer."[33] Nobody? Macaulay the historian seems to be enjoying ubiquity as well as omniscience.

This manner does Macaulay a disservice. It was doubtless, as Sir Charles Firth has observed, the secret of his public success. It permitted him to realize, and greatly surpass, his expressed ambition to "produce something which shall for a few days supersede the last fashionable novel on the tables of young ladies."[34] His cavalier and casual way of citing his authorities, which has the same origin, may irritate the scholar, but it did not trouble the reader to whom Macaulay was principally addressing his work. Yet the accuracy of his lofty simplicities and of his liberal allusions to pamphlets and novels and diaries and road maps was guaranteed by an immense and voracious study of obscure sources, unpublished documents, and earlier historians.[35] Most writers have read less than they get credit for; Macaulay had read more.

---

31 Macaulay, *History of England* [ix], in *Works*, 2:225.
32 Macaulay, *History of England* [ix], in *Works*, 2:232.
33 Macaulay, *History of England* [viii], in *Works*, 2:121.
34 Quoted in Trevelyan, *Macaulay*, p. 621.
35 For details, see Firth, *Commentary on Macaulay's History*, chaps. 4, 5. Macaulay's critics, including Sir Leslie Stephen, readily acknowledged his diligence and his learning.

The confident manner was the way to the public's heart. The first two volumes sold 13,000 sets in four months; volumes three and four, twice that number in half the time.[36] In about a quarter of a century, Longmans sold more than 140,000 sets of the *History* in Great Britain alone. This meant an average of 6,000 sets a year for a population of over twenty million—though an unprecedented figure for a work of history, Macaulay reached a relatively small reading public. He could therefore write for people he, in a sense, knew and to whom he did not have to explain everything, much though he loved to explain everything. Popular as he intended his *History* to be, he could presuppose relatively cultivated and well-informed readers who caught literary allusions and historical instances without needing the prompting of a condescending footnote.

But, while Macaulay found his general reading public immensely supportive, his expansiveness rested, as it were, on a narrow social base. Somewhat uneasily, but, in the end, triumphantly, he made himself a part of England's intellectual aristocracy; his certainty, on the surface so unruffled, reflects his sense that he was on the right track, in the right place, and not alone. Macaulay could hear reassuring supportive echoes wherever he turned. He was a meritorious officer in a select and influential army, all of whose generals were cousins. This is not a farfetched metaphor. In nineteenth-century England, intellectual leadership was the business of a few extended families. A few ramified clans translated the classics, edited the journals, headed the colleges, reformed the schools, advanced the sciences, and wrote the laws. There was some circulation within this elite, and much adroit renewal: the leading families rarely let a promising recruit get away. They

---

[36] See Trevelyan, *Macaulay*, p. 622.

co-opted him, or her, by marriage. The intellect was on the march in England, and these were its shock troops.[37]

Thomas Babington Macaulay struggled to be in the vanguard, carrying the flag. His life is a splendid instance of the careers open to the talented from the middling classes. He came from a respectable family of exemplary piety, with few connections, and average income—indeed, had its piety been less absorbing, its income would have been more ample. Macaulay made his way into the favor of the Whig aristocracy, though not without qualms and hesitations, and was created Baron Macaulay in 1857, for his literary attainments. He remained a bachelor, but his beloved sister Hannah married Charles, later Sir Charles, Trevelyan, who was to become a distinguished public servant and civil service reformer. Charles' son, Macaulay's nephew, George Otto, later Sir George, Trevelyan, became a fine modern historian and his uncle's first biographer; Sir George's son, aptly named George Macaulay Trevelyan, became a famous historian in his own right and master of Trinity College, Cambridge, which his even more famous great-uncle had attended. G. M. Trevelyan married the daughter of the novelist Mrs. Humphry Ward, who was Matthew Arnold's niece, thus joining the Macaulays to the Arnolds who, in turn, formed connections with the Huxleys and the Penroses.

It was a clan but not a sect, a brittle troop of high-strung individualists. Many of them achieved eminence in their fields—in economics, in literature, in art criticism, in govern-

---

[37] For the march of intellect, see R. K. Webb, *The British Working Class Reader, 1790–1848: Literacy and Social Tension* (1955), p. 13. About the intellectual aristocracy, discussed in this paragraph and below, I have learned much from Noel Annan, *Leslie Stephen: His Thought and Character in Relation to his Time* (1952), especially p. 3; and from Annan's splendid essay, "The Intellectual Aristocracy," in *Studies in Social History: A Tribute to G. M. Trevelyan*, ed. J. H. Plumb (1955), pp. 241–287.

ment, less in the church, but impressively in history—and they did not always agree. Nor were they all Whigs of Macaulay's persuasion, or of any persuasion. But they offered him an intelligent audience and a foretaste of immortality. Macaulay longed for immediate popularity. But, sounding like Stendhal, he liked to caress in his mind the applause of the ages: "Corragio," he wrote in his Journal in 1850, "and think of A.D. 2850."[38] Unlike Stendhal though, Macaulay found his public in his lifetime. At home in his world, sure of the understanding of the elite and the approval of the larger public, Macaulay was naturally confident about his work and hopeful for the future.

That was the public Macaulay. There was also a private Macaulay, and he is far more elusive.[39] To the extent that his formal style was meant to protect, rather than express, his character, it gives his biographer little help—it is at this point, when style becomes a mask rather than remaining a face, that the study of style reaches its limits, and independent evidence becomes indispensable. Yet his style is not wholly uninstructive for the private Macaulay. It becomes indiscreet when, instead of being confident, it proclaims confidence. It gives involuntary testimony with such favorite words as "voluptuary": he characterized himself, if unwittingly, in characterizing the Earl of Dorset as an "intellectual voluptuary."[40]

[38] Journal, January 12, 1850, in Trevelyan, *Macaulay*, p. 536.

[39] It was only after his nephew G.O. Trevelyan's masterly life and letters appeared in 1876 that the private side of Macaulay's temper first emerged. "No reader of Macaulay's works," notes Sir Leslie Stephen, "will be surprised at the manliness which is stamped no less plainly upon them than upon his whole career. But few who were not in some degree behind the scenes would be prepared for the tenderness of nature which is equally conspicuous." Stephen, "Macaulay," p. 343. "Manliness" is a term others also applied to him, including Trevelyan and Taine.

[40] See Macaulay, *History of England* [viii], in *Works*, 2:129. For other uses see two passages in Chapter 9, in *Works*, 2:193–194.

Macaulay: *Intellectual Voluptuary*

Perhaps the best opening to the inner Macaulay is the point I have already made: Macaulay was a performer anxious to please. Now, the person he wanted to please most, whom he addresses, if unconsciously, all the time, is his father. John Clive, in his penetrating biography of the young Macaulay, both begins and concludes with the historian's father, and justly so. Zachary Macaulay was prominent in what Sydney Smith, the wit, called the Clapham sect, a party of earnest Evangelicals devoted to the religion of the heart and the improvement of the world. William Wilberforce, the anti-slavery agitator, was its most famous member. The group was small, its influence enormous. The Claphamites relied on arguments that plain Christians, weary and suspicious of theological refinements, could understand: the experience of conversion, the primacy of Scripture, the sincerity of belief, the need for action. They occupied strategic posts in English society: some were Members of Parliament; some were pros-perous merchants; some, like Zachary Macaulay, were respected public servants. Tom Macaulay grew up in the midst of this sect, early familiar with the good, sober talk of men of affairs and early imbued wtih the heavy obligations of sainthood. He was a precocious child, a notable prodigy, anxiously loved by his mother, adored by his sisters, and spoiled by his astonished acquaintances. His father loved him in his own Claphamite way; not without affection, he undertook to keep his son's ego within bounds—it would not do for sinful Christians to be proud.

The Claphamites' devout, unwearied quest for self-improve-ment entailed close and candid attention to the imperfections of others. This was not cant or self-indulgence: criticisms were unsparing but mutual, and to proffer them responsibly was among the Evangelicals' highest duties. Young Macaulay felt the lash of paternal admonition all too often. As an apprentice Evangelical, he might have smitten the other's cheek; as a dutiful son, he did not dare—and in fact did not wish—to retaliate. In 1824, already a young man of great promise, Tom Macaulay delivered a powerful oration against the slave trade before the Society for the Mitigation and Abolition of Slavery, which his father had founded the year before. It was a great occasion; the Claphamites were there in force, and even a member of the royal family consented to grace the platform. The speech was a triumph, a foretaste of the parliamentary speeches Macaulay would deliver only a few years later. Applause was prolonged and enthusiastic, and the father had tears of pride in his eyes. But as the two walked home together, Zachary Macaulay told his son, "By the way, Tom, you should be aware that when you speak in the presence of royalty, you should not fold your arms."[41] That this sort of severity was hard for the father to sustain seems likely; that a rebuff at such a moment was a devastating affront to the son is certain. This was sadistic propriety masquerading as parental wisdom.

It is the way of the world that men try hardest to please those significant figures whom they please the least. Easy victories bring little satisfaction; repeated failures encourage reiterated effort, to the moment of ultimate gratification or ultimate resignation. As Macaulay grew up, went to Cambridge, and entered the world, he continued to pacify his father, to seek his elusive applause. After he lost his religious faith, Macaulay moderated his language in controversy for his father's sake, stopped for a time sending contributions to a high-spirited quarterly because its tone offended his father,

---

[41] See Clive, *Macaulay*, p. 72. For a slightly different account of the incident, see the appendix in Trevelyan, *Macaulay*, pp. 721–722.

was desolated when he failed in mathematics at Cambridge because he feared his father's reproaches—his mother, in any event, begged her husband to spare the son at least for a while. Even after he had been in politics for some years, when he was in his thirties, Macaulay would take positions in which he did not quite believe because he hoped they would make Zachary Macaulay happy. He felt himself fortunate, he told his sister Hannah in 1831, that he had managed to soften ambition "into a kind of domestic feeling." This, he wrote, "I owe to my dear mother, and to the interest which she always took in my childish successes. From my earliest years, the gratification of those whom I love has been associated with the gratification of my own thirst for fame, until the two have become inseparably joined in my mind."[42] This letter demonstrates that with Macaulay, as with others, infantile patterns survived, suitably transmogrified, in the man. It makes plain that among his intimate audience, his mother was easy to please. What it leaves unsaid is that the most important target of his desperate anxiety was his father.

One powerful ingredient in Macaulay's inner life, then, was his yearning for his father's approval. Another ingredient, quite as powerful, was his passionate love for two of his younger sisters, Hannah and Margaret. Even remembering the unbridled effusiveness of much nineteenth-century correspondence, the profuse employment of extravagant epithets, and the easy equating of affection with love, we cannot escape the conclusion that Macaulay's feelings for his sisters were extraordinary in their intensity and erotic in their essence.[43] He called his love for them his "greatest enjoyment" and his "strongest feeling"; he addressed Hannah as "my

---

[42] July 6, 1831, quoted in Trevelyan, *Macaulay*, pp. 165–166.
[43] See Clive, *Macaulay*, p. 267.

dear girl, my sister, my darling—my own sweet friend," and told her how he pined "for your society, for your voice, for your caress." While he bravely steeled himself for the inevitable day that his sisters would marry, when they did, he suffered bouts of depression resembling breakdowns; in the midst of his gratifying political activities and arduous legal labor, he wept, professed that his heart was broken, and declared that, when Hannah married Trevelyan, "the work of more than twenty years" had "vanished in a single month."[44]

This is not the voice of a man deficient in sexual passion, but of one who has steered his sexuality into a sheltered harbor. To love one's sister was safe; it was a love inhibited in its aim—unless, of course, one was Byron. But why should Macaulay pour all his passion into this kind of ungratified —if gratifying—incest? At this point, conjecture must supply the want of adequate evidence. Macaulay's love for his father was a prolonged strain, the intermittent but protracted siege of an impregnable fortress punctuated by desertions from so impossible a task, by "idle reading," and by sloppy attire. Significantly, his sister Hannah recalled later in life that Macaulay's faults "were peculiarly those that my father had no patience with."[45] On the other hand, Macaulay's love for his mother included large portions of voluptuous regression; he would fondly recall the motherly touch, her lavish intimate care during illnesses he welcomed for the sake of her closeness.[46] Ambivalence is the lot of humanity, and Macaulay had his share, but it was in his relation to his father that it emerged most visibly, though rarely into

[44] For these passages, see Clive, *Macaulay*, pp. 266–272, 281, 284–285.
[45] See Trevelyan, *Macaulay*, p. 48; William A. Madden, "Macaulay's Style," in *The Art of Victorian Prose*, ed. George Levine and William Madden (1968), p. 151n.
[46] On this point see Clive, *Macaulay*, p. 34.

open consciousness. Behind the screen of the son's poignant affection there was rage and, I think, rivalry.

Another bit of evidence adds a significant piece to the mosaic of Macaulay's character: his volubility. Macaulay was a great talker, and, like other great talkers, a bad listener. He was given to one-sided conversations and rapid-fire delivery. Sydney Smith was once asked how he had spent the night. "Oh, horrid, horrid, my dear fellow!" he replied. "I dreamt I was chained to a rock and being talked to death by Harriet Martineau and Macaulay."[47] Others had this nightmare in their waking hours. When a delegation of Quakers waited on Macaulay to protest against his malicious caricature of William Penn in the *History*, Macaulay complacently noted in his journal that he had completely routed them: "They had absolutely nothing to say," a remark we are entitled to take literally.[48] But the compulsive talker, though the target of easy jokes, is a wounded being, driven by his neurosis either to blurt out dreadful secrets, or to get in a word edgewise before he is interrupted. I would suggest that the great orator was unconsciously terrified that no one was listening to him. His offerings had been spurned and so, half in hope and half in despair, he made them over and over again. The only arena in which Macaulay could permit himself to be a voluptuary was in the realm of the intellect.

---

[47] See R. K. Webb, *Harriet Martineau: A Victorian Radical* (1960), p. 11.
[48] Firth, *Commentary on Macaulay's History*, 272–273, to which I also owe this malicious reading of Macaulay's words.

The Liberal

FOR Macaulay, psychological needs and social realities happily coincided. No one wholly escapes his early past, least of all Macaulay. What loomed large for Macaulay the young boy, and what was symbolized by the heroic stature of his pious and exigent father, was the Evangelicalism of the Clapham sect. As his religious beliefs faded, as he extricated himself from the mire of biblicism, he retained the energy of the Claphamites, their detestation of evil and their solemn desire to aid good causes. In fact, his dramatic perception of history as a combat between two clearly delineated forces translated the Evangelicals' view of things into secular terms.[49] Similarly, to celebrate progress in history, and to insure its future advance, was to translate early injunctions into mature conduct.

Such translations are commonly called a secular religion, but this term, which has been used to explain the most incongruous phenomena, merits the historian's suspicion. A fervent conviction that emerges after a religious belief has gone may be its functional replacement; it may give the sense of exaltation, the certainty of salvation, or the pleasure of ritual that the now discarded faith once gave. But the two may be independent of one another; and, even if they are psychological equivalents, it remains a difficult question just which half of the term—*secular* or *religion*—deserves emphasis. Normally, it is *religion* that has borne the weight. But *secular* has its own claims. What may matter is not that a set

---

[49] Amid a large literature, G. M. Young, *Victorian England: Portrait of an Age* (2nd edn., 1953), retains its vitality on this and many other matters.

of convictions resembles, or even replaces, a religion with its irrational tenacity and its resistance to empirical evidence, but that it permits a scientific appraisal of the world. Secularization is never a small step.[50]

With Macaulay, certainly, the emphasis must be on the adjective. The precise contours of his religious views have not been fully traced, but he obviously detested religious enthusiasm, rejected miracles and the literal inspiration or even the symbolic supremacy of the Bible, and softened the stern doctrine of original sin into the anthropological commonplace of human fallibility. Macaulay was reticent about his beliefs—understandably so. The coarse candor and widespread freethinking of the eighteenth century had been replaced, decades before the accession of Victoria, by a new emphasis on respectability and a measure of public piety among the ruling orders. It was not until 1858, the year before Macaulay's death, that the House of Commons admitted a member—Lionel de Rothschild—unable to take the oath, previously required, that he was a Christian. And it was only in the following year that Darwin's shattering *Origin of Species* appeared. Before then it had been neither prudent nor common to profess oneself an agnostic, let alone an atheist, and even later it remained rare. Lacking public professions, the student of Macaulay must depend on the tenor of his work, and on a rare philosophical remark—and that one marginal—that has been drafted to do heavy duty for the understanding of Macaulay: "But," the eighteenth-century skeptic Conyers Middleton had written, "if *to live strictly and think freely; to practise what is moral and to believe what is*

[50] See my essay "Rhetorics and Politics in the French Revolution," in Peter Gay, *The Party of Humanity: Essays in the French Enlightenment* (1964), pp. 162–187, especially pp. 165–170. As my late friend Henry L. Roberts once wrote: "It must be admitted that a 'secular religion' is not an altogether obvious entity." *Russia and America* (1956), p. 19.

rational, be consistent with the sincere profession of Christianity, then I shall acquit myself like one of its truest professors." Underlining the critical passage, Macaulay added a note, *"Haec est absoluta et perfecta philosophi vita."* For Macaulay, then, the absolute and perfect life of the philosopher amounted to strict living and free thinking, moral practice and rational belief. If that is Christianity, Macaulay was a Christian. But it is not, and, it is reasonable to conclude, neither was Macaulay.[51]

While Macaulay did not make a god of God, he did not make a god of progress either. His confidence in progress was grounded in realities that offered daily tributes to optimism. Whether one accepted Macaulay's definition of what constitutes progress or not, few—even among devout and sophisticated Christians—had any question that progress itself is desirable. And once one accepted his definition, there could be no doubt that the evidence for progress was overwhelming. Macaulay's style fits into this progress with ease. The amplitude of his periods, his accumulative prose, aptly mirrors the improvements all around him. Its very leisureliness demands time for reading. It breathes and presupposes opulence. It suggests comfortable chairs, warming fires, expensive slippers, China tea, efficient servants, long weekends, and high dividends. In this expansive culture, money was time, and Macaulay's *History* a fitting companion to the long novel, the long poem, and the long dinner.[52] For Macaulay, the

[51] The passage from Middleton has been much quoted; I am citing it from Clive, *Macaulay,* p. 489. It is fair to add that Macaulay when challenged at a public meeting at Leeds, angrily told his questioners, "Gentlemen, I am a Christian." Trevelyan, *Macaulay,* p. 204. My interpretation stands.

[52] Taine was moved to similar metaphors. "Seated in an arm chair, with our feet on the fender, we see little by little as we turn over the leaves of the book, an animated and thoughtful face arise before us. . . ." *History of English Literature,* trans. H. van Laun (1873), p. 627.

message of progress was more than a psychological weapon, it was also a report on contemporary history.

Macaulay was not wholly naïve about the signs of the times. G. M. Young has called him an Augustan,[53] and the implication that he was, in his style of thinking as much as in his style of speaking and writing, a son of the eighteenth century, is highly suggestive. In decisive ways, Macaulay was not a beginning but an end. But he was heir to more than the English Augustans. He was heir also to the Western Enlightenment, both in his belief in progress and in his reserve. The philosophes, as I noted in my essay on Gibbon, surrounded their confidence with caution, and believed that all progress must somehow be paid for. Macaulay reiterated, in his speeches, his essays, his *History*, that it is better to be cultivated than barbaric, better to live in cities than in hovels, better to have the truths of science than the fancies of religion. But "rude" ages, he acknowledged, had advantages—candor and spontaneity—that advanced cultures tend to dissipate. Gains to reason meant losses for poetry. And the forward march of civilization is not likely to go on unchecked forever.[54] A new barbarism may come, and some future traveler may visit what are now the monuments of Western greatness to see only their ruins.

But these were shadows in a panoramic picture essentially bright. As Macaulay insists in his *History* and often elsewhere, life, despite grievous setbacks, had improved and is improving. In the famous peroration to Chapter 3 of his *History*, Macaulay proffers this conviction in the most concentrated

---

[53] Young, *Victorian England*, p. 8n. John Clive rejects this designation, as I do, though for other reasons; he sees Macaulay as being far more sympathetic to the Romantics than has generally been acknowledged. Clive, *Macaulay*, p. 79.

[54] See above, p. 50; and Clive, *Macaulay*, pp. 77–78, 107.

form. He deplores the inclination to imagine "the England of the Stuarts as a more pleasant country than the England in which we live." Nostalgia is human; it springs from mankind's "natural impatience of the state in which we actually are," which disposes us to exaggerate the happiness of bygone times. This very discontent is a source of improvement, because, "if we were perfectly satisfied with the present, we should cease to contrive, to labour, and to save with a view to the future." Yet, natural as it is, nostalgia is an illusion, a mirage. Minds have softened and matured; diseases have been extirpated and life has been lengthened; fathers, husbands, teachers, and jailers have grown far more humane; games and politics alike are infinitely less coarse under Victoria than they had been under William. Most impressive, the poor are fewer in number and better off than ever before. "Every class doubtless has gained largely by this great moral change: but the class which has gained most is the poorest, the most dependent, and the most defenceless."[55]

Much as Macaulay loved the classics, and intimately as he knew them, he found himself in the camp of the moderns in whatever battles the ancients and moderns were still fighting. He derided the fashion of praising ancient poets simply because they were ancient, and he invidiously compared the poetry of Plato with the philosophy of Bacon. Indeed, Bacon was, in Macaulay's eyes, a decisive turning point in human history. He had created a system of thought that permitted mankind to glimpse the power of practical thought—the unlimited potential of reason, reasonably employed, to make life not just a little prettier but a great deal better. In a vast

---

[55] Macaulay, *History of England* [iii], in *Works*, 1: 332–333. For similar views, see "Southey's Colloquies," in *Works*, 5:330–368; and "Lord Bacon," in *Works*, 6:135–245, especially the second, analytical half of the essay.

essay on Bacon—almost a book—that added up to over 50,000 words, Macaulay in 1837 rehearsed once more the benefits of true philosophy: longer life, better health, faster communications, in short, greater power over nature.

Macaulay cheerfully acknowledged the materialistic edge to this kind of appraisal. Bacon's philosophy principally benefited what cultivated men were pleased to disdain as the low side of life. It improved existence without producing—or promising—Utopia. It sustained the body, even if it did not perfect the spirit. Yet, as the essay itself testifies, Macaulay by no means underestimated the force of the spirit: after all, it was Bacon's philosophy that had fathered the scientific and industrial revolutions. But, fond as Macaulay was of the father, he was even fonder of the offspring. "The wise man of the Stoics would, no doubt, be a grander object than a steam-engine. But there are steam-engines. And the wise man of the Stoics is yet to be born." His choice of metaphor is anything but accidental; Macaulay, far from being afraid of the machine, unhesitatingly celebrates it. He recognized and welcomed the transforming power of the railway; its fatal impact on the stagecoach and its invasion of the English landscape did not give him pause. If it had harmful effects, they were consequent not upon the invention of the machine but rather upon the unregulated activities of the financiers; Macaulay spoke in behalf of governmental regulation of the railways in order to protect a national asset.[56] Surveying the archaic English legal system, Macaulay compared it unfavorably with the industrial system—a system more modern, more aesthetically satisfying than the antique jumble of rules under which Englishmen were tried in court. "Can there be a

[56] Speech on the Ten Hour Bill, May 22, 1846, in *Works*, 8:360–376, especially 362.

stronger contrast," he asked rhetorically, "than that which exists between the beauty, the completeness, the speed, the precision with which every process is performed in our factories, and the awkwardness, the rudeness, the slowness, the uncertainty of the apparatus by which offenses are punished and right vindicated?"[57] No wonder Macaulay should find the Great Exhibition of 1851 dazzling and exceedingly romantic; no wonder that Ruskin should find Macaulay naïve.

But glorious and palpable as progress was, Macaulay did not find it to be automatic. He joined the demand of the Evangelical that men should do good to the confidence of the liberal that they can do good: effort is necessary but it can be effective. It was this principled posture, rather than social origins or social ambition, that made Macaulay proudly confess himself a Whig: "I entered public life a Whig;" he told the electors at Edinburgh in 1839, "and a Whig I am determined to remain." But he immediately added that he used the name "in no narrow sense." It defined, not loyalty to a book or a favorite statesman, not even to a party for its own sake, but to a set of values that this party embodied. Arbitrary rule, corrupt politics, religious intolerance, inhumane laws were all unmitigated evils, and it was the Whigs who had, despite some regrettable lapses, opposed them all. In his characteristic vein, Macaulay enumerates the progressive posture of the Whigs for the past two centuries and more; the phrase "It was that party," uttered seven times, is the knot that securely holds the pearls of Whig policy together on a string of humane endeavor. And now, as under Elizabeth, the Stuarts, and the Hanoverians, the Whigs remain faithful to their purpose: "To the Whigs of the nineteenth century we

[57] Speech on Parliamentary Reform, June 5, 1831, in *Works*, 8:32.

owe it that the House of Commons has been purified. The abolition of the slave trade, the abolition of colonial slavery, the extension of popular education, the mitigation of the rigour of the penal code, all, all were effected by that party; and of that party, I repeat, I am a member."[58] It was electioneering talk of this sort, which he blithly imported into his essays and into passages of his *History*, that moved Leslie Stephen to observe that Macaulay "was not only a thorough Whig, but pretty much convinced that all *but* Whigs were fools."[59]

For the debater and reformer, this stance had its advantages; for the historian it presented pitfalls hard to avoid. It compelled Macaulay, much against his conscious intention, to mitigate as only human the failings of those he admired while he pilloried as detestable the failings of those he detested.[60] His historical sympathy was by no means always dormant; on many occasions his liberal sense of justice, susceptibility to paradox, and sheer immensity of information made him notice what he might have liked to overlook. His long essay on Bacon, for one, dwells with almost painful relish on Bacon's cruelty and corruption, and excuses them not one bit. Yet often enough (to borrow an anachronistic device from Mommsen) Macaulay falls into the error of perception that the *New York Times* detected in its correspondents covering the Republican Convention of 1952,

---

[58] Speech at Edinburgh, May 29, 1839, in *Works*, 8:158–159.

[59] "Macaulay, Thomas Babington," in *Dictionary of National Biography* (edn., 1949), 12:411.

[60] At the same time, Macaulay found historians—other historians—who were "advocates" thoroughly unsatisfactory on that ground. He criticized Hume as an "accomplished advocate," and he used this term of opprobrium for a practice he himself was guilty of: extenuating the failings of his own side and exercising great severity against the other. See Firth, *Commentary on Macaulay's History*, p. 23.

when they regularly called the managers of Eisenhower's campaign the "Eisenhower organization," and the managers of Taft's campaign the "Taft machine." The Whigs were Macaulay's Eisenhower, the Tories his Taft.

Whiggism left its tracks across the entire range of Macaulay's historical exploration. At the very time that Ranke was proclaiming the historicist principle that would oblige historians to see every epoch as equally close to God, Macaulay saw the past partly as a prologue to the present, a time to get away from and improve upon. What imperiled his historical work was not so much that he made partisan moral judgments, but that he made moral judgments at all. Yet, once again, it is important to recognize Macaulay's capacity for distance and objectivity. The past was a moral drama, and, as a drama, it was interesting for its own sake. No reader of his history can miss his noble, and often strikingly successful, efforts to transport himself to the seventeenth century, and to take his readers with him on his voyage. Again and again, Macaulay visualizes events through the eyes of the past and assesses them with its standards. "Like Macaulay's Victorian reader," one recent student of Macaulay's style has observed, "what we remember when we finish the book is the 'going back,' the displacement in time, and the re-living of events the most memorable aspects of which have little to do with the history of England's material, moral, and intellectual progress."[61]

This testimonial to Macaulay's history-mindedness—for displacement in time and reliving of events is precisely that— is valuable precisely because it forms part of an indictment, from a critic convinced that Macaulay's way of "losing himself

---

[61] Madden, "Macaulay's Style," p. 150.

in the past" is the product of a psychological malaise, the studied avoidance of troubling emotional problems which Macaulay "chose not to confront."[62] That Macaulay was driven by demons of denial, that his style functioned among other things as a suit of armor against intolerable realities, is a proposition to which I have devoted much of this essay. But we cannot have it both ways: critics used to take what they considered Macaulay's present-mindedness as a symptom of his political passions; critics are now taking what they consider his past-mindedness as a symptom of his fear of life. Whether Whig or neurotic, Macaulay, it seems, cannot win. This has been so for a long time; as far back as Gladstone, readers have taken Macaulay's style as a mirror of his defects rather than of his virtues.[63]

I submit that a more generous estimate is possible and would be more just. Macaulay, I think, was right to think of himself as something better than a professional Whig. He was, in the largest sense of that difficult modern word, a liberal. His parliamentary speeches, his essays, insofar as they touch on such matters, and his *History*, are a voluble testament to his decency. The causes he stood for and supported with all his considerable dialectical skills—Catholic emancipation, removal of Jewish disabilities, educational reform, intellectual liberty, and, after a time of hesitation and self-instruction, state intervention in setting limits to the working day—were causes characteristic for a humane and generous-

[62] Madden, "Macaulay's Style," pp. 149, 151. George Levine agrees: "He converted history into romance without violating any of the canons of truthfulness, and he dwelled in the unreal world all the time he argued the superiority of the real world from which he was retreating." Levine, *The Boundaries of Fiction: Carlyle, Macaulay, Newman* (1968), p. 158.

[63] Gladstone thought that Macaulay's style was a "mirror which reflects the image of himself," lacking perspective, balance, and breadth. See Madden, "Macaulay's Style," p. 127.

minded man. Like many liberals in his time, Macaulay was prone to bouts of hysteria over the threat of red socialism, but his fears did not compel him to repudiate the causes in which he believed; they simply confirmed his earliest political impulse, to work for the timely and far-reaching reforms that would make revolution unnecessary.

Macaulay's proverbial clarity deserves the same complex response. It was in part a sign of superficiality, in part evidence for his inability to grasp the tragic dimension in things, in part the didactic streak that urged him to teach when, at least as a historian, his principal task should have been to understand. But it was a sign also of his impatience with cant and obfuscation, his desire to get to the bottom at least of those things that he recognized to be deep. It expressed the expansive energy that characterized the age in which he lived. I am not arguing, with so many, that the vices of Macaulay's style were his own, its virtues the virtues of his age. In both the historian and the age, virtues and vices were thoroughly intermingled. But that he should have been clear, hopeful, energetic, and opulent is scarcely vicious. His gravest sin, venial rather than mortal, is complacency, and he had some reason even for that. We see more deeply now than Macaulay, but then our world is a far sadder place than his. That his style is a style as inappropriate to our time as it was appropriate to his is a reflection far less on his time than on ours.

4

Burckhardt

The Poet of Truth

The Condottiere

A<small>N</small> old anecdote (one of those that is nowhere and yet everywhere true) describes it roughly as follows." The narrator is Jacob Burckhardt; the old anecdote appears in the strategic opening section of his *Kultur der Renaissance in Italien*; the situation it describes is the anomalous dependence of Italian rulers on their hired soldiers of fortune, the *condottieri*.

Once the burghers of a city—apparently Siena is meant—had a general who had freed them from foreign pressure. They consulted daily how to reward him, and concluded that no reward they had in their power was great enough, not even if they made him lord of the city. At last one of them rose and suggested, "Let us kill him and then worship him as the patron saint of the city." And that, we are told, is how they dealt with him, much as the Roman senate did with Romulus—*Eine alte Anekdote, von jenen, die nirgends und doch überall wahr sind, schildert dasselbe ungefähr so: Einst hatten die Bürger einer Stadt—es soll Siena gemeint sein—einen Feldherrn, der sie von feindlichem Druck befreit hatte; täglich berieten sie, wie er zu belohnen sei, und urteilten, keine Belohnung, die in ihren Kräften stände, wäre gross genug, selbst nicht, wenn sie ihn zum Herrn der Stadt machten. Endlich erhob sich einer und meinte, "Lasst uns ihn umbringen und dann als*

Stadtheiligen anbeten." Und so sei man mit ihm verfahren, ungefähr wie der römische Senat mit Romulus.[1]

This chilling story offers a sudden horrifying glimpse into a mental world in which ingenuity alone rules. These Italian city fathers are not just cruel or cynical—they are beyond all moral constraints. But the story also offers a glimpse, puzzling rather than horrifying, into the mental world of the historian who relates it. Burckhardt's source is Stefano Infessura's sixteenth-century "Roman diary," a compendium of rumors, historical dates, eyewitness reports, written partly in Latin, partly in Italian, a litany of treaty breaking, treacherous promises of safe-conduct, poisoned dinners, of unrelieved, lighthearted slaughter. At the time Burckhardt chose to quote this curious document, he was a mature and responsible scholar, occupying a respected chair of history at the University of Basel. And it was a work of history he was writing, not a romance; he was reporting on a voyage of exploration unprecedented for cultural history, and, precisely because of his daring, he needed to be cautious. The story, which Burckhardt practically copied, down to the formula indicating it to be hearsay—*sunt qui dicunt*—is, in all likelihood, a traditional *topos* illustrating the lengths to which man's ingratitude can go.[2] Burckhardt was ready to admit that it might not be strictly true, but rather, as his reference to Romulus indicates, an archetypal anecdote. Why employ so tainted, or at least, undependable, an informant as this?

That is the first question this story raises. Burckhardt's unblinking—I am tempted to say, affectionate—report on its

---

[1] Jacob Burckhardt, *Die Kultur der Renaissance in Italien: Ein Versuch,* ed. Walter Goetz (1925), pp. 21–22; [*The Civilization of the Renaissance in Italy: An Essay,* trans. S. G. C. Middlemore, 1878 (ed. L. Goldscheider, 1945), pp. 13–14].

[2] See Stefano Infessura, *Diario della Citta di Roma,* ed. Oreste Tommasini (1890), p. 105.

imaginative sadism raises a second question. A historian's choice of subject, and even more, his handling of it, is a deeply emotional affair. However successful he may eventually be in eliminating his person from his conclusions, his initial selection and strategic approaches are part of his most private biography. There are times, to be sure, when they are principally responses to the wishes of a professor or the blandishments of a publisher. But in general, the character of the historian and the character of his history stand in an intimate, if subterranean, relationship. There is, of course, no reason why they need to be identical twins; the historian's identification with his material may be the candid salute of recognizing his like or the involuntary expression of an unconscious affinity. It may also be a compensation or a wish: a sinner dwelling on purity, a servant on masters.

Certainly with Burckhardt, the contrast between the extravagant violence on which he concentrates and the sober moderation of his life is striking. Outwardly, at least, his existence was tranquil, securely circumscribed. Jacob Burckhardt was, except for his genius, a typical Swiss patrician. He was born in Basel in 1818, he died in Basel in 1897, and he treated the three years he taught at Zurich as a kind of genial exile, a time mainly for hard intellectual labor. He studied in Berlin, with Ranke and other luminaries, but he obtained his doctorate back home, in Basel. When he was away from Basel, he missed it; after he returned in 1858 to assume his chair at the university, he would take long walks over familiar ground, happy to see his lovely Rhine valley with the Vosges mountains looming in the background—the land, in short, where he had been born and raised.[3] There were times, especi-

---

[3] See Burckhardt to Heinrich Meyer-Oechsner, c. June 9, 1858, in *Briefe*, ed. Max Burckhardt, 7 vols. to date (1949–1969), 4:26. I will return to the question of research and results below, in the Conclusion.

ally in his younger years, when he ached to get away from his native city; its obscurantist piety and petty gossip oppressed him. But his intermittent rebelliousness gave way in his mature years to a mood of contentment. Not without some turmoil, which spilled over into anguished letters to friends, he abandoned the faith of his fathers, denounced religious orthodoxy as a form of laziness, made fun of his fellow citizens for "shitting piety—*Frommscheisserei*"[4] and came to regard himself as an unbeliever; yet, while he was willing to inflict some pain on his devout family, he retained more than a touch of conservatism in his skepticism, and a believer's awe before the eternal and the inscrutable. He was a stylist, with a connoisseur's eye and a craftsman's hand for good writing, but he published little, devoting most of his energies, as a dutiful burgher, to his lectures in Basel.[5] He traveled widely and with open eyes: his first trip to Italy, when he was nineteen, gave his life a center that, despite some later doubts, he never lost, a core of commitment around which his fantasies could crystallize—*dort, nur dort, finden sich die Centra, um welche herum meine Phantasiebilder sich crystallisieren können.*[6] But when he went to Paris at twenty-five, for a summer of study, he was repelled by the ambiguous fascinations of a modern metropolis.[7] While his travels enlarged his historical perspectives, they strengthened his inclination to see potential horror in what he judged to be an emerging mass society. The more he saw the world, the more he feared it as brash, unsettled, materialistic; he deeply distrusted those hallmarks of

---

[4] To Eduard Schauenburg, January 24, 1846, in *Briefe*, 2:193.

[5] ". . . *ein nützlicher Bürger* . . ." To Gottfried Kinkel, September 14, 1844, in *Briefe*, 2:123.

[6] To Friedrich von Tschudi, November 18, 1839, in *Briefe*, 1:125.

[7] See his letters from Paris, especially to Johanna Kinkel, August 21–25, 1843, in *Briefe*, 2:38–43.

modernity: the big city, the speeding railroad, and the Social-ist movement. Basel gave Burckhardt the quiet, settled life he craved; with his extensive correspondence, his ruminative walks, his exhausting schedule of lectures, he found, at home, the haven he needed far more than the forays that took him from his moorings. Burckhardt's Basel was not Renaissance Siena; *that* was one of its merits.

For all its managed tranquility, Burckhardt's style of think-ing was not free from strains that, however inconspicuous in his time, have emerged as grim ironies in ours. Burckhardt repudiated philistinism with the tight-lipped disdain of the cultural aristocrat cornered by the mob, and he denounced mass society with a loathing that his colleague, Nietzsche, would make into a philosophy; all his life, with increasing intensity, he defended *Bildung* and *Kultur*. But he preserved a substantial dose of parochial prejudices, including anti-Semitism, that disclose the hold of provincial perspectives on such liberated a thinker as Burckhardt. It is customary, and just, to admire Burckhardt's prescient fear of a new barbarism, his acute prediction of the coming reign of the "terrible simplifiers." But his smug contempt for contemporary Jews—for their supposed noisiness and parvenu tastes, and even for "Papa" with his "well-known nose"—though intended to stigmatize one supposed version of modern barbarity, actually served the cause of another, far more terrible barbarity.[8]

Despite all this, there is a deep consistency about such a life. Even Burckhardt's anti-Semitism fits: the Jews were "nervous" and Burckhardt wanted above all to be quiet. It is a biographer's cliché, reinforced by the teachings of modern

[8] See his letter to Max Alioth, July 24, 1875, in *Briefe*, 6:42. And see George L. Mosse, *Germans and Jews: The Right, the Left, and the Search for a 'Third Force' in Pre-Nazi Germany* (1970), pp. 58–60.

[145]

psychology, that man is a bundle of contradictions. Nothing seems easier, nothing is more common, than to draw up parallel pairs of antitheses and, tying them together, call them the portrait of a personality. That was, as I have noted, Macaulay's way of seeing—or, rather of not seeing—character;[9] it is too melodramatic and far too neat to facilitate psychological perception. Burckhardt too had his polarities. An emotional man yet a retiring bachelor, a master of the pen who realized himself mainly in the spoken word, a clear-eyed pessimist who loved the world, a parochial cosmopolitan—these are tensions which, together, do not add up to incoherence. On the conscious level, in any event, it was Burckhardt's unflagging love and deepening concern for humanistic culture that provided his existence with a vital center. And, precisely as a cultivated humanist, he had an abiding respect for style, but for style that served the truth rather than self-display. In 1842, after he was certain of his vocation as a historian, he observed in a revealing letter that while people freely talk about the art of history—*man spricht immer von einer Kunst der Geschichtsschreibung*—most have no idea what it takes to be interesting; as for himself, he wrote, he had taken a vow to write in a readable style all his life—*Ein Gelübde habe ich mir gethan: mein Lebenlang einen lesbaren Styl schreiben zu wollen.*[10] It is significant that when Burckhardt thought of a historian's readable style he took Ranke to be a master, but he also judged Ranke's relation to the truth not to be quite clean—*nicht ganz sauber*; Ranke had sacrificed a great deal of the truth, a very great deal, to his magnificent power of description—*er hat seiner herrlichen Darstellung viel, sehr viel aufgeopfert.*[11] Whatever the place of that doubt-

[9] See above, p. 111.
[10] To Gottfried Kinkel, March 21, 1842, in *Briefe*, 1:197.
[11] To Heinrich Schreiber, October 2, 1842, in *Briefe*, 1:217.

Jacob Burckhardt

From *Jacob Burckhardt: Eine Biographie* by Werner
Kaegi, Benno Schwabe & Co., Basel, 1950

ful story about Siena's *condottiere* in his work, it is clear that
Burckhardt had no intention of making Ranke's sacrifice.

For Burckhardt, style was truthful expression. But how was
he to find modes of expression appropriate to the vast and
problematic theme he had chosen for himself? As we all
know, in the mid-1850s, when Burckhardt began to ponder
his masterpiece, the Renaissance was uncharted territory.
There were some sketchy maps, drawn in broad strokes by
imaginative travelers guessing the contours of this *terra in-
cognita*. A hundred years before Burckhardt, Voltaire had
hailed the great age of literary and artistic revival in Italy at
the time of the Medici as a dawn after a long Scholastic
night—a vista partly glimpsed through his own quick and
lucid intelligence, partly borrowed from near-contemporaries
like Vasari. And in Burckhardt's own time, in the 1840s,
Michelet had written—poured out, would be the better word
—a brilliant paragraph on that great mental revolution, man's
self-discovery and his discovery of the world, that made these
earlier centuries so memorable. Burckhardt, of course, knew
and acknowledged these intuitive explorations.[12] His enterprise was different in kind. He was confirming intuition with
scholarship, elaborating hints into a portrait; he was creating
with one stroke what it is given to few historians—very few—
to create: a new field of study. A paragraph does not make a
historical period. What Michelet had hinted at with his
breathless diction, Burckhardt elaborated in animated and persuasive detail: an autonomous historical epoch with its own

[12] See Burckhardt, *Kultur der Renaissance*, p. 284 [p. 184].

physiognomy, its rich articulation and inner coherence, its unmistakable mental style.

Burckhardt had no hesitation, in fact he rather took pleasure, in underscoring the difficulties of his task. As a first caution, he subtitled his book an essay—*Ein Versuch*—and in the opening sentence he expanded his caution into a warning: "This work bears the title of a mere essay in the true sense of that word, and the author is thoroughly aware that he has undertaken an exceedingly large task with very moderate means and energies—*dass er mit sehr mässigen Mitteln und Kräften sich einer überaus grossen Aufgabe unterzogen hat.*" This disclaimer was a mark of true modesty rather than the kind of covert boasting with which so many writers try to disarm criticism in advance.[13] Burckhardt recognized, better than anyone, how much he had felt compelled to omit. Between 1858, when he began to write, and 1860, when he published the book, he told his friends that his compass was shrinking. He was simply too busy with his lectures to write anything but " 'Renaissance fragments' on a greatly reduced scale." Only a "capitalist," he commented wryly, someone who has all his time at his disposal, could make his work more than a partial and tentative essay.[14]

But an essay, though by definition a tentative statement, can claim, on the same grounds, room for maneuver. It is the most personal of genres; it concentrates responsibility on the writer. To read *Die Kultur der Renaissance in Italien* is not to hear the voice of history—as Fustel de Coulanges' listeners were invited to hear in his lectures—but the voice of Burck-

---

[13] Burckhardt, *Kultur der Renaissance*, p. 3 [p. 1]; "There is nothing in the world I fear more," he wrote to Paul Heyse on August 14, 1858, "than being overestimated." *Briefe*, 4:31.

[14] To Paul Heyse, August 14, 1858, in *Briefe*, 4:29–30.

hardt. Of course, since style is in some measure the historian, every work of history is to that measure personal, and it has been my interest in this book to disengage the personal from the conventional and the social layers of language. But in his *Kultur der Renaissance,* the personal voice is immediately recognizable because it is highly audible and wholly unapologetic. We do not have to tease it out because it is the author's chosen vehicle. The reader encounters Burckhardt everywhere —in his adjectives, his epigrams, his introductory paragraphs, his transitional devices, his robust judgments of men, ideas, and actions.

Burckhardt as cicerone is knowledgeable, articulate, and opinionated. He fears neither epithets nor superlatives. In his *Kultur der Renaissance,* statues are beautiful, speeches are brilliant, despots are vicious; Niccolo Machiavelli is the greatest dilettante who ever wrote on the art of war, Leon Battista Alberti ranked first in everything that is praiseworthy. Burckhardt never leaves any doubt about his own views. Reflecting on the unbridled power of the fourteenth-century despots, he is reminded of that strange, briefly successful demagogue Cola di Rienzi: "In times like these," he thought to found a new rule over Italy "on the frail enthusiasm of the corrupt urban population of Rome"; but by the side of the Renaissance tyrants of his day, Cola seems, to Burckhardt, from the outset a poor, lost fool—*von Anfang an ein armer verlorener Tor.*[15] Again: Dante, even if he had not written the *Divina Commedia,* would be a milestone marking the boundaries of medieval and of modern times; in him, mind and spirit take a sudden mighty step toward the recognition of their secret inner life—*Auch ohne die Divina Commedia wäre Dante ein*

---

[15] Burckhardt, *Kultur der Renaissance,* p. 14 [p. 9].

Markstein zwischen Mittelalter und neuerer Zeit. Geist und Seele tut hier plötzlich einen gewaltigen Schritt zur Erkenntnis ihres geheimen Lebens.[16] Burckhardt takes care to place his facts into a wide historical frame; he notes not just what they are, but what they mean. Men's ability to perceive the beauty of landscape is always the consequence of long and complex cultural processes.[17] And he finds it instructive—*lehrreich*—to see the hold of astrology on the Renaissance mind; neither education nor enlightenment, he insists, could do anything against this delusion—*Wahn*—because it was supported by the authority of the ancients and satisfied passionate fantasies and the fervent wish to know and determine the future.[18]

In his large definitions and sweeping epigrams, Burckhardt is as visible as he is in his specific judgments. The sense of honor—*Ehrgefühl*—which played such a prominent role in the moral economy of Renaissance man, was, Burckhardt writes, a "mysterious compound of conscience and selfishness which is left to modern man even after he has lost, through his own fault or not, all else: faith, love, and hope—*die rätselhafte Mischung aus Gewissen und Selbstsucht, welche dem modernen Menschen noch übrig bleibt, auch wenn er durch oder ohne seine Schuld alles übrige, Glauben, Liebe und Hoffnung eingebüsst hat.*"[19] Alert and conscientious, Burckhardt warns, clarifies, anticipates possible misunderstandings: the modern reader may underestimate the Humanists because their books now seem sources of boredom—*Quellen der Langenweile*—yet much that now appears commonplace was for them and their contemporaries a new view of things,

---

[16] Burckhardt, *Kultur der Renaissance*, pp. 289–290 [p. 188].
[17] Burckhardt, *Kultur der Renaissance*, p. 274 [p. 178].
[18] Burckhardt, *Kultur der Renaissance*, p. 482 [p. 314].
[19] Burckhardt, *Kultur der Renaissance*, pp. 405–406 [p. 263].

laboriously acquired, about which no one had talked since the ancients—*Vieles, was uns in ihren Schriften als Gemeinplatz erscheint, war für sie und ihre Zeitgenossen eine mühsam neu errungene Anschauung von Dingen, über welche man sich seit dem Altertum noch nicht wieder ausgesprochen hatte.*[20] And Burckhardt conceals his feelings as little as his opinions or conclusions. What happens in Milan in 1529, when the three dreadful sisters—*die drei furchtbaren Geschwister*—war, starvation, and pestilence, join forces with the extortionate exactions of the Spaniards, is truly and deeply moving—*wahrhaft erschütternd.*[21]

Burckhardt, then, offers himself as his reader's guide. His voice firm and his hand on his guest's arm, he takes him through the glittering and crowded palace of the past, pausing here and appraising there, advancing unerringly, on a preconceived plan, from room to room and floor to floor, and punctuating the itinerary with little orienting gestures: "But to return to Rome . . . ," and "I shall come back to this later. . . ." He points to the masterpieces—the virtue of Pope Pius II, the versatility of Leon Battista Alberti—with an appreciative sweep of the hand. But he also notices the most inconspicuous details—the enormous attention to the ideal of feminine beauty, the craze for classical first names—savoring their workmanship and interpreting their larger significance. And, unlike more insecure guides, Burckhardt candidly communicates his uncertainties and confesses his patches of ignorance. Who can penetrate the depths, he asks, where the character and destiny of peoples take their form; where the inborn and the acquired join to produce a second, a third nature? Where even mental gifts which at first glance one

[20] Burckhardt, *Kultur der Renaissance*, p. 221 [p. 144].
[21] Burckhardt, *Kultur der Renaissance*, p. 462 [p. 301].

thought native turn out to be relatively recent? Is it only
since the thirteenth century that the Italian has possessed
that vivacity and certainty, that capacity for playing with all
things in word and form, that has characterized him ever
since? Or did he acquire these traits before? Burckhardt asks
these questions, and then comments, with a shrug of scholarly
despair, that if we do not know such things as these, how
then are we to assess that infinitely rich and refined network
of veins, through which spirit and morality incessantly flow
back and forth?—*Wessen Auge dringt in die Tiefen, wo sich
Charaktere und Schicksale der Völker bilden? wo Ange-
borenes und Erlebtes zu einem neuen Ganzen gerinnt und
zu einem zweiten, dritten Naturell wird? wo selbst geistige
Begabungen, die man auf den ersten Blick für ursprünglich
halten würde, sich erst relativ spät und neu bilden? Hatte z.
B. der Italiener vor dem 13. Jahrhundert schon jene leichte
Lebendigkeit und Sicherheit des ganzen Menschen, jene mit
allen Gegenständen spielende Gestaltungskraft in Wort und
Form, die ihm seitdem eigen ist? Und wenn wir solche Dinge
nicht wissen, wie sollen wir das unendlich reiche und feine
Geäder beurteilen, durch welches Geist und Sittlichkeit un-
aufhörlich ineinander überströmen?* It seems odd at first
glance, in a book so filled with confident opinions, for Burckhardt to conclude that while we may judge individuals, we
would do well to leave nations alone with talk of "general
tendencies"—*aber die Völker möge man mit Generaltenden-
zen in Ruhe lassen.*[22] But such displays of modesty are functional: they give the cicerone all the more authority when he
is being authoritative.

The passages I have quoted suggest the flexibility of Burck-

---

[22] Burckhardt, *Kultur der Renaissance*, p. 404 [pp. 261–262].

hardt's diction. They also suggest its prevailing manner of informality. Burckhardt does not resort to the ironic antitheses of Gibbon, the dramatic anticipations of Ranke, the rhythmic reiterations of Macaulay. He simply talks. The Renaissance palace he has constructed and is guiding his readers through is classical in its proportions, harmonious in its outlines. But it is casually strewn with possessions; its walls are hung with paintings in the Renaissance fashion, jostling one another frame to frame; its furniture is placed for comfort rather than formality. It is not immediately apparent how cunningly Burckhardt has planned his guided tour, piling effect on effect with the most deliberate forethought; it appears to be a ramble. Again and again, Burckhardt addresses his reader directly; he replaces the stagy distance that most other historians affect with a consistent show of intimacy: "Should we add at this point . . .—*Sollen wir hier noch beifügen?*" and "Let us start with . . .—*Beginnen wir damit*" are two such overtures on a single page.[23] They are everywhere, and they turn *Die Kultur der Renaissance* into a long, if one-sided, conversation.

Burckhardt reinforces the appearance of an informal report through his persistent use of the present tense. This is not precisely the historical present—the device that lends an often factitious vitality to past events. It is, rather, the means by which the historian shows himself to the reader performing the act of analysis. The Sforza clan, Burckhardt notes, has this particular interest: we seem to glimpse its striving for the dukedom from the very beginning—*Dieses Geschlecht Sforza gewährt überhaupt das Interesse, dass man die Vorbereitung auf das Fürstentum von Anfang an glaubt durch-*

---

[23] Burckhardt, *Kultur der Renaissance*, p. 405 [pp. 262–263].

schimmern zu sehen.[24] Again, the serious appeals to national feeling that begin to resound in early sixteenth-century Italy move Burckhardt to conclude: local patriotism substitutes for national sentiment without replacing it—*Von dem Lokalpatriotismus kann man etwa sagen, dass er die Stelle dieses Gefühles vertritt, ohne dasselbe zu ersetzen.*[25] The engagement of the writer with the reader is as intimate as the engagement of the writer with his subject; the historian stands at the intersection of historical reality and historical communication.

Style—this is my preliminary conclusion to which I will return at the end—is the bridge to substance. The story about Siena's ingratitude *must* be told. It is true nowhere, as Burckhardt hints, but true everywhere as well—true certainly in the Renaissance. It is extravagant, but then the Renaissance was an age of extravagance, and only the improbable—perhaps the impossible—can convey its demonic quality. The Renaissance, as Burckhardt spreads it out before his reader, was a time of unceasing turmoil, of freedom as dreadful as it was exhilarating. So much in their world was new that men lived in a state of perpetual moral confusion; Italy was in a grave moral crisis, from which the best of men saw no escape— *immerhin aber fand Italien um den Anfang des 16. Jahrhunderts sich in einer schweren sittlichen Krisis, aus welcher die Bessern kaum einen Ausweg hofften.*[26] Life was more tragic than it was in the theatre of the time; true tragedy, which found no place on the stage, stepped with mighty steps through palaces, streets, and public squares—*Die wahre Tragödie, welche damals auf der Szene keine Stätte fand,*

---

[24] Burckhardt, *Kultur der Renaissance*, p. 23 [p. 14].
[25] Burckhardt, *Kultur der Renaissance*, p. 119 [p. 80].
[26] Burckhardt, *Kultur der Renaissance*, p. 405 [p. 263].

schritt mächtig einher durch die Paläste, Strassen, und Plätze.[27] And it is the kind of tragedy that modern man found particularly poignant and indeed particularly relevant to his condition: the tragedy of the will.

Will, to be sure, celebrated its victories in the age of the Renaissance, mainly in that greatest of Renaissance inventions, *l'huomo universale.* Burckhardt dwells almost with awe on one of these, Leon Battista Alberti, who was athlete, scientist, mathematician, painter, sculptor, architect, musician, psychologist, essayist, poet, wit, student of manners, and man of the world with equal competence and equal grace. It goes without saying, Burckhardt concludes his recitation, that the most intensive willpower pervaded and sustained Alberti's whole personality; with the greatest of Renaissance men, he too could say that humans can do everything on their own as soon as they will to do it—*Es versteht sich von selbst, dass eine höchst intensive Willenskraft diese ganze Persönlichkeit durchdrang und zusammenhielt; wie die Grössten der Renaissance sagte auch er: "Die Menschen können von sich aus alles, sobald sie wollen."* And, towering as Alberti was, he was a mere beginner compared to Leonardo da Vinci, a man of such gigantic proportions that we will never more than divine them from a great distance—*Die ungeheueren Umrisse von Lionardos Wesen wird man ewig nur von ferne ahnen können.*[28]

An age that produces such titans deserves the most extravagant of epithets. The Renaissance that Western man experienced was the time of a great awakening, the greatest since the early Greeks. "In the Middle Ages," Burckhardt wrote in a much-quoted passage,

[27] Burckhardt, *Kultur der Renaissance*, p. 309 [p. 202].
[28] Burckhardt, *Kultur der Renaissance*, p. 132 [p. 87].

both sides of human consciousness—the side turned to the world and that turned inward—lay, as it were, beneath a common veil, dreaming or half awake. The veil was woven of faith, childlike prejudices, and illusion; seen through it, world and history appeared in strange hues; man recognized himself only as member of a race, a nation, a party, a corporation, a family, or in some other general category. It was in Italy that this veil first melted into thin air, and awakened an *objective* perception and treatment of the state and all things of this world in general; but by its side, and with full power, there also arose the *subjective*; man becomes a self-aware individual and recognizes himself as such—*Im Mittelalter lagen die beiden Seiten des Bewusstseins— nach der Welt hin und nach dem Innern des Menschen selbst— wie unter einem gemeinsamen Schleier träumend oder halbwach. Der Schleier war gewoben aus Glauben, Kindesbefangenheit und Wahn; durch ihn hindurchgesehen erschienen Welt und Geschichte wundersam gefärbt, der Mensch aber erkannte sich nur als Rasse, Volk, Partei, Korporation, Familie oder sonst in irgendeiner Form des Allgemeinen. In Italien zuerst verweht dieser Schleier in die Lüfte; es erwacht eine objective Betrachtung und Behandlung des Staates und der sämtlichen Dinge dieser Welt überhaupt; daneben aber erhebt sich mit voller Macht das Subjective, der Mensch wird geistiges Individuum und erkennt sich als solches.*[29]

But this great awakening, though undeniably a blessing, was also a curse. It was an experience, with its "mighty surging," that Italians did not wholly enjoy; they were "compelled to endure" it.[30] The exfoliation of all human powers in the Renaissance, pushing toward extremes in objectivity and subjectivity alike, rarely, very rarely, issued in harmony. The universal men, the Albertis and Leonardos, were far from representative of their age; they were its glory and embodied

[29] Burckhardt, *Kultur der Renaissance*, p. 123 [p. 81].
[30] Burckhardt, *Kultur der Renaissance*, p. 429 [p. 279].

the ideal against which others measured themselves, only to recognize themselves as failures.

With inner harmony a rare achievement, Renaissance individualism produced excesses whose tragic contradictions were often pushed to their fatal extremes. In fact, it is the law of individualism as it emerges in the Renaissance that inherent contradictions work themselves out in public: "Good and evil lie strangely mixed together in the Italian states of the fifteenth century—*In ganz merkwürdiger Mischung liegt Gutes und Böses in den italienischen Staaten des 15. Jahrhunderts durcheinander.*"[31] Renaissance man takes pride in cultivating that side of his personality he thinks most characteristic; he pursues the kind of literature he finds most interesting; he wears the clothes he fancies will express him most fully. This very need for self-expression often results in aggressiveness, in eccentricity and ruthlessness for their own sake. Artists are among the most highly articulated individuals, but tyrants and *condottieri,* too, develop their individuality "to the highest degree."[32] While the imagination of Renaissance man presides over striking inventions and exuberant originality, it presides quite as much over crime and cruelty. Burckhardt calls attention to the "vehemence of weakness—*Heftigkeit der Schwäche*" which is unable to exercise any self-control. And this perversion of strength—*Ausartung der Kraft*—at times assumes colossal proportions and gives crime in the Renaissance its highly personal coloration.[33]

The lust for fame, Burckhardt argues, follows this cult of personality like a shadow. Having shrugged off piety and humility, Renaissance man seeks to prove his individuality

---

[31] Burckhardt, *Kultur der Renaissance*, p. 16 [p. 10].
[32] Burckhardt, *Kultur der Renaissance*, p. 124 [pp. 81–82].
[33] Burckhardt, *Kultur der Renaissance*, p. 420 [p. 273].

by seeking renown; fame—the esteem of others—is the mirror that confirms self-esteem. And, like the cult of personality, the search for fame produces consequences admirable in some instances, terrifying in others. While the poet or the painter longs for a public coronation or a papal commission that will give him immortality, others, lacking such talent or such pacific inclinations, will seek public notice in less innocent ways. Renaissance man had no doubt that it was better to be infamous than to be unknown. "How many," Burckhardt exclaims, quoting Machiavelli, "who could not gain distinction by praiseworthy acts, strove for it through disgraceful acts!" Among thoughtful historians—*besonnene Geschichts-schreibern*—several have recorded "striking and terrible" enterprises undertaken solely from the "burning desire to do something great and memorable—*das brennende Verlangen nach etwas Grossem und Denkwürdigem.*" If the Renaissance has blown away the medieval veil of faith and prejudice, it has woven a modern veil: the paean written by the hired hack, the myth invented by the official chronicler. Yet once in a while, the truthful historian draws aside this new veil and allows us to see, in their truly frightful magnitude, "the most colossal ambition and thirst after greatness—*Durst nach Grösse*—independent of object or outcome." The stupendous crimes of the Renaissance are thus, for Burckhardt, no mere degeneration of ordinary vanity; they are something downright demonic—*etwas wirklich Dämonisches*—the result not of free choice but of obsession, characterized by the most extreme methods, and by total indifference to the success of the enterprise.[34]

While, in accord with its inner law, the perversion of

---

[34] Burckhardt, *Kultur der Renaissance*, p. 142 [p. 93].

individuality produces an antidote, the feeling of honor, this radical counterpoison kills as much as it cures. For there are many who confuse the harping on honor with the lust for fame, and the restraint that the one would impose is wiped away by the exigence of the other. The feeling of honor— *Ehrgefühl*—may prevent crimes or encourage them; it is compatible not only with egotism and vice, but with immense self-deception—*ungeheurer Täuschungen.*[35] The Middle Ages were not the only time in which men saw the world through veils of illusion.

Burckhardt carries his analysis of Renaissance individualism through to the end. Among the checks on egotism, unbridled wit is among the most effective. Gigantic men make gigantic targets, and the Renaissance wits had a wide and crowded field for the exercise of their destructive talents, as they humbled conceit and punctured pretentiousness. But while wit was the scourge of vice, it often became vicious itself: there was much "heartless and pointless" malice in the age; there were libels and attempts at blackmail as gross as the crimes they professed to expose. In Aretino, Renaissance wit reaches the heights of deflating power and the depths of venality, typical of both in this age of excess.[36]

Not even the Renaissance scholars escape Burckhardt's cool judgment. The development of individuality entails, among those given to literature, the most patient cultivation of literature and the arts. This cultivation takes time—it is far from easy to acquire the ancient languages, to study obscure astrological or magical texts, to search for manuscripts, to improve one's handwriting, and to perfect the art of conversation. But to develop this side of human capacities is often

---

[35] Burckhardt, *Kultur der Renaissance*, p. 406 [p. 263].
[36] Burckhardt, *Kultur der Renaissance*, pp. 145–156 [pp. 95–103].

to court isolation or exile. The rise of individual ways of thinking and study was paradoxically fostered by the absence of political freedom; it was the fourteenth-century despotisms that gave the Humanistic private scholar his first great opportunities. Thus the ripest Renaissance scholarship was often the bitter harvest of internal migration or compulsory exile. The price of individualism—Burckhardt insists on this—is high, almost prohibitive.

Nor is it a price men have ceased to pay. The triumphs and tragedies of Renaissance individualism continue to work in the modern world. From his early years onward, Burckhardt was a prophet. A *Kulturpessimist* of the most unrelieved sort, he foresaw, as I have said, a world of dictatorship, conformity, materialism, and unconquerable vulgarity. But in his historical writings, he kept his passion for prophecy in check. As he told Nietzsche, then his gifted young colleague, in acknowledging Nietzsche's *Unzeitgemässe Betrachtung* on history, "My poor head has never been capable of reflecting, even remotely, on the first principles, aims, or desirable direction—*letzten Gründe, Ziele und Wünschbarkeiten*—of historical science, as you are able to do."[37] But one first principle on which he did reflect was that the past is not simply past, but that it has a certain continuity with the present.[38] Renaissance individualism was the heritage of modern man, his opportunity and his fate. As Burckhardt wrote to the king of Bavaria while he was engaged on his book, and told his readers in its last sentence, his "mere essay" was a book about the birth of modernity; the Italian Renaissance was the

---

[37] To Friedrich Nietzsche, February 25, 1874, in *Briefe*, 5:222.
[38] To Louise Burckhardt, April 5, 1841, in *Briefe*, 1:164–167; to Karl Fresenius, June 19, 1842, in *Briefe*, 1:206–209, an important letter from which I shall quote again.

mother, and must be called the leader, of the modern epoch—
die Führerin unseres Weltalters.[39] In view of Burckhardt's
assessment of this modern epoch, that was a most ambiguous
compliment.

Many readers have treated Burckhardt's *Kultur der Renaissance* as a celebration, as a gorgeous pageant depicting super-
human individuals performing glorious deeds. This, as my
exposition should make plain, is a misreading. But, like many
misreadings, it deserves our attention, for Burckhardt is not
wholly free from responsibility for it. Section 1, "The State
as a Work of Art," is an animated chamber of horrors.
Burghers who kill that they might worship, despots who train
dogs to tear apart their starving subjects, princes who murder
their guests and popes who steal for their children, satanic
monsters like Cesare Borgia who luxuriate in their lust for
blood—these figures dominate the opening scenes of Burckhardt's drama. They make up the first act he invites his
readers to witness, the last they will forget. Burckhardt, significantly enough, here draws on malicious gossip, uncertain
traditions, sensational diaries; it is as though he has given his
historian's skepticism a holiday for the sake of good, that is to
say terrible, stories. In an early letter, in fact, Burckhardt
offers amusing and instructive evidence that there were moments when he refused to inhibit his will to believe: visiting the
room at the Wartburg in which Luther had lived for a time
in protective captivity and translated the Bible, Burckhardt
sees the famous ink spot on the wall that for centuries guides

---

[39] Burckhardt, *Kultur der Renaissance*, p. 527 [p. 341]; to Maximilian II,
May 25–27, 1858, in *Briefe*, 4:23.

have displayed to tourists. Burckhardt is fairly sure that the spot is a recent addition—*Der Tintenfleck an der Wand mag nachgemacht sein*—but he finds Luther's own story, that he threw his bottle of ink at an apparition of the devil, irresistible, and so he believes it—*Luther selbst sagt, er habe dem Teufel das Tintenfass zugeschleudert, und ich glaube es.*[40] From crediting this obvious if charming forgery to crediting the Borgias with all the devilish actions that tradition ascribes to them is a small, psychologically easy step.

Such willed credulity hints at the unholy, if unconscious, pleasure that Burckhardt took in the monsters he delineates with such affectionate patience. His use of the untranslatable epithet, *Gewaltmensch*, for Alberti, which suggests a man of violence as much as a man of power, is a related and revealing symptom of a secret infatuation with enormities which Burckhardt condemned with the greatest vehemence yet relates with the greatest relish. To say that Burckhardt experienced subterranean longings for lawless sensuality is only to say that he was human. But Burckhardt denied these urges more energetically than do most others. He led, as we know, the most orderly, most self-protective life possible. He refused flattering calls to other universities, he refused even to lecture in faraway places lest he divert energies from his routine, which was to prepare lectures for his audiences in Basel. He treated all attempts to marry him off with a lighthearted show of indifference; he preferred Italy, he wrote, to the most glowing dark eyes.[41] A repressed bachelor, a small-town patrician, a duty-ridden academic, he was a voluntary spectator to life. Such a man would find the study of a period as

---

[40] To Louise Burckhardt, April 5, 1841, in *Briefe*, 1:169.
[41] See Burckhardt's letter to Gottfried and Johanna Kinkel, January 11, 1846, in *Briefe*, 2:190; to the same couple, September 12, 1846, in *Briefe*, 3:38.

extravagant, as emotional as the Renaissance a richly rewarding experience. This was an age that reveled in the qualities
Burckhardt lacked; it openly displayed all the sensuality—
both of sex and of cruelty—that Burckhardt chose, or felt
compelled, to do without. To write the history of the Renaissance, then, was to live vicariously, to act out on paper what
it would have been intolerable to act out in reality. Burckhardt
and Macaulay seem an incongruous pair in many ways, but
they had this in common: they were both intellectual voluptu-
aries. Burckhardt must have felt it a supreme gratification to
be a *condottiere*, if only a *condottiere* of the mind.

The Poet

G OETHE, one of the writers whom Burckhardt admired
most, once said that each of his works was the frag-
ment of a great confession. With Burckhardt, too,
each book was a piece of autobiography, not in the trivial
sense that a book reflects its author simply because he was its
author, but in the graver sense of being an agent and proof
of self-liberation. Burckhardt's essays of his student years—
the early 1840s—were his means for coming to terms with
Ranke's way of thinking and even Ranke's way of writing:
the stylistic reminiscences that audibly echo his great, if
problematic, teacher, are touching signs of Burckhardt's efforts
at winning independence.[42] His book on Belgian art, published

---

[42] "*Mein Weg ist aber: durch die Abhängigkeit zur Unabhängigkeit.*" To
Friedrich von Tschudi, March 16, 1840, in *Briefe*, 1:144. I have already
quoted this striking declaration in the Introduction, p. 11.

in 1842, was a declaration of autonomy, a first hint at the role that the history of art might play in the history of culture.[43] Then, in the dozen or so years between the conception of his *Zeit Constantins des Grossen* and the publication of his *Kultur der Renaissance*, with his unique guide to Italian art, the *Cicerone*, a stepping stone from one to the other, Burckhardt achieved final mastery over his material and his style. The book on the age of Constantine, published in 1852, is Burckhardt's final reckoning with Christianity, a personal debate with a personal adversary. It stands against piety, edification, and hypocrisy. It is the last reverberation of a private struggle that Burckhardt had fought out years before in his correspondence and in family discussions, but which he still lacked the sovereignty to treat with the serenity of true distance. His style, though already characteristic in its vigor and its intimate tone, is in transition; it is often stiff, reflecting some final caution. Burckhardt, as he himself told his readers in the preface, still prefers to "do too little than too much."[44] Burckhardt's *Cicerone*, published in 1855, breathes lighter air; it is Burckhardt's tribute to his Italian experience, to the virility and the sunny freedom that more sober, more repressed, travelers from Northern Europe have always hailed as Italy's peculiar gift to humanity. Burckhardt's perspective is large, his judgment of art firm and candid. He has won his inner freedom, one feels, and reached his mature style; the historian about to discover a new historical period stands before us. As Burckhardt's self-confidence grows, the

[43] On this point, see Werner Kaegi, *Jacob Burckhardt: Eine Biographie*, vol. 2, *Das Erlebnis der geschichtlichen Welt* (1950), pp. 465–466.
[44] Jacob Burckhardt, *Die Zeit Constantins des Grossen*, ed. Felix Stähelin, in *Jacob Burckhardt-Gesamtausgabe* (1929), 2:2. A comparison of the architecture of Burckhardt's *Constantin* and *Kultur der Renaissance* yields some interesting resemblances (both begin with politics, for example) and some striking differences (the later book is also the far more classical).

informality of his rhetoric, the range of his dicta, the depth of his perception keep pace. In his tastes, his attitudes, and his preoccupations, the Burckhardt who wrote the *Kultur der Renaissance* is the same historian who wrote the *Zeit Constantins des Grossen* a decade before; in his style he is, for all the clear anticipations in his earlier writings, a different man. By the late 1850s, as his sentences and his paragraphs show, his power of orchestration has reached its full range.

Interestingly enough, one note Burckhardt sounds through all of these writings is his unvarying admiration for the personal quality that Machiavelli had called *virtù*—that peculiar mixture of versatility, energy, and ruthlessness we tend to associate, especially after reading Burckhardt, with the *Gewaltmenschen* of the Renaissance. Whether Burckhardt in his fantasies imagined himself possessing this quality is something we will never know; that he admired it, and needed to admire it, is written over the pages of these books. Constantine, who, in Burckhardt's interpretation, is a wily, bold, and amoral politician who uses religion to save a crumbling empire, is just such a man; Burckhardt sees in Constantine, much as Gibbon did, a "terrifying but politically magnificent human being—*furchtbaren, aber politisch grossartigen Menschen.*"[45] And he lavishes his most unmeasured epithets of contempt on Eusebius, calling him the most loathsome of panegyrists— *widerlichsten aller Lobredner*—for concealing Constantine's true qualities behind his tendentious, dishonest eulogies to the supposed ideal Christian ruler.[46] Constantine deserved to be admired, but not for the actions and the character that Eusebius lent him. The greatest among Italian artists are

---

[45] Burckhardt, *Constantin,* p. 296. Gibbon applies his favorite epithet, "artful," to Constantine. See Gibbon, *History of the Decline and Fall of the Roman Empire,* 2:290.

[46] Burckhardt, *Constantin,* p. 296.

more fortunate than the first of the Christian emperors; while Constantine's true greatness is concealed behind the fog of piety, the artists' true greatness survives for all to see, in their buildings, their statues, their paintings. Michelangelo, that towering genius, the modern artist par excellence in his untiring search striving for new possibilities—*Er sucht stets neue Möglichkeiten zu erschöpfen und kann deshalb der moderne Künstler in vorzugsweisem Sinne heissen*; Raphael, that supreme expression of psychological health and normal personality; Leonardo, who made the contingent appear natural and inevitable, that mighty spirit—*ein ganz gewaltiger Geist*—these are the immortals to whom Burckhardt could unashamedly pay the tribute of his superlatives. For him, the secularist, they were intimations of eternity embodied in the single exceptional individual.[47] It is no accident that Burckhardt should have admired Rubens beyond most other painters, Rubens the versatile and robust genius—diplomat and man of letters as much as painter—who produced an *œuvre* immense in its quantity and overpowering in its energy. Burckhardt defended Rubens in his first writings and returned to him in a late manuscript, *Erinnerungen aus Rubens,* published, in obedience to his request, after his death. His Rubens is an *Übermensch,* though fortunately not a hateful one; a being of tremendous power, with admixtures of the coarseness and wildness that Burckhardt characteristically finds essential for the sake of completing the picture of this natural phenomenon—*Auch das Derbe und Wilde wird man einer solchen nicht bloss nachsehen, sondern es von ihr im ersten Augenblick erwarten, damit die Erscheinung eine vollständige sei.* Pointedly, Burckhardt observes that sensitive souls might find Rubens' figures too full-blooded—*Delikate Leute nehmen*

[47] Jacob Burckhardt, *Der Cicerone,* ed. Heinrich Wölfflin, in *Jacob Burckhardt-Gesamtausgabe,* vols. III–IV (1933), 4:74, 249–250, 271.

an dem Blutreichtum seiner so glänzend gesunden Gestalten Anstoss—but plainly this strapping good health, far from troubling Burckhardt, satisfies something in him. In an extravagant and moving final paragraph Burckhardt bestows the supreme accolade: he associates Rubens with Homer. The two, he writes, were the greatest storytellers our old globe has ever known—*die beiden grössten Erzähler, welche unser alter Erdball bis heute getragen hat.*[48] Judgments such as these permit us to estimate Burckhardt's investment in that vast tapestry, the culture of the Renaissance. It is to that book that his earlier writings served as a preparation, of that book that his later manuscripts were an echo. *Die Kultur der Renaissance* sublimates his innermost urges to perfection.

To recognize the component of sublimation in a work of history is not to minimize its formal qualities or to deprecate its claims to objectivity; it is, rather, to discover the historian's temperamental starting point. Sublimation, after all, is a long and winding river, which picks up tributaries in its course, and its mouth often little resembles its source. The demands of craft, the habits of training, the contributions of experience enlarge and modify the historian's original endowment and youthful intentions. Burckhardt certainly did not offer his published work as the direct reflection of his primitive dispositions; he cherished control in art as much as in life, in thinking about culture as in writing about history. For poetry and politics alike, form was the supreme necessity.[49] If Burck-

---

[48] Jacob Burckhardt, *Erinnerungen aus Rubens*, ed. Heinrich Wölfflin, in *Jacob Burckhardt-Gesamtausgabe* (1934), 13:391, 517.

[49] " *Studiren Sie die Form und suchen Sie darin strenge zu werden,*" he advised one correspondent. To Emma Brenner-Kron, May 21, 1852, in *Briefe*, 3:155. In one remarkable passage, Burckhardt declared his desire for poetic expression, for the unconscious breaking forth, in consciously artistic form—*den poetischen Ausdruck hätte ich gerne, das Unbewusste, welches in künstlerisch bewusster Form hervorbricht.* To Albert Brenner, May 24, 1856, in *Briefe*, 3:249.

hardt trusted intuitions and valued emotions, he insisted on testing the first and disciplining the second. Much as he feared the growing power of the philistine, he feared even more the uncontrolled spontaneity of "genius," which, he was sure, was worse than philistinism. In a paternal correspondence with a young student, Albert Brenner, he conceded that their century showed the typical symptoms of a democratic epoch, but he warned against defiant "ultra-Byronesque" postures as a remedy more lethal than the disease. And he pleaded with Brenner that, if he really thought himself a demonic character, not to take pleasure in that notion, not for a moment— *Wenn Sie sich wirklich für eine dämonische Natur halten, so verlange ich nur Eins: dass Sie sich in diesem Gedanken niemals, keinen Augenblick, gefallen mögen.*[50] In one of his last letters he underscored once again his hostility to the charismatic leader: as he told the church historian Ludwig von Pastor, he had never accepted Nietzsche's vision of the *Übermensch*, and always dreaded "*Gewaltmenschen*" and "*outlaws*" as the very scourges of God—*flagella dei.*[51]

While his published writings reasonably enough express the same political convictions, they also leave clues to Burckhardt's ambivalence. The great criminals of the Renaissance were scourges, *Gewaltmenschen*, but so, after all, was his admired Alberti. Burckhardt's unconscious left its traces in his books; it prompted him to record with a certain sympathy the forces straining, like the secret energies of the id, beyond the bounds of good and evil. But this did not induce him to prize immorality or irrationality, either in the history he was living through or the history he was writing about. *Die Kultur der Renaissance* was not a work of self-indulgence or of sheer

---

[50] March 16, 1856, in *Briefe*, 3:247.
[51] January 13, 1896, in *Briefe*, ed. Walther Rehm (1946), pp. 93–94.

self-expression. It was a work of diligent research and meticulous construction.[52]

The stylistic architecture of Burckhardt's masterpiece stands as a monument to his passion for design, his imperious need to give shape to the disparate materials surviving from the past. There is a good deal of violence in Burckhardt's *Kultur der Renaissance,* much strain and tension, but they are all subsumed under the grand composition of his vast, crowded, but harmonious canvas. There are two types of temperament among historians: there are those who revel in the uniqueness of unduplicable events and those who crave the beauty of organic coherence. Burckhardt obviously belongs to the second of these; the six sections of his published book, with their little introductory essays and their measured progression represent a radical and magnificent simplification of his original scheme.[53] Section follows section with a persuasive logic that gives the book its perspicuity and a certain air of inevitability.

The shape of Burckhardt's *Kultur der Renaissance* was an aesthetic choice designed to make a substantive point: the Renaissance was, in Burckhardt's view, a coherent entity pervaded by a common spirit. And at this point, Burckhardt's style reveals not merely his psychological dispositions but also dominant cultural attitudes with which Burckhardt was perfectly in tune. For well over half a century before he published the book, historians had been preoccupied with the

---

[52] On the opening page of his masterpiece, Burckhardt notes the difficulty facing the cultural historian: "It is the most essential difficulty of cultural history that it is compelled to break up a large mental continuum—*grosses geistiges Kontinuum*—into single, often seemingly arbitrary categories, if he wants to portray it at all." Burckhardt, *Kultur der Renaissance,* p. 3 [p. 1].

[53] See Kaegi, *Jacob Burckhardt,* vol. 3, *Die Zeit der klassischen Werke* (1956), pp. 668–669, 690.

notion of *Zeitgeist* or *Volksgeist* and had sought evidence for an animating, all-pervading spirit in the cultures of the past. To no one's surprise, they found what they were looking for, reading single facets of culture—religion, politics, morals, art —as manifestations of a larger unity. In recent years, skeptics have objected that this perception was vitiated by a vast circular argument: once the historian starts with the conviction that everything he studies is part of an organism, all he needs to do is to explain in what respect each segment participates in, and expresses, the whole.[54] The most blatant contradictions and most irrepressible conflicts could be fitted into the *Zeitgeist*: Hegel saw spiritual, and Marx material, conflicts not as embarrassing evidence contradicting, but as indispensable elements confirming, their scheme. Segments that fitted with other segments proved the pervasiveness of the *Zeitgeist* because they fitted; segments that did not fit proved it with equal ease, because the contradictions gave life to the whole and were anyway resolved through the play of the dialectic. In this view of history, everything served to confirm organicism, nothing was capable of disproving it. Such reasoning was the very reverse of scientific thinking—it was a metaphysical game.

To some measure, it was a game in which Burckhardt participated. He repudiated Hegel in particular and philosophy in general, but the Hegelian idea appeared in the writings of classicists and art historians he respected; and the idea of total order was, as I have said, in any case congenial to him. He was perfectly capable of perceiving the coexistence of pagan and Christian convictions, or the struggle between tradition

---

[54] The most trenchant criticism, to which I am much indebted though I do not accept it all, has recently come from E. H. Gombrich; his *In Search of Cultural History* (1969).

and innovation, in the men of the Renaissance: his complex characterizations of Petrarch and of Pope Pius II brilliantly demonstrate this capacity. But his memorable slogans and decisive epithets made it easy to read his work as though he saw simplicity where there was complexity, and high fences between historical epochs when there were, in fact, wide bridges. By sharply confronting "medieval man" with "Renaissance man," Burckhardt did nothing to take distance from the prevailing notion of a *Zeitgeist*. Yet, though both temperamentally and professionally predisposed to see more coherence in culture than was actually there, Burckhardt was too knowledgeable a scholar, and too suspicious of metaphysics, to rest content with such myths. After all, myths, even the science of mythology, as he once told a correspondent, made him dizzy.[55] Moreover, Burckhardt was not wholly wrong. The various aspects of culture, though often lying side by side with little contact, even more often in conflict and always in flux, yet coexist within a certain range of possibilities that permit the historian to make cautious generalizations. Burckhardt discovered a pattern of ideas and conduct that deserved to be distinguished as a distinct period. "Renaissance man" was not a Hegelian myth but what would later be called a Weberian ideal type. This was a triumph of historical insight, not a psychological or methodological error. Burckhardt's architecture was perhaps too uniform, but it was not arbitrary.

But if the *Kultur der Renaissance* was a triumph of architecture, a work of research and design, was it also a work of science? Burckhardt, we know, was committed all his life to the enjoyment, the study, and the making of form. His cul-

55 To Friedrich Salomon Vögelin (September 17, 1866), in *Briefe*, 4:227.

tural competence was impressive; in a century of specialists, he retained something of the versatility of Renaissance man. He was a serious poet, an accomplished sketcher, a talented musician, a voracious reader of modern literature, a knowledgeable critic with pronounced preferences and even more pronounced dislikes, and the best-informed gallery-goer of his age. Such an amateur—something far better than a dilettante —did not choose his stylistic devices at random.

Nor could he be indifferent to their effect. Despite all his disclaimers, he reflected with a good deal of seriousness about the relation of beauty to truth, of style to content. It was as a conscientious historian devoted to the discovery of the truth that he came to distrust the scientific pretensions of Ranke and to find the political passivity and professed neutrality of Ranke's historicism both unworkable and undesirable. "It is high time," he told his friend Paul Heyse in 1852, "that I free myself from that general, falsely objective, passive acceptance of everything and everybody—*dem allgemeinen, falsch objektiven Geltenlassen von allem und jedem*—and to become pretty intolerant once again."[56] At the same time, he did not want to be an entertainer, a mere storyteller. The general public, he wrote derisively, had been permanently overstimulated by the rush of events and the mass of print; it only wants brilliantly written, piquant scenes from the past, preferably without documentation or verification—*eine Reihe brillant geschriebener, pikanter Parthien aus der Geschichte, ohne Urkunden und Belege.* No honest historian—*ehrlicher Historiker*—could give the age what it wanted: tendentious history—*Tendenz-Geschichte*—in tune with its tendentious poetry and tendentious art. Whoever had honest intentions with history could never unconditionally affirm such history—

---

[56] August 13, 1852, in *Briefe*, 3:161.

Burckhardt: *The Poet of Truth*

*Wer es mit der Geschichte ehrlich meint, wird zu einer
Geschichte mit Tendenz nie unbedingt Ja sage können.*[57]
Whatever the practical obstacles to his program, Burckhardt's
ideal seems straightforward enough. Even his rejection
of Ranke's *Selbstauslöschung* seems nothing less than a far-
seeing recognition of the bias concealed behind the historicist's celebration of power. Considering the consequences of
Ranke's tolerance, Burckhardt's intolerance is welcome. But
then Burckhardt complicates matters by calling history a form
of poetry. As he began to think about the philosophy of
history, casually but daily—*ein zwar nur beiläufiges, aber
tägliches Denken über die Philosophie der Geschichte*—Burckhardt came to see the most exalted poetry in history—*die
höchste Poesie in der Geschichte.* In Rankean fashion, indeed
in Rankean language, Burckhardt acknowledged the truth of
the ancient saying that God is the greatest of poets—*unser
Herrgott der grösste Dichter sei.*[58] For him at least, history
was, and remained, poetry in the highest possible degree—*die
Geschichte ist und bleibt mir Poesie im grössten Masstabe.*[59]
Yet, while history was poetry, poetry was not history. In one
of his lectures, Burckhardt appreciatively quoted Aristotle's
familiar saying that poetry is more philosophical and deeper
than history, and added his gloss: poetry does more for our
understanding of human nature than does history—*Die Poesie
leistet mehr für die Erkenntnis des Wesens der Menschheit.*
That is why, for Burckhardt, the poet's gift was far greater
than the historian's, even at its best, could ever be.[60]

---

[57] To Heinrich Schreiber, October 2, 1842, in *Briefe*, 1:217.
[58] To Friedrich von Tschudi, March 16, 1840, in *Briefe*, 1:145. It is
worth noting here that the German words *"Dichter"* and *"Dichtung"* refer,
not to poets alone, but to all imaginative writers and writings.
[59] To Karl Fresenius, June 19, 1842, in *Briefe*, 1:208.
[60] See Jacob Burckhardt, *Weltgeschichtliche Betrachtungen*, ed. Albert
Oeri, in *Jacob Burckhardt-Gesamtausgabe* (1929), 7:52.

The contradiction, though apparent, is only superficial. Burckhardt recognized poetry and history to be distinct literary genres; it was mainly in their reach for knowledge that they were alike. Both place the highest value on direct perception—*Anschauung*: a contemplative, intuitive grasp of reality. Like the poet, the historian handles his material with devout respect and a kind of productive receptivity. As he encounters some great monument of the past, which though it stands in eternal silence yet eloquently speaks of the human spirit, the historian feels a shudder of awe—*einen ehrfurchtsvollen Schauer*.[61] For all his moral distance from Ranke, Burckhardt's religious humility before the past sounds Rankean echoes. If the chariot of history runs over the unfortunate, the historian records and accepts the event.[62] Historical life takes a thousand forms; capable of infinite complexities, it appears in all possible guises. The human spirit, free or unfree, speaks at times through the multitude, at times through great individuals; it is full of optimism or pessimism as it founds and destroys states, religions, cultures—*das geschichtliche Leben, wie es tausendgestaltig, komplex, unter allen möglichen Verkappungen, frei und unfrei daherwogt, bald durch Masse, bald durch Individuen sprechend; bald optimistisch, bald pessimistisch gestimmt, Staaten, Religionen, Kulturen gründend und zerstörend*. And men must pay their passive tribute—*unvermeidlich unseren passiven Tribut bezahlen*—as they confront it contemplatively—*beschauend gegenübertreten*.[63]

For Burckhardt's historical procedures, *Anschauung* is absolutely central. Yet this mixture of contemplation and intuition, though essentially passive, is also thoroughly objec-

---

61 To Karl Fresenius, June 19, 1842, in *Briefe*, 1:206.
62 On this point, see Gombrich, *Cultural History*, p. 21.
63 Burckhardt, *Weltgeschichtliche Betrachtungen*, in *Gesamtausgabe*, 7: 5–6.

tive. Though private in its origins, it is turned to the outside world, toward historical reality. Burckhardt himself noted in 1863, a little ruefully, that he was growing quite prosaic in his study of history—*Ich werde allgemach gar prosaisch bei der Erforschung der vergangenen Zeit.*[64] Eight years before, as he was beginning to steep himself in the Renaissance, he acknowledged that he was being tormented by the spirit of science—*ein wissenschaftlicher Quälgeist.*[65] And when the *Kultur der Renaissance* was finally before the public, he modestly told an old friend to whom he had sent a copy, that he might smile and shake his head over so much dilettantism, but should at least admit that the author had spared no effort and no sweat—*Mein lieber alter Freund wird vielleicht über den Dilettantismus der Arbeit mit einigem Lächeln den Kopf schütteln, aber doch gewiss zugeben, dass Autor es an Mühe und Schweiss nicht hat fehlen lassen.* There was *one* word of praise, Burckhardt added, that he would like to hear: that he had vigorously resisted many opportunities for letting his imagination roam freely, and had instead held fast to the testimony of the sources—*Einen Lobspruch vernähme ich auch noch gern aus Ihrem Munde, dass nämlich Autor vielen Gelegenheiten, die Phantasie spazieren zu lassen, kräftiglich widerstanden und sich hübsch an die Quellenaussagen gehalten hat.*[66] His imagination was exigent, lusting for freedom of action; a source of insights and of trouble, it needed to be cherished and disciplined. Werner Kaegi has shrewdly read Burckhardt's characterization of Machiavelli as a self-portrait: Machiavelli, Burckhardt writes, was endangered neither by false claims to originality nor by the fraudulent spinning out of ideas, but by a strong imagination, which he obviously

[64] To Emanuel Geibel, October 10, 1863, in *Briefe*, 4:137.
[65] To Albert Brenner, October 17, 1855, in *Briefe*, 3:226.
[66] To Heinrich Schreiber, August 1, 1860, in *Briefe*, 4:53.

tamed with great difficulty—*einer starken Phantasie, die er offenbar mit Mühe bändigt*.[67] When in the mid-1860s Burckhardt was asked to collaborate in the revision of Kugler's famous history of art, he showed himself most reluctant, and one of the reasons he offered was that he had no time now to travel to museums: "To compile descriptions from books about things I have not seen for myself becomes more and more intolerable to me."[68] Generally Burckhardt used the word *Anschauung* not in the spiritual but in the literal sense of visual inspection. A critically important aspect of his method was seeing for himself.

By appreciating the cognitive power of *Anschauung*, Burckhardt hints at a psychology of research that William Whewell in England and Claude Bernard in France were developing in his lifetime. It was a psychology wholly contrary to the Baconian myth of induction—to the picture, that is, of the scientist constructing his theories through the laborious piling up of single instances, the amassing of brick after brick of fact. Whewell and Bernard argued instead that scientists arrive at their theories in precisely the opposite way, by beginning with a hunch, often of comprehensive scope. "A hypothesis," Bernard wrote, "is . . . the obligatory starting point of all experimental reasoning. Without it no investigation would be possible, and one would learn nothing: one could only pile up barren observations."[69] In the sciences, then—in all

---

[67] Kaegi, *Jacob Burckhardt*, 3:710–711; see Burckhardt, *Kultur der Renaissance*, p. 80 [p. 55].

[68] To Paul Heyse, December 6, 1864, in *Briefe*, 4:169.

[69] Quoted in P. B. Medawar, *The Art of the Soluble: Creativity and Originality in Science* (1969), p. 170. For this epistemological view and its history, see the lucid exposition in Medawar, *Induction and Intuition in Scientific Thought* (1969); and for a leading current exposition, see the important writings of Sir Karl Popper, especially, *The Logic of Scientific Discovery* (1934; trans., 1959), and *Conjectures and Refutations* (1963).

sciences, including history—intuition stands at the beginning of inquiry.

This psychological account of scientific procedure is the opposite of primitivist; it offers no support for the familiar notion that children, peasants, or madmen have readier access to truth than more privileged human beings. Burckhardt's use of "intuition" or "poetry" is in fact unfortunate, because these terms as commonly employed minimize the components of knowledge and skill essential to the effective working of the scientific imagination. The scientist's intuition is a net dropped into a stocked pond; the emptier the pond, the less satisfactory the haul. And, besides knowledge, this kind of intuition requires training, for without that the scientist cannot subject his guesses to adequate tests or fit them into existing bodies of theory. The amateur will not see what the experienced researcher sees, and even if he were to see it by chance, he would not know what to do with it. Scientific vision is nine-tenths experience. And finally, this vision requires revision. The hunch of the scientist, unlike the intuition of the Romantic, is far from infallible or unerring. It demands self-criticism and the criticisms of others. Intuition must survive ordeals before it may join the exclusive club of theories.

Unwilling to be tarred with the brush of philosopher, Burckhardt only adumbrates this epistemological position, and does so in his own graphic vocabulary. "Even a half-mistaken historical perspective," he wrote in 1859, "is worth a great deal more than no perspective at all"—his way of saying that a preliminary hypothesis is essential to all research.[70] Earlier, he observed that he, the poetic man, must

---

[70] To Wilhelm Vischer, the Younger, June 20, 1859, in *Briefe*, 4:40.

get some fodder or he will starve to death—*Der poetische Mensch muss auch hie und da etwas zu "ässen" haben, wenn er nicht draufgehen soll*—his way of saying that without receiving steady reinforcements of knowledge, the most intuitive of researchers cannot go on.[71] From the beginning of his career as a historian Burckhardt had insisted that he had no capacity for abstract thinking or for speculation; his substitute—*Surrogat*—was to sharpen his *Anschauung* day by day, and stick to the material, to nature and history—*Ich klebe von Natur am Stoff, an der sichtbaren Natur und an der Geschichte.*[72]

Thus, for Burckhardt, poetry and history, beauty and truth —in short, art and science—were far from being the mortal enemies of positivist philosophy, disputing one another's territory across extensive, heavily fortified borders. They were, rather, allies, almost inseparable twins. Burckhardt experienced this mutually reinforcing alliance as a psychological necessity;[73] but beyond that, he found it an indispensable presupposition for his historical method. With his reverence for the real, he protested that the poetry he felt working within him was anything but fanciful or romantic—*nicht etwa romantisch-phantastisch*; he was sure that *such* a genre would do the historian no service at all—*was zu nichts taugen würde.*[74] It was, rather, a way of seeing the past, and a way of conveying one's vision to the public. And poetry was so effective because the reality it discovered and delineated was itself

---

[71] To Gottfried and Johanna Kinkel, January 11, 1846, in *Briefe*, 2:189.
[72] To Karl Fresenius, June 19, 1842, in *Briefe*, 1:206.
[73] As he told a friend, he needed a historical and, in addition, a beautiful terrain, otherwise he would die—*ich bedarf eines historischen und dazu eines schönen Terrains, sonst sterbe ich.* To Hermann Schauenburg, March 22, 1847, in *Briefe*, 3:58.
[74] To Karl Fresenius, June 19, 1842, in *Briefe*, 1:208.

poetic. It is because the world of history is a gigantic poem that the poet—a certain kind of poet, responsive and responsible to reality—was best equipped to be its student.[75]

I therefore find it impossible to discuss Burckhardt's substance apart from his style, or his style apart from his substance. The past is intensely dramatic, enormously rich, finely differentiated; hence the historian must be, in his manner of perception as in his manner of presentation, colorful, free from artifice, precise—and personal. In an early letter, Burckhardt had deplored his inability to make an impact on the public through the drama—*Gegen aussen, auf das Publicum möchte ich nie anders wirken als durch das Drama. Und das ist mir versagt.*[76] Yet more than he would ever know, his wish was gratified, above all in the writings of his maturity. For, like Ranke, Burckhardt came to perceive the past as a great drama; he would do it full justice in that drama he entitled *Kultur der Renaissance in Italien*. To call history a drama is easy; the metaphor came to the pen of Macaulay as it has to that of countless other historians. But, like Ranke, Burckhardt took the designation seriously—it was, as we have seen, not the only debt he owed to his German teacher.

Yet the very quality of perception that seems to unite teacher and pupil actually separates them. Ranke's drama was an optimistic melodrama, with villains clearly marked as villains and designed, by the Divine Playwright, to serve the cause of the hero. Ranke's piety permitted him to visualize the Father making everything come right in the end. Burck-

[75] To paraphrase Schiller's famous saying that world history is the universal judgment—*Die Weltgeschichte ist das Weltgericht*: for Burckhardt, world history was a universal poem: *Die Weltgeschichte*, he might have said, *ist das Weltgedicht*.

[76] To Gottfried Kinkel, January 27, 1844, in *Briefe*, 2:71. In italics in the original.

hardt's skepticism permitted him no such comfort. His historical vision was, as I have shown, essentially ambivalent: the indeterminacy of his favorite word *Gewaltmensch* and his dualistic view of individualism vividly exemplify his conviction that civilization is essentially problematic and fearfully fragile. Half a century before Freud, Burckhardt saw destruction at its very heart. Burckhardt's style, though never vulgarly mimetic, beautifully reflects his dramatic yet Stoical vision: his sense of interminable conflict lit up by personal greatness, of gigantic and unconclusive confrontations lent tragic depth by his sturdy refusal to offer a hope he himself did not feel. Only high culture is immortal, though it too is exposed to the accidents of time, the barbarity of conquerors, and the heedless violence of the mob. Yet it is only through the work of individuals that history achieves its power to console, and, like the cultural heroes Burckhardt celebrated, he too was an incurable individualist. "I will never found a school—*Ich werde nie eine Schule gründen!*" Burckhardt wrote to his friend Paul Heyse at the height of his powers.[77] He meant the remark as a lament. Looking back, we may take it instead as Burckhardt's most solid claim to immortality.

[77] To Paul Heyse, November 30, 1862, in *Briefe*, 4:125.

Conclusion

On Style in History

I SAID at the beginning that I intended these essays as a contribution to the persistent debate over the definition of history. One striking conclusion on which they converge is that the straightforward dichotomy between art and science is quite untenable. Gibbon, among the most self-aware men of letters that historical literature has known, firmly made his work part of the philosophes' program of turning history into a science. Ranke explicitly argued that there is a profound affinity and necessary alliance between *Dichtung* and *Wissenschaft*. Macaulay did not pronounce on the matter, but his writings stand in the tradition of Gibbon: he wanted to be read and to be believed; he admired, if I may put it this way, Bacon and Shakespeare in equal measure. And Burckhardt, as I have shown in some detail, thought a certain kind of poetry not merely the associate but the very foundation of prosaic history. From the perspective of these historians, and indeed from that of the modern historical profession in general, art and science are not neatly segregated from each other; they share a long, meandering frontier which scholarly and literary traffic crosses with little impediment and few formalities. Nor do the two between them engross the terrain of possibilities. A craft may bear the characteristic markings both of art and of science; to include it under one rubric may not exhaust its definition. Or it may be neither, except in the loosest application of the terms; to expel it from one in no way guarantees it a haven in the other.

It will therefore become necessary to trace the boundaries and specify the character of science and of art. But this much, I think, I can conclude with confidence now: history is an art much of the time, and it is an art by virtue of being a branch of literature. I say "much of the time," for the widespread complaints against inartistic historical writing are perfectly justified. Clio, G. M. Trevelyan found it necessary to remind the public at the beginning of this century, is also a muse; history, H. R. Trevor-Roper found it necessary to insist more recently, no longer speaks to the general public because it has lost its grip on literature.[1] Some of the laments we hear are the helpless response of the philistine confronted with the daunting apparatus of scholarship, but it remains true that much historical work is innocent of even a nodding acquaintance with the writer's art. We have all encountered those dreary, dutiful chronicles piling up mounds of facts that everyone knows or nobody wants to know; those narrow, earnest monographs choking in their garlands of ibids and parched in their deserts of charts. We have wondered at those mountainous and learned French theses that do strive for distinction but founder in literary incoherence, with their style borrowed at once from the frenzy of Michelet and the un-

---

[1] See G. M. Trevelyan, "Clio: A Muse" (1903), in *Clio, A Muse* (1913), and somewhat abridged in *The Varieties of History, From Voltaire to the Present*, ed. Fritz Stern (1956), pp. 227–245. H. R. Trevor-Roper, *History: Professional and Lay* (1957).

gainly informativeness of the railway timetable.[2] Whatever else it may be, history is not an art all of the time.

I have no wish to sentimentalize the past, least of all the past of historical writing. Trevelyan's much-quoted polemic against historians who forget their obligations to literature in whoring after the false god of science has an impressive pedigree. Literary historians in ancient Greece and Rome conducted a running battle with pedantic annalists; in the end, the historians won, subjected history to the stringent discipline of rhetoric, and pronounced the anathema against scholars who breached the rules of style appropriate to the dignity of history. Again, in the Renaissance, humanist historians denounced the "barbarity" of their Scholastic forebears and applied this derisive epithet to a failure of taste rather than a failure of decency; they never doubted that medieval historians had been unable to write proper history because their culture had prevented them from imitating such classic literary models as Livy.[3] And in the Age of Enlightenment, the philosophe-historians mocked the erudite scholars of the seventeenth and early eighteenth centuries not just for the mortal sin of being Christians but also for being pedants, a sin which, though only venal, was in their eyes discreditable enough. Tacitus, Guicciardini, and Voltaire all wanted to be accurate historians, but they also wanted to be interesting; they rec-

---

[2] In justice I should note two splendid exceptions, Emmanuel Le Roy Ladurie, *Les paysans de Languedoc*, 2 vols. (1966); Pierre Goubert, *Beauvais et les Beauvaisis de 1600 à 1730* (1960).

[3] See Stephen Usher, *The Historians of Greece and Rome* (1969); Felix Gilbert, *Machiavelli and Guicciardini: Politics and History in Sixteenth-Century Florence* (1965); Donald R. Kelley, *Foundations of Modern Historical Scholarship: Language, Law, and History in the French Renaissance* (1970); Hanna H. Gray, "Renaissance Humanism: The Pursuit of Eloquence," *Journal of the History of Ideas*, 24, no. 4 (October–December 1963), 497–514.

ognized that the road to interest traversed the land of art, and that some of their most learned contemporaries failed to take it. Thus the unliterary presentation of historical material has a long and respectable tradition behind it, almost as long—and almost as respectable—as the tradition that began with Herodotus and Thucydides. We can read the history of history in several ways, but one profitable way is as an inconclusive debate between the proponents of beauty with truth and the proponents of truth without beauty. The contest is intermittently confused by bouts of politeness: each protagonist ceremoniously suggests to the other that dispute is really redundant, since science need not be dull and art need not be inaccurate. But contentious or courteous, the debate, it seems, goes on.

One political reality that has made the debate particularly confusing is the curious alliance between scientists and skeptics. In the last two centuries, as the claims of historical scientists have grown more emphatic, the very different claim that objective knowledge is impossible has become louder as well, and it has often been made by the same historians. The irenic posture of most eighteenth- and nineteenth-century historians has not survived into our time; what we have today is a spectrum of views ranging from the certainty that history is a strict science to the incompatible certainty that it is wholly literature, to the more widely held conviction that it is neither of these. A forceful expression of one modern attitude is V. H. Galbraith's declaration that "there is no essential connexion" between history and literature, "however much and long they have been associated. By all means," he adds, "write like Macaulay and Gibbon—if you can—but however one writes and whatever one writes about, the basic aim should be to arrive at the bare truth. Truth and rhetoric are bad bedfellows."[4] In its righteous insistence on the historian's duty to truth, and to that alone, Galbraith's dictum is a bracing declaration of faith. But to treat style as decoration is to give advice that is at once bad and dated. It is bad because to write like somebody else cannot be good style: Gibbon and Macaulay, after all, much as they modeled themselves after admired ancestors, wrote like themselves. And it is dated, because it reverts to the classical and neo-classical conception of style as the application of rhetoric to subject matter. If we have learned anything since the Romantics—or, for that matter, since Buffon—it is that style is not the dress of thought but part of its essence.[5] It is, after all, significant that while in the course of centuries history has shed many of its partners and defied most of its masters, it has never surrendered its profitable affection for literature. It seems a little late in the day to disrupt a liaison that has persisted for such a long time and has been so agreeable to both partners.

The study of style, then, suggests that the historian has not finished his work once he has understood the causes and the course of events. Historical narration without analysis is trivial, historical analysis without narration is incomplete. Monographs need not be artistic, though in skillful hands they can have their own aesthetic quality. But the house of history, to which monographs are so indispensable, must be

---

[4] V. H. Galbraith, *An Introduction to the Study of History* (1964), p. 3.

[5] Dryden wrote in the preface to his *Annus Mirabilis*: ". . . the first happiness of the poet's imagination is properly invention, or finding of the thought; the second is fancy, or the variation, deriving or moulding of that thought . . . the third is elocution, or the art of clothing or adorning that thought so found and varied in apt, significant and sounding words." Quoted in Graham Hough, *Style and Stylistics* (1969), p. 3. Some isolated instances apart (my epigraph from Burton records one such), this was the standard view; it makes Buffon's famous remark all the more remarkable.

not only secure, but handsome as well. Otherwise, though it may stand, neither casual tourist nor cultivated connoisseur will take the trouble to visit it.

But if history is often an art, what kind of art is it? Here the trail, easy to follow so far, becomes less legible. The assertion that the historian's principal loyalty is to the truth—an assertion that no one has ever disputed—does not instantly differentiate it from other literature. The stylistic techniques that historians employ to state their truths resemble strikingly the techniques that novelists and poets employ to present their fictions. And conversely: it is one of the proudest boasts of imaginative authors—of all but fabulists and sometimes even of fabulists—that they are conveying truth through their work. Aristotle's much-quoted observation that poetry is truer than history has found many echoes; Burckhardt was only the most famous of historians to give it his humble assent.

But we do well, I think, to hesitate before we equate the truth of poetry with the truth of history. We are here in the hands of analogy, and analogy is a seductive, which is to say dangerous, guide. Sigmund Freud used to say that he envied novelists and poets—*Dichter*—for their rapid, almost instinctive grasp of hidden psychological processes, but he never confused his science of psychology with the art of poetry; intuitive divination might at times provide a breathtaking shortcut to the truth, but never a substitute for the patient pursuit of causal connections or the rigorous test of scientific demonstration. But because fiction and history have style in common, it becomes critical at this point to specify in what the truth of fiction consists. Fiction can certainly offer veracity of detail; novelists and poets are no strangers to research. Balzac tells his readers perhaps more than they care to know about the printing business in *Les illusions perdues*; Melville piles up exhaustive technical information about whales and whaling in *Moby-Dick*; Thomas Mann dwells with undisguised relish on the causes and treatment of tuberculosis in his *Zauberberg*. In themselves, these facts are reportage; detached from the fiction in which they perform their function, they would be pieces of journalism or scholarship or even history. But they exist to provide plausible settings for imagined characters, to ease the reader's entry into the fictive world the writer has constructed for him. Truth is an optional instrument of fiction, not its essential purpose.

Most makers of fiction, to be sure, are shackled by chains of probability and coherence. "Information is true if it is accurate," E. M. Forster once said. "A poem is true if it hangs together."[6] The storyteller's initial choices constrict the choices he can make later. In *La nausée*, Jean-Paul Sartre follows the mental crisis of Roquentin, a twentieth-century Frenchman troubled by uncertain academic aspirations and immured in a provincial town for his research. What he eats, whom he meets, how he talks, even what nauseates him, must all be appropriate to his location in time, place, and station. The arm of coincidence must never be allowed to grow too long. Yet what is remarkable about fiction, as distinct from history, is not its limits but its license. It is true that what Dickens can permit David Copperfield and his friends to say, wear, believe, or experience is far from infinite. To establish a character is to sign a contract. But will David's mother marry Mr. Murdstone or not? Does Mr. Murdstone beat David? And does David bite Mr. Murdstone? On these and countless other matters Dickens' implicit con-

[6] Quoted in George Watson, *The Study of Literature: A New Rationale of Literary History* (1969), p. 29.

tract with his readers is conveniently silent. A writer may stir a drop of fantasy into his realism; he may give Sherlock Holmes an invented address in a real street, or supply the Statue of Liberty with a sword in place of a torch. But the reader would find fault with Conan Doyle or Franz Kafka only if these novelists had been writing police reports—or histories.

There are times, of course, when fiction assumes some of the burdens of history. A novel about Henri IV or a play about Queen Victoria requires an intimate commerce with facts in which a novel about Tom Jones or a play about Barbara Undershaft need not engage. Yet even in these historical fictions, the obligations of literature differ from those of history. Shakespeare's historical plays stand as a reminder of how readily historical personages lend themselves to myth making, and the more remote the event from our passionate and partisan concerns, the more malleable the past in the poet's hands. Doubts arise, to be sure, if the myth is too tendentious or self-serving; when Rolf Hochhuth tells lies about Winston Churchill we are not inclined to palliate them on grounds of poetic license; when Shakespeare denigrates Richard III as an unrelieved villain we may enjoy his poetry without accepting his verdict; when Schiller has St. Joan dying on the battlefield, our temptation to laugh becomes irresistible. Yet within generously drawn political or aesthetic boundaries, readers of fiction suspend their disbelief in behalf of the writer's invention, even when he is inventing reality. They do not insist on verifying his evidence as he moves beyond documents to imaginary conversations or unknowable thoughts. They allow Solzhenitzyn to invade Stalin's mind with a freedom that a historian can envy but not imitate.

The truth of such privileged portraits as Solzhenitzyn's exploration of Stalin's mind in *The First Circle* is a combination of the particular and the general. If Solzhenitzyn had portrayed Stalin as a lovable, much-maligned philanthropist, he would have failed to convince anyone: Stalin, his readers would say, was not like that. And if Solzhenitzyn had portrayed Stalin as a mechanical monster, with no regions of fear or madness, he might have secured emotional assent qualified by reservations: human beings, his readers would say, are not like that. The proofs for Solzhenitzyn's portrait lie outside his fiction, in his readers' knowledge of history and of human nature.

Imaginative writers normally claim that their fictions penetrate to truths of a high and general kind. The writer sees life with an embracing sympathy or a perceptive eye; he empathetically identifies himself with many conditions and comprehends the dilemma of life which it is the supreme task of melodrama to deny and escape.[7] Novelists have said many penetrating things about social relations and private conflicts, about the travail of faith, the subtleties of rank, the power of money, the temptations of the flesh. Fielding offered as his bill of fare nothing less than human nature. But these free-floating truths emerge from a context of untruths. Indeed, to make a story too probable, to derive it too closely from newspaper accounts, as realists have been known to do, is to turn bad history into bad fiction. In my judgment, the experi-

---

[7] To quote but one representative statement, from George Watson: "To have studied and understood *Othello* is to have absorbed information about the moral world; and anyone who has observed with care the steps by which the heroes and heroines of Henry James's novels take or fail to take their decisions could not avoid learning what few men could otherwise know about what a considered decision in all its stages is like." Watson, *The Study of Literature*, p. 46.

ments of writers like Truman Capote and Norman Mailer with new genres—documents as novels and novels as documents—have only served to confound two distinct realms, to the benefit of neither. Oscar Wilde presciently condemned such innovations when he visualized the novelist working "at the Librairie Nationale, or at the British Museum, shamelessly reading up his subject," and falling "into careless habits of accuracy."[8] However much we may love stories for the truths they reveal, we love them even more for the lies they tell. "A copy of the universe," Rebecca West has said, "is not what is required of art; one of the damn things is ample."[9] Precisely. But what is not required of art is required of history: to discover, no matter how shocking the discovery, what the old universe was like rather than to invent a new one. The difference is nothing less than decisive.

To establish the distinction between the truths of fiction and the truths of history helps to specify the kind of art that history is, or can be. But it throws no light on the other, more problematic, part of the question at issue: does its commitment to truth make history even remotely into a science? Can it aspire to the kind of objectivity without which any science cannot live? On this point, the evidence of my essays on four stylists is equivocal, even contradictory; it offers support, indeed, to two opposed positions. The first

[8] Oscar Wilde, *Intentions* (1891), in *The Artist as Critic: Critical Writings of Oscar Wilde*, ed. Richard Ellmann (1969), pp. 293–294.
[9] Quoted by D. Terence Langendoen, "The Problem of Linguistic Theory in Relation to Language Behavior: A Tribute and Reply to Paul Goodman," *Language as a Human Problem, Daedalus* (Summer 1973), p. 198.

of these is better known than the second, but still worth setting out. It holds that the study of style is a study in limitations. Clearly, like other historians, these four masters saw the historical world as *their* historical world. And clearly, it is their style that supplies the most incriminating evidence for their ineradicable, unconscious parochialism. Gibbon the ironist, Ranke the believer, Macaulay the liberal, Burckhardt the poet —each of these looked on the past from his angle of vision which only partly intersected that of the others.

This sweeping skepticism, which questions the very possibility of objective history, finds sustenance in a well-known theory of perception that is the psychological counterpart of the sociological theory of false consciousness. It is very popular with historians—largely, I suspect, because it rescues them from the imputation of naïveté. Its proponents argue that perception is largely projective, and motivation determinative of results. Notions like the "innocent eye," they insist, or of the mind as a passive and accurate camera, are nothing better than misconceived metaphors, the delusions of simpleminded positivists or equally simpleminded Realists. Every perception is a construction; the simplest observation (as Goethe said long ago) is already a theory. Facts are never neutral; they are impregnated with value judgments. The child hears not just a sound, but a loving or a scolding voice; the adult looking at a painting translates its two-dimensional lines and colors into a representation of three-dimensional reality. Reinforcing the pressures of social location or cultural presuppositions, the accidents of time and place and affiliation create mental sets that act like so many distorting lenses. What is more, to observe and to reflect are at the same time to act; the historian studies the past that he may influence, no matter how modestly, the world around and the world within him. The control he seeks may be no more than self-control, a reassuring sense of familiarity or hope in a bewildering or threatening environment. But his historical inquiries, like all inquiries, are always the response to some need, and always directed to some purpose; interest is built into his most primitive acts of perception and appears in suitably disguised form in his most urbane presentations. And the evidence for this position is ample and seems irrefutable: different reports on the same realities, different interpretations of the same events, and, as always, different styles.

In sharp contrast, the natural sciences, this line of argument goes on, have discarded their biases in the course of their triumphant career; rising above class or nation or anthropomorphism, they have gained distance with their repeatable experiments, falsifiable theories, and dispassionate vocabulary. Whatever the metaphysical status of the realities the scientist studies—and philosophers of science continue to debate the question—natural scientists have their chemical analyses, their counter readings, and their mathematical formulas. In the midst of such wealth (to recall Ranke's saying from a different context) the historian is poor. He may have information no reasonable critic will dispute: he may know the precise date of a battle or the correct wording of a charter. He has techniques, often quite sophisticated, enabling him to expose forgeries and make jumbled numbers intelligible. The prestige of natural science continues to haunt his waking dreams. Like the natural scientist, the historian also governs his domain of certainty. But it is pitifully small. He aspires to tell true stories, but there are so many ways of telling the same story that the very meaning of "the same" is imperiled. The historian's strategies of exposition are all, consciously or unconsciously, strategies of persuasion. Style, therefore, just

[196]

because it is the mark of the historian's distinctiveness and distinction, is also the proof of his unconquerable subjectivity.

This pessimistic assessment of the historian's claim to objectivity has long been the stock-in-trade of historiography, which, as I have suggested, justifies its existence with the argument that historians are doomed to limited perspectives; it is the wrestling with these limits, the offering of new, larger interpretations that prove to be limits in turn, that give the writing of history its history. There is nothing very bold about this view. In perceiving their task to be the analysis of perspectives, historiographers have drifted with prevailing currents in the theory of knowledge. For over two centuries, epistemologists have been propelled by an un-masking animus; they have been intent on exposing the un-challenged prejudices, the unrecognized preconceptions, the comfortable ignorance built into the pursuit, and concealed in the very possibility, of knowledge. This critical current was usually one-sided, combative, polemical. Though it drew on classical sources, it rose with the antitheological and antimetaphysical crusade of the Enlightenment, and crested in the sociology of Marx, the epistemology of Nietzsche, and the ontology of the historicists. Since the mid-nineteenth cen-tury, historians have reiterated that progressive historians write progressive history and bourgeois historians bourgeois history, and that, like their controlling assumptions, the style of these historians is the expected, indeed the inescapable, style of their party or their class. And they have reinforced their skeptical epistemology with a relativist metaphysics, questioning the objective existence of facts as distinct from the historian who interprets them. Historical facts, Carl Becker wrote, are not out there, in the world of the past, but in here, in the mind of the historian. And the popular conclusion has been summarily put by E. H. Carr: "The belief in a hard core of facts existing objectively and independently of the interpretation of the historian is a preposterous fallacy, but one which it is very hard to eradicate."[10]

The tenor of Carr's conclusion suggests how much authority this position carries among historians today. Most consider it beyond discussion. Yet it is precisely this preposterous fallacy I wish to defend. My essays permit a drastically different and far more hopeful set of conclusions. I am not disposed to deny—how could I?—that the historian's mental set or secret emotions often cause partial blindness or involuntary distortions, but I would argue that they can also provide a historian with a clear view of past actions that other historians have been too ill-prepared to understand, too indifferent even to see. As Burckhardt put it, transmitting a bit of ancient wisdom: if our eye were not in some way sunlike, it could not see the sun—*Unser Auge ist sonnenhaft, sonst sähe es die Sonne nicht.*[11] Passion, notorious as the historian's most crippling liability, may become his most valuable asset. Not all consciousness is false consciousness.

This position, too, finds impressive support in modern psychology, both in psychoanalysis and in the psychology of perception, and to my mind its findings, which have had little impact on the historical profession, are conclusive. Perception is part of the total person, and the dominant direction of the person may be, not toward myth or self-protection, but

[10] E. H. Carr, *What Is History?* (1962), p. 6.
[11] Jacob Burckhardt, *Weltgeschichtliche Betrachtungen*, ed. Albert Oeri, in *Jacob Burckhardt-Gesamtausgabe* (1929), 7:6, 6n.

toward mastery and reality. To equate motive with distortion, or even with limitation, is demonstrably illegitimate; there are motives and ideals driving the inquirer toward the efficient comprehension of the outside world. The need that generates inquiry may be sublimated into disinterestedness. Even empathy, the very emotion that the modern historian is ceaselessly enjoined to cultivate, has its objective component. Qualities are as inherent in the object as size.[12]

I cannot exaggerate the significance of this psychological point of view for the historian. As he trains his senses and his conceptual apparatus to become more sensitive and accurate instruments, as he ascends from the self-indulgent and self-centered realm of the pleasure principle to the austere atmosphere of the reality principle, what he sees and what there is match more and more closely. Ranke's celebrated wish to relate the past as it actually happened is neither a fatuous fantasy nor a concealed ideology. It is a difficult but perfectly realistic expectation. And I might add that while historians' distortions are richly documented, historians' accurate and effective perceptions are richly documented as well: convergent reports on the past, reduction in the range of acceptable interpretations, and precise expressiveness in style.

While normally, then, the historian of history proceeds from apparent objectivity to concealed subjectivity, I propose that he can profitably reverse this procedure and move from subjectivity to understanding. Read in this fashion, these four essays are more than reports on the limitations that bias imposes and style reveals; they are reports as well on the

---

[12] There are "aspects of objects perceived as emotionally significant without being subjective in character. That is, they are not delusive projections but features of things, and an aspect of knowledge of physical events." George S. Klein, *Perception, Motives, and Personality* (1970), p. 65.

special capacity of each of these historians to see historical realities inaccessible to others. I have suggested that the feline malice animating Gibbon's parallel clauses exhibits his insensitivity to the oceanic feeling for mixed motives. But his ironic vision equipped him to penetrate the fraudulent machinations of Roman politicians, and the all-too-human pettiness of the Church Fathers. I have argued that the dramatic devices shaping Ranke's prose reveal his implicit conformity and conservatism. But his dramatic vision gave Ranke an unprecedented appreciation of the complex confrontations among the great powers. I have treated the bourgeois amplitude of Macaulay's rhetoric as a symptom of a prosperous and expansive English social system. But his optimistic vision allowed Macaulay to discard the nostalgia that obstructed the perception of others and to value, without embarrassment, the improvements in England's social, cultural, and economic life. I have traced Burckhardt's informal and emphatic way of writing to his unconscious identifications with the magnificent personalities of the Renaissance. But it was this empathetic vision that for the first time encompassed the enormous vitality of the Renaissance and its historic uniqueness.

The most rigorous test of this analytical strategy would be a look at the cognitive style[13] of a historian who is at once a scholar, a man of letters, and a known partisan. I do not want to write yet a fifth essay, but there is one historian who combines these qualities in heroic proportions, and whose historical work will prove a bulwark against skepticism. Theodor Mommsen, the only historian (if we except Winston Churchill) ever to win the Nobel Prize for Literature, was an unsurpassed scholar, a distinguished stylist and, by his

---

[13] For this term, see Klein, *Perception, Motives, and Personality*, pp. 8–10.

own testimony, a lifelong *animal politicum*.[14] The general public knows Mommsen as the author of the *Römische Geschichte*, a work notable for its analytical lucidity and narrative vigor. But the historical profession knows Mommsen preeminently as a meticulous inquirer and inventive academic entrepreneur, who inspired younger men with his enthusiasm for the sources. Yet, though relentless in his pursuit of detail, Mommsen was richly endowed with historical imagination, and filled grievous lacunae in abundant yet fragmentary documents with brilliant conjectures and inspired emendations. For Mommsen, as for Burckhardt, the imagination was the mother of history as well as of poetry—*die Phantasie, welche wie aller Poesie so auch aller Historie Mutter ist*.[15]

In a much-quoted address, Mommsen insisted that the historian is born not made.[16] But Mommsen himself certainly worked on his style, taking pleasure in the felicity of his prose; he cultivated his taste by reading *belles lettres*— French novels and English poetry—all his life. In the manner of Burckhardt, Mommsen was a gifted, if occasional, poet and, in Burckhardt's manner, he responded sensitively to the emotional and aesthetic side of his experience. Mommsen's *Römische Geschichte* displays his literary culture, but what is of central interest here are his notorious anachronisms.

[14] The phrase comes from a passage in his will, written in 1899, but not printed until 1948: "I have never had, and never aspired to political position and political influence; but in my innermost being, and I think with the best that is within me, I have always been an animal politicum and wished to be a good citizen—*bin ich stets ein animal politicum gewesen und wünschte ein Bürger zu sein*. That is not possible in our nation, in which the individual, even the best, never gets beyond serving in the ranks, and beyond political fetishism." Quoted in Alfred Heuss, *Theodor Mommsen und das 19. Jahrhundert* (1956), p. 282.

[15] Quoted in Albert Wucher, *Theodor Mommsen: Geschichtsschreibung und Politik* (1956), p. 21n.

[16] "Rede bei Antritt des Rektorates," October 15, 1874, in *Reden und Aufsätze* (3rd printing, 1912), pp. 3–16.

Mommsen's first readers made much of his "subjective way of writing history." Even more than his clarity and vigor, it was his putting ancients into modern dress, those "Liberals" and "Junkers" who march through his pages, that was the most distinctive aspect of his style from the beginning.[17]

Mommsen justified his practice with a certain self-consciousness. "There is a lot to be said about that modern tone," he wrote to his friend Wilhelm Henzen in 1854, the year that the first volume of his *Römische Geschichte* appeared. He insisted that he had no intention of cajoling the public. True, direct allusions had offered themselves by the hundreds, but he had scorned them all. Yet he had found it essential to make the ancients climb down from their imaginary pedestals and to place them once again into the real world, where men love and hate, work and play, invent fantasies and tell lies. "That is why the consul had to become the mayor—*und darum musste der Konsul ein Bürgermeister werden.*" He might have overdone it, but he was confident that his intentions, at least, were "pure and right—*rein und richtig.*"[18]

We have no cause to question the purity of Mommsen's intentions, though we may doubt that his desire to endow faded historical figures with new life exhausts his reasons for introducing Junkers and Agrarians onto the Roman stage. When he undertook to write the *Römische Geschichte*, the stirring and dismaying events of the revolutions of 1848 lay in his immediate memory. Mommsen had been engaged in those revolutions as partisan and publicist, and had been briefly deprived of his academic post during the first period of

---

[17] For their reception, see the citations in Wucher, *Mommsen*, chap. 3.

[18] Mommsen to Henzen, November 26, 1854. Quoted in Ludo Moritz Hartmann, *Theodor Mommsen. Eine Biographische Skizze* (1908), pp. 62–63.

reaction. He was—in .the German fashion—a liberal; he hated the rural oligarchy and distrusted military and clerical power alike. In the years that followed the first three volumes of his *Römische Geschichte,* despite his immense and wide-ranging activity as professor of ancient history and superintendent of numerous scholarly enterprises, he found time to serve first in the Prussian, then in the German legislature. Nor was he a latter-day Gibbon, a silent senator. He was contentious, outspoken, and fearless. Politics was in his bones, on his mind—and under his pen.

It would seem only natural for such a political being to see the past principally in political terms and to invest the political struggles in that past not merely with the urgency, but with the very shape, of the present. And this is the charge that Mommsen's critics leveled against him during his lifetime and have leveled ever since: Mommsen worshipped the Caesar of ancient Rome because he longed for a Caesar in his own time; disgusted with modern demagogy, he smuggled his offended feelings into his assessment of the Republican opposition to Caesar.[19] Mommsen was sensitive to such criticisms. In the second edition of his third volume, which delineates the ascent of his hero, Mommsen added a long passage firmly denying that his admiration for Julius Caesar meant admiration for Caesarism, and turned the criticism against his critics: his glorification of Caesar, precisely because he was so great a statesman with so noble an aim, should actually be read as a devastating critique of his modern authoritarian disciples.

---

[19] Writing an obituary on Mommsen, the English historian Francis Haverfield noted: "Probably he had met his Cicero: there were many in 1848 who talked admirably and acted feebly." *English Historical Review,* 19 (1904), 84. In Wucher, *Mommsen,* p. 92n.

Mommsen protested in vain; his disclaimer, though as explicit and eloquent as he could make it, has not carried conviction.[20] It was indeed eminently plausible to argue that Mommsen's anachronisms are symptomatic of partisanship. Yet this verdict on Mommsen's historical perception trivializes his accomplishment. Near the end of his life Mommsen said once again what he had often said and always acted on: the vital nerve of the scholarly enterprise is inquiry free from all presuppositions—*Unser Lebensnerv ist die voraussetzungslose Forschung.*[21] This was anything but rhetorical self-justification: Mommsen's view of antiquity was something more than a mere outlet for the frustrated passions of a defeated liberal. Mommsen's Roman experience was shared by many other northerners—Englishmen, Netherlanders, Germans—facing, for the first time, the sources of their classical culture. Italy was the sunny playground of their schoolboy imagination, and the reality, though overlaid by medieval and modern accretions, was more intense than their most lavish fantasies. To be overwhelmed by Italy: that had been the experience of Goethe, duly recorded—and dutifully reexperienced by countless Germans. But others had experienced it as well, historians as much as poets. Gibbon, unsentimental as he was, had felt the Italian magic, and so had Ranke and Burckhardt. When Mommsen went to Italy in 1844, his emotions were in good company. "Italy!" he wrote, "holy soil of nature, art, history! The first trip through your very own sea, the first step on your holy soil!" After he reached Rome, he wept. And when he came back to Italy thirty years later, he traveled

---

[20] But note the more favorable appraisals in the more recent literature by Heuss and Wucher (see notes 14 and 15 above.)

[21] "Universitätsunterricht und Konfession" (1901), in *Reden und Aufsätze,* p. 432.

through the country like an old lover recalling his first love—a metaphor, I must add, that is Mommsen's own.[22] Mommsen's emotion for the Roman past was a palimpsest, whose layers only the most delicate reading can discriminate. It was composed of memories reinforced by his thirst for political action; this thirst, in turn, was fed by memories; and both stood under the severe discipline of his scholarly probity.

In sum—and this, of course, is the point of this exploration—Mommsen's passions gave him insights denied to earlier historians of the Roman Republic. Modern research has pulverized the Roman party contest, and has shown the parties to have been interest groups clustering around family alliances.[23] Mommsen doubtless oversimplified the struggle, giving Cicero's sweeping terms *optimates* and *populares* more credit than they deserved. Yet it was because he participated in the politics of his day—with partisan convictions but with open eyes—that Mommsen saw the politics of ancient Rome with a vividness unavailable to earlier historians, and with as much objectivity as the historians' techniques then in existence would permit. Gibbon had thought his captaincy in the Hampshire militia not useless to the historian of the Roman Empire, and in the same way, Mommsen's political activities proved not useless to the historian of the Roman Republic. And his chosen style was the perspicuous and dependable map of his discoveries.

[22] See Lothar Wickert, *Theodor Mommsen: Eine Biographie*, vol. 2, *Wanderjahre: Frankreich und Italien* (1964), pp. 43, 55f. A fascinating book could be written on the impact of Italy on great historians.

[23] See especially Lily Ross Taylor, *Party Politics in the Age of Caesar* (1949). Another historian whom it would be very interesting to examine from this perspective would be Jules Michelet, whose gift for empathy was enormous. "I am accomplishing a hard task," he wrote in 1849, "that of reliving, remaking, and suffering the Revolution. I have just passed through September and all the horrors of death: massacred at the Abbey, I am going

The dramatically divergent potentialities inherent in the historian's mental set raise the interesting prospect of similar polarities in the other dimensions, culture and craft, from which the historian also draws his motives, his materials, and his style. Most cultures, at most times, with their rewards for compliance and their horror of subversion, confine the historian's choice of subject matter and mode of judgment within defined boundaries of social decorum and political acceptability. No braver than most men, few historians have courted the martyrdom of the heretic. We have often been told, and rightly, that most historians preside over the construction of the collective memory. And they are not architects whose patrons have given them a free hand. They are under pressure to design an impressive, even a glorious facade that may bear only a tangential resemblance to the structure of events concealed behind it. Memory, we know, is the supple minister of self-interest, and collective memory is in this respect, as in others, like the memory of individuals. Most collective memory is a convenient distortion or an equally convenient amnesia; it has all too often been the historian's assignment to assist his culture in remembering events that did not happen, and in forgetting events that did. The culture wants a past it can use.[24] This cosmetic activity, I need hardly add, is rarely

before the Revolutionary Tribunal, that is, to the guillotine." Quoted in Emery Neff, *The Poetry of History* (1947), p. 149.

[24] When I was giving this conclusion its final revision, I recalled an essay by my late friend, Richard Hofstadter, which anticipates this argument in substance, and even in phrasing. I reprint the passage here: "Society and special interests in society call upon him [the historian] to provide them with memory. The kind of memory that is too often desired is not very different

venal or even conscious; to paraphrase George Bernard Shaw, historians do not need to be paid to do what they are eager to do for nothing. The parochial or nationalist productions by respectable practitioners show only too plainly that the historian is most insidious as a purveyor of cultural biases when he does not recognize them to be biases, but shares them and takes them to be established conclusions rather than unexamined prejudices.

But this is only the depressing, if admittedly the more prominent, side of a two-sided story. There have been times when societies have called, not for reassuring tales, but for harsh truths about their past. Then the historian exchanges the embroidered robe of the appointed panegyrist for the white coat of the independent anatomist. Paradoxically—it is, as we shall see, not the only paradox of his profession—the historian can be most useful when he is most free. Yet whatever beneficial consequences flow from the historian's pursuit of truth, they are available only to a relatively open society, which permits professional fraternities to set their own standards and tolerates intelligent and organized discontent. Cosmopolitans in a parochial culture, skeptics in a religious culture, socialists in a capitalist culture can feel free to undertake historical investigations that aim at veracity rather than beautification; outsiders often command a high and wide prospect, above the assumptions and values generally taken for granted. Critical history, of course, carries its own risks;

---

from what we all provide for ourselves—that is, memory that knows how to forget, memory that will rearrange, distort, and omit so much as is needed to make our historical self-images agreeable. In a liberal society the historian is free to try to dissociate myth from reality, but that same impulse to myth-making that moves his fellow men is also at work in him." Hofstadter, "History and the Social Sciences," in *Varieties of History*, ed. Stern, pp. 359–360.

it often substitutes new myths for old, or mistakes unmasking for truth and indignation for demonstration. But the point remains that culture may at times actually foster disinterested historical inquiry. And history records enough instances of such moments to permit the hope that these are perhaps exceptional, but by no means abnormal, interludes in man's age-old effort to deceive himself and oppress others.

Nineteenth-century liberal culture was the time when the ideal of a historical science uninhibited in its researches and free from all presuppositions celebrated its most notable triumphs. It is striking to see Burckhardt, whose assessment of his century was notoriously sour, judging it to be exceptionally well placed for the study of history. The easy accessibility of all literatures and all modes of thought, the relative indifference of states to the results of historical research, the impotence of established religions to interfere with the free airing of their past, seemed to him the most prominent reasons why his time was propitious for historians.[25] Liberalism, to be sure, suffered from complacency, as Macaulay's detractors were among the first to point out. It smuggled self-satisfaction into historical interpretation through the theory of progress, and cheerfully counted all earlier cultural achievements as imperfect prefigurations of its own. But liberalism also generated a refreshing atmosphere of self-criticism. It made Marx possible, though, I should add, it held Marx's critique of liberal historians at bay until well into the twentieth century. Yet, however self-serving the liberal ideal, and however flawed its application, it had its share in producing an intellectual climate congenial to the pursuit of objectivity.

It is not an accident—and this brings me to the dimension

[25] See Burckhardt, *Weltgeschichtliche Betrachtungen*, in *Gesamtausgabe*, 7:9–19.

of craft—that the nineteenth century should also have witnessed the transformation of history into a profession. It was then, as I have said, that the historian moved into his own house, the university. Practically all the leading historians of the age—Ranke and Burckhardt, Michelet and Fustel de Coulanges, Mommsen and Maitland—were professors; and another, Macaulay, could have been a professor had he not preferred to write history instead. I have already suggested that this move exacted its price. Craft in that century, as before or since, imposed its own constraints on the free exercise of the inquisitive spirit: its generally cautious and sometimes servile relation to power, its often smug orthodoxies and respectable points of view, and its stubborn resistance to radical new vistas. But it also developed its internal impulse toward autonomy, a capacity for detachment from the society that in general it served. Professionalism at its best braced the historian to resist the egregious, and to recognize the subtlest, pressures for conformity that culture could bring to bear on the individual historian.

Professionalism can do, and has done, more than this. Just as it intervenes to regulate the historian's traffic with his culture, it intervenes to regulate his traffic with himself. In establishing standards of proof and presentation—the full footnote, the honest bibliography, the accurate citation—it compels the historian's sources, reasoning, and conclusions into the glaring light of public scrutiny and serves to discriminate what he owes to others from what he has contributed on his own. The judgment of the professional forum is always candid and often cruel, and it prepares the way for more inclusive and more accurate historical interpretations. Like so much else in the discipline of history, the struggle for objectivity is a collective affair.

The share of professionalism in epistemological clarification is far more extensive than has usually been recognized. In serving as the systematic critic of personal perceptions, it acts as a kind of public superego, strengthening and extending the self-criticism that any responsible practitioner builds into his proceedings in the course of his training and his practice. And this pressure toward objectivity is realistic because the objects of the historian's inquiry are precisely that, objects, out there in a real and a single past. Historical controversy in no way compromises their ontological integrity. The tree in the woods of the past fell in only one way, no matter how fragmentary or contradictory the reports of its fall, no matter whether there are no historians, one historian, or several contentious historians in its future to record and debate it.

If this sounds like naïve Realism, I can only plead that I mean it to be Realism, though not of the naïve variety. One reason why interpretation has been generally treated as an exercise in subjectivity is that historians have illegitimately imposed one meaning of *interpretation,* smuggled in from the arts, on another meaning, appropriate to history. In the arts, interpretation is the interpreter's choice among a valid set of alternatives, as in an actor's interpretation of a role or a conductor's interpretation of a score. Charles Beard used the word in this permissive sense when he called attention to his precise title, *An* Economic Interpretation, rather than *The* Economic Interpretation; he insisted that he had used the indefinite article to show his awareness that his was far from being the only possible interpretation. With the same ill-placed modesty, Burckhardt offered his interpretation of the Renaissance as only one of several, all equally legitimate. But this usage (of which, I must confess, I too have been guilty) begs the very question an interpretation is designed to answer.[26] For the historian, an interpretation is a general explanation of events, nearly always providing a hierarchy of causes. To the extent that it is correct, any conflicting interpretation is false.

It is, of course, a matter of common knowledge that historical events are usually burdened with more than one interpretation. But I want to offer two glosses on this undeniable fact of the historian's life. Interpretations may supplement rather than contradict one another, just as different maps of the same territory may be equally correct without being in conflict at any point. The coexistence of interpretations, in short, is possible and even likely if these interpretations are, in the benign sense of that word, partial.

But when interpretations contradict each other, the historian cannot resign himself to these conflicts on the ground that they are inherent in his material, or in the nature of historical research. It is precisely the conflicts of interpretation that are the measure of how unsatisfactory the knowledge of the historical discipline is on this point. Physicists, seeking to reconcile incompatible theories of the origin of the universe, or the nature of particles, take such conflicts as a spur to further work rather than a reflection on the inescapable perspectivism of human knowledge. It is in any event reassuring to note that the pendulum of historical interpretations does not always swing with the same vehemence. New facts, better readings of old facts, the elimination of discredited views all bring about a reduction in its oscillations. Interpretations, to be sure, do not always tend toward the inertia of total

---

[26] See Charles Beard, *An Economic Interpretation of the Constitution of the United States*, 2nd edn. (1935), "Introduction to the 1935 Edition"; Burckhardt, *Kultur der Renaissance in Italien*, p. 3 [p. 1]; Peter Gay, *The Enlightenment: An Interpretation.* I suppose "*the* Interpretation" would have sounded immodest; but it would have been what I meant.

agreement; the impress of great events in the present encourages historians to take a new look at the past and discover the importance of what had been thought insignificant before, or the insignificance of what had been thought important. Or the impulse from neighboring disciplines may give a fresh push to the pendulum by throwing old certainties into doubt or by making unsuspected connections.

I am not suggesting that this process will ever end; the landscape of the past is too remote, too obscure, or, in modern history, too overcrowded for that. In fact, such a conclusive interpretation—the map that will never need revision—is unrealizable in principle. One commonplace way of stating that principle is to say that every generation must rewrite the histories of its predecessors. The commonplace is true, but not for the reason usually offered in its behalf. It holds true, rather, because events have posterities that may continue to the end of time—or, at least, the end of all historical writing. The meaning of an event for its posterities, as distinct from its contemporary meaning or its causes, is perpetually open to revision. As new generations reappraise the French Terror or the Great Depression, these events acquire new meanings, and these in turn become subject to inquiry and interpretation. History, in a word, is unfinished in the sense that the future always uses its past in new ways. But this argument in no way damages the point that an interpretation is an attempt to offer an objective account of an objective past—and it is, in any case, the task of the profession to make it so. In sum, like the realms of culture and of private character, craft has a Janus face, looking not merely toward subjectivity but toward science.

This has important bearing on style. Style, as I have argued, is the man, much of the time, and, as I have also argued, man is compounded of several dimensions. Style is the vector of their complex, sometimes conflicting, pressures. Culture and craft between them supply the possibilities and restrict the range of expression; character makes choices among the available options and lends the touch of individuality that becomes the historian's stylistic signature.[27] Whether style, then, is a clue to incurable subjectivity or to scientific objectivity, or to a mixture of the two, is a question that we can never answer in advance.

There still remains one more obstruction to the definition of history. I have noted what kind of art history can claim to be; I want now to specify what kind of science it is. Since Wilhelm Windelband's celebrated address of 1894, historians have sharply separated *Geschichte* from *Naturwissenschaft*. In Windelband's vocabulary, history seeks to understand unique events; it is idiographic. Natural science, in contrast, aims at general laws; it is nomothetic.[28] Historians of a wide range of persuasions have accepted this distinction; they have argued that historians seeking general laws have ceased to be historians and have turned into retrospective sociologists, nostalgic demographers, or pretentious metaphysicians. But the argument is false, or at least incomplete. The so-called hard sciences like astronomy or molecular biology are often concerned to explain singular events that are in nature like

[27] "It seems useful to visualize the motivational field as having a center and a periphery determined by the adaptive relevance of component motives, the peripheral ones including not only those irrelevant to the specific adaptive purpose but also repressed motives." Klein, *Perception, Motives, and Personality*, p. 61.

[28] See Wilhelm Windelband, "Geschichte und Naturwissenschaft" (1894), in *Präludien*, 2 vols. in 1 (7th and 8th edn., 1921), 2:136–160.

the events the historian fits himself to understand. And other natural sciences, like geology, generally concentrate on individual events, and thus resemble history more often and more closely than, say, physics.[29] On the other side, historians, even if they do not seek to establish general laws, freely use them in their interpretations, especially their causal interpretations, and in their logic of proof. The historians' great debate over the place that history should occupy in the spectrum of the sciences has been bedeviled by their identification of science with the most abstract, most severe, among its branches. This has induced them to beat a despairing retreat into *belles lettres*, or to undertake a manic effort at aping the natural sciences, even in style—with disheartening results. What makes a science into a science is its incessant pressure for objectivity and its verifiable propositions; what defines it is not its capacity to generate laws but its reliance on laws in its explanations, laws that may actually be borrowed from other disciplines—as they are, in history, mainly from psychology.[30] In all of these defining characteristics, history is—almost—a science. It is (to borrow Lévi-Strauss' phrase) the science of the concrete.

We are now in position to amend Bury's famous dictum and say: history is almost a science and more than a science.

[29] See for these issues, above all, Ernest Nagel, *The Structure of Science: Problems in the Logic of Scientific Explanation* (1961); and Carl G. Hempel, *Aspects of Scientific Explanation and Other Essays in the Philosophy of Science* (1965).

[30] They are—I should perhaps say: they should be. I am in any case convinced that the principal auxiliary science for history is psychology, in particular the branch known as ego psychology, developed by Heinz Hartmann, Anna Freud, and Erik Erikson from the work of Freud, a distinct move toward realizing Freud's greatest ambition: to construct a general psychology, applicable to "normal" persons as much as to neurotics. Once again, I want to refer to my forthcoming book, *Three Variations on the Theme of Cause: Manet, Gropius, Mondrian.*

This definition is admittedly paradoxical. But that makes it all the more precise, for the historian's craft, especially in its modern, professional incarnation, is pervaded by paradox. There is, first of all, the pair of incompatible injunctions that are required baggage for every apprentice historian: he is told to empathize with the past, but, at the same time, to preserve distance from it. If he neglects the first, he will never leave the present but parade in his writings contemporary actors dressed up in period costumes. And if he neglects the second, he will never leave the past, becoming not its student but its accomplice. This paradox denotes the tense yet productive coexistence of engagement and detachment that differentiates him from the novelist on one side and the physicist on the other. This is not the only way in which the modern historian resembles the psychoanalyst, who must sympathetically penetrate the most secret recesses of his patient's life, yet remain, as Freud poignantly put it, a stranger to his patient forever.

This paradox arises because, unlike the scientist of nature, the scientist of the human past is of the same stuff as his materials. That is what makes history into the most fragile of the sciences, susceptible to all the germs carried by the winds of doctrine, and vulnerable to the charges of prejudice or ideology that are so familiar. The critical distance that other modern scientists take for granted is, for the historian, a laborious victory over sympathy and anxiety. The emotional empathy that is irrelevant to other scientists is a quality he must patiently cultivate. Though one among the sciences, history faces problems no other science shares to the same degree.

The dual nature of history—at once science and art— emerges even more strikingly in the related paradox that history is at the same time a progressive discipline and a timeless treasure house of classics. Nowadays the historian will not begin his studies of ancient Rome with Gibbon or Mommsen; they are no longer the last word. Yet *The Decline and Fall of the Roman Empire* and the *Römische Geschichte* are imperishable masterpieces which no amount of fresh facts or revisionist interpretations will eject from the pantheon. What makes them immortal is more than their sheer literary merit, great though that is. Their view of the past embodies truths that have been confirmed by other historians and have become a permanent cultural possession. These books, and others like them, are like exquisitely drawn if somewhat old-fashioned maps: delightful to consult, a model to later map-makers, and still useful for showing others the way.

It is the historian's style that gives his map its distinct form. But the art of that style is of a very special kind. A few flourishes apart, it must not interfere with the historian's science. His literary devices are not separate from historical truth, but the precise means of conveying it. It is this aim that principally dictates his stylistic choices. The objective function of Gibbon's irony, whatever its psychological origins, is to give appropriate expression to the irony pervading Roman history. The objective function of Burckhardt's energy, whatever its origins, is to express the energy informing the age of the Renaissance. The historian's use of elevated diction, compression or elongation of time spans, synecdoche, ana-phora, indirect free style, or whatever other devices he may use, perform reportorial functions. To use words for their own sake, to make jokes that are not instrumental to the presentation, to employ emphasis in the interest of drama not inherent in the material, are sheer self-indulgence, mere fine writing.

On Style in History

The relation of style to truth has been obscured by the all too patent fact that a work of history is not a copy of the real world. It is a report, often with aesthetic merit. The linear nature of written literature compels the historian to present in sequential fashion structures that exist concurrently. But that is an inconvenience the historian shares with the astronomer and the sociologist. While the stylist's shaping hand appears to be imposing order on disparate, often seemingly disconnected past realities, his act of ordering is formal, exacted by the requirements of presentation. The order itself is something the historian does not make; he finds it. So controversial an activity as the carving out of a historical period is not a construction but a discovery. The order, the period, are there.

Historians are always making the happy discovery that their rhetoric differs from the rhetoric of the chemist or the biologist. But this does not entail the expulsion of history from the family of the sciences. It simply makes the historian's science special, with its own way of telling the truth. What should prevent the historian from offering his findings in the dry, deliberately graceless manner of a paper, say, in clinical psychology, is not literary aversion but his recognition that such a mode of presentation would be not merely less delightful than a disciplined narrative—it would also be less true. Style is the art of the historian's science.

BIBLIOGRAPHY

I have compiled this bibliography with no intention of being comprehensive, let alone complete; I have listed and briefly commented on the writings I cite in the text, and on others that have made a difference in my thinking.

Introduction: *Style–From Manner to Matter*

Stylistics and Linguistics

Erich Auerbach, *Mimesis: The Representation of Reality in Western Literature* (1946; trans. Williard R. Trask, 1953). A classic bridge from philology to sociology spanning Western literature from Homer to Virginia Woolf; enormously perceptive and justly influential.

Charles Bally, *Le langage et la vie* (1925; 3rd edn., 1951). A pioneering study in modern stylistics, concentrating on ordinary speech.

Wayne C. Booth, *The Rhetoric of Fiction* (1961)'. Clearheaded examination of literary strategies of novelists; applicable to other modes of writing.

E. H. Gombrich, *Art and Illusion: A Study in the Psychology of Pictorial Perception* (2nd edn., 1961). A brilliant attack on the notion of the "innocent eye," and a documented account of the various ways in which the seer contributes to what he sees. (But see Gibson and Klein titles in Conclusion, pp. 237, 238.)

Charles F. Hockett, *A Course in Modern Linguistics* (1970). A highly recommended general introduction to the field.

Graham Hough, *Style and Stylistics* (1969). Short but lucid introductory essay with useful summaries of the classic works; a short bibliography.

J. Middleton Murry, *The Problem of Style* (1922; edn. 1960). Though hardly profound, it has some interesting observations.

C. K. Ogden and I. A. Richards, *The Meaning of Meaning* (1923; 10th edn., 1949). A well-known early statement in modern semantics.

Ferdinand de Saussure, *Course in General Linguistics* (1915; trans. Wade Baskin, 1959). The wellspring of modern linguistics; its basic distinction between *langue* and *parole* was important to this essay.

Meyer Schapiro, "Style" (1953), most accessible in *Aesthetics Today*, ed. Morris Philipson (1961), pp. 81–113. Brilliant and comprehensive survey of all the meanings of style. Indispensable.

Leo Spitzer, *Linguistics and Literary History: Essays in Stylistics* (1948). Important collection of exemplary and civilized studies with a suggestive introduction on "Linguistics and Literary History."

Stephen Ullmann, *Style in the French Novel* (1957; 2nd edn., 1964).

——, *The Image in the Modern French Novel* (1960).

——, *Language and Style: Collected Papers* (1964). All highly informative and highly suggestive studies; Ullmann's reading of literary texts is exemplary for the historian.

Style in History; History of Style

H. Hale Bellot, *American History and American Historians: A Review of Recent Contributions to the Interpretation of the History of the United States* (1952). An intelligent survey. (See also Higham title, p. 221.)

Herbert Butterfield, *Man on His Past: The Study of the History of Historical Scholarship* (1955). Contains some illuminating essays, especially good on the emergence of the German school. (See also Ranke section, pp. 224–227.)

E. H. Carr, *What Is History?* (1962). An enormously popular set of lectures, essentially preaching an untenable relativism—though with some self-protective reservations.

R. G. Collingwood, *The Idea of History* (1946). The classic statement of the modern Idealist position; in this context, Collingwood's excessively neat but immensely revealing *Autobiography* (1939) deserves to be read.

F. M. Cornford, *Thucydides Mythistoricus* (1907). An important early statement of the proposition that Thucydides' history followed the conventions of Greek drama. (But see Finley and Ullman titles in this section.)

John H. Finley, *Thucydides* (1942). An important modification of Cornford's thesis; the book embodies the findings of Finley's articles, including especially "The Origins of Thucydides' Style," *Harvard Studies in Classical Philology*, 50 (1939), 35–84.

Peter Gay, *A Loss of Mastery: Puritan Historians in Colonial America* (1966). A set of lectures on one type of seventeenth-century history-writing.

Bibliography

———, *The Enlightenment: An Interpretation*, vol. 2, *The Science of Freedom* (1969), pp. 368–396. A brief interpretation of history-writing in the eighteenth century.

Clifford Geertz, "Ideology as a Cultural System," in *Ideology and Discontent*, ed. David E. Apter (1964), pp. 47–76. Much the most rational and most comprehensive interpretation of a heatedly debated notion. (See also Lichtheim title in this section.)

G. P. Gooch, *History and Historians in the Nineteenth Century* (1913; 1959). Though thoroughly old-fashioned, a comprehensive survey of the classic century of history-writing.

John Higham, with Leonard Krieger and Felix Gilbert, *History* (1965). A searching essay on the development of history-writing in the United States; aided by supplementary, equally searching, essays on European history in America and on some major European historians.

Richard Hofstadter, *The Progressive Historians: Turner, Beard, Parrington* (1968). A civilized trio of essays; doing justice both to the sociology and the psychology of history.

John Holloway, *The Victorian Sage: Studies in Argument* (1953). An interesting study of the relation of rhetoric to philosophy in writings of Carlyle, Disraeli, and other great Victorians.

M. L. W. Laistner, *The Greater Roman Historians* (1947). In a sizable literature, stands out as a good survey.

George Lichtheim, "The Concept of Ideology" (1965), reprinted in Lichtheim, *The Concept of Ideology and Other Essays* (1967). A well-informed historical survey.

Karl Mannheim, *Ideology and Utopia: An Introduction to the Sociology of Knowledge 1929–1931*, trans. Louis Wirth and Edward A. Shils (1936). The classic statement.

———, *Essays on the Sociology of Knowledge*, ed. Paul Kecskemeti (1952). An important posthumous collection on special aspects of the sociology of knowledge.

Friedrich Meinecke, *Historism*, 2 vols. (1936; trans. J. E. Anderson, 1972). A subtle and elegant tracing of the historicist strand as it emerged in reaction to the Enlightenment in eighteenth- and early nineteenth-century Germany, culminating in Ranke. Important and, to my mind, totally misleading.

Robert K. Merton, "The Sociology of Knowledge," "Karl Mannheim and the Sociology of Knowledge," in Merton, *Social Theory and Social Structure*, (rev. edn., 1957), pp. 456–488, 489–508. Two lucid appraisals.

J. G. A. Pocock, *The Ancient Constitution and the Feudal Law; A*

Study of English Historical Thought in the Seventeenth Century
(1957). A model of how the social roots of historical style should
be exposed and appraised.

Sir Ronald Syme, *Tacitus*, 2 vols. (1958). A powerful and exhaustive
account of Tacitus, deliberately written in a Tacitean style.

James W. Thompson, *A History of Historical Writing*, 2 vols. (1942).
There are other general histories, but this is probably the best,
though none too good; a full history of history remains to be written.

B. C. Ullman, "History and Tragedy," *Transactions of the American
Philological Association*, 73 (1942), 25–53. A sensible modification
of Cornford's extreme position, it argues that while ancient history
borrowed from the drama, it had scientific elements.

René Wellek, A *History of Modern Criticism*, 1750–1950, 4 vols. to
date (1955–1965). In the absence of a complete history of styles
this magisterial history of literary criticism can serve as an immensely informative substitute.

1: Gibbon: *A Modern Cynic among Ancient Politicians*

By Gibbon

The Autobiography of Edward Gibbon, ed. Dero A. Saunders (1961).
The most accessible version of Gibbon's memoirs, which present
something of a bibliographical nightmare. A careful critical edition
is that by Georges A. Bonnard (1966).

The English Essays of Edward Gibbon, ed. Patricia B. Craddock
(1972). A carefully edited collection.

Essai sur l'étude de la littérature, in *Miscellaneous Works of Edward
Gibbon, Esq.* ..., 2nd edn., ed. John Lord Sheffield, 5 vols. (1814),
4:1–93. This five-volume collection also contains most of Gibbon's
minor writings; its correspondence is now superseded (See below,
under Norton).

*Gibbon's Journal to January 28, 1763. My Journal, I, II, III, and
Ephemerides*, ed. D. M. Low (1929). Definitive.

*Gibbon's Journey from Geneva to Rome: His Journal from 20 April
to 2 October 1764*, ed. Georges A. Bonnard (1961). Definitive as
well.

The History of the Decline and Fall of the Roman Empire, ed. J. B.
Bury, 7 vols. (1896–1902). The best critical edition, though some
of its notes are now out of date.

The Letters of Edward Gibbon, ed., J. E. Norton, 3 vols. (1956).
Another definitive edition.

Bibliography

The Library of Edward Gibbon, Introduction by Geoffrey Keynes (1950). Fascinating information about a great collector and reader of books.

On Gibbon

J. B. Black, The Art of History (1926). Civilized essays on the four great eighteenth-century historians, including one on Gibbon; Hume, Voltaire, and Robertson are the other three.

Harold L. Bond, The Literary Art of Edward Gibbon (1960). Very helpful stylistic analysis.

Leo Braudy, Narrative Form in History and Fiction: Hume, Fielding and Gibbon (1970). Interestingly places Gibbon into company with a philosopher and a novelist.

C. N. Cochrane, "The Mind of Edward Gibbon," University of Toronto Quarterly, 12, no. 1 (October 1942), 1–17; 12, no. 2 (January 1943), 146–166. A careful survey of Gibbon's philosophical position.

Lewis P. Curtis, "Gibbon's Paradise Lost," in The Age of Johnson: Essays Presented to Chauncey Brewster Tinker, ed. Frederick W. Hilles (1949), pp. 73–90. An elegant essay on Gibbon's style, seeing Gibbon as the aristocratic educator.

Giuseppe Giarrizzo, Edward Gibbon e la cultura europea del settecento (1954). A wide-ranging study, living up to its title.

James William Johnson, The Formation of English Neo-Classical Thought (1967). Culminates in a long chapter on Gibbon.

Michael Joyce, Edward Gibbon (1953). Short and clear.

D. M. Low, Edward Gibbon, 1737–1794 (1937). Remains the best biography.

Shelby T. McCloy, Gibbon's Antagonism to Christianity and the Discussions That It Has Provoked (1933). Detailed and specialized.

Arnaldo D. Momigliano, "Gibbon's Contribution to Historical Method" (1954), in Momigliano, Studies in Historiography (1966), pp. 40–55. A very important essay.

Thomas P. Peardon, The Transition in English Historical Writing, 1760–1830 (1933). A judicious monograph, which places Gibbon into his time.

Joseph Ward Swain, Edward Gibbon the Historian (1966). Inferior to earlier studies, especially Low's.

H. R. Trevor-Roper, "Edward Gibbon after 200 Years," The Listener, 72, no. 1856 (October 22, 1964), 617–619; 72, no. 1857 (October

29, 1964), 657–659. Warmly appreciative of Gibbon the historian and, more surprisingly but persuasively, of Gibbon the man.

On Gibbon's World

J. B. Brumfitt, *Voltaire, Historian* (1958). A reliable monograph.

M. L. Clarke, *Greek Studies in England, 1700–1830* (1945). Survey of classical learning in Gibbon's day.

David C. Douglas, *English Scholars, 1660–1730*, rev. edn. (1951). An important, illuminating study of the much neglected generations of scholars who preceded Gibbon.

Peter Gay, *The Enlightenment: An Interpretation*, 2 vols. *The Rise of Modern Paganism* (1966); *The Science of Freedom* (1969). An attempt to offer a comprehensive interpretation of Gibbon's century; both volumes have full bibliographies.

Arnaldo D. Momigliano, "Ancient History and the Antiquarian," in Momigliano, *Studies in Historiography*, pp. 1–39. Another of Momigliano's penetrating essays.

Jean Seznec, *Essais sur Diderot et l'antiquité* (1957). Moves far beyond its announced subject to provide understanding of links between the eighteenth century and classical antiquity.

Jürgen von Stackelberg, "Rousseau, d'Alembert et Diderot traducteurs de Tacite," *Studi Francesi*, no. 6 (September–December 1958), 395–407.

————, *Tacitus in der Romania: Studien zur literarischen Rezeption des Tacitus in Italien und Frankreich* (1960). Together establish the heritage of Tacitus in France. A full study for his influence on England remains to be written, though Auerbach and Bond are most useful.

2: Ranke: *The Respectful Critic*

By Ranke

Sämmtliche Werke, ed. Leopold von Ranke, Alfred Dove, and others, 54 vols. (1867–1890). The most comprehensive, though not wholly complete edition; the masterpieces have been published separately or in collections of selected works.

Deutsche Geschichte im Zeitalter der Reformation, ed. Paul Joachimsen, 6 vols. (1926). Notable for including some posthumous fragments, like the "Luther-Fragment" of 1817 (6:313–399), and the so-called "Frankfurt Manuscript" of 1837 (6:403–469). Other

Bibliography

posthumous publications are conveniently listed in Rudolf Vierhaus, *Ranke und die soziale Welt* (1957), pp. 251–252.

Das Briefwerk, ed. Walther Peter Fuchs (1949). A good collection of Ranke letters.

Neue Briefe, ed. Bernhard Hoeft and Hans Herzfeld (1949). A valuable companion volume.

Aus Werk und Nachlass, vol. 1, *Tagebücher*, ed. Walther Peter Fuchs (1964). Immensely revealing.

On Ranke

Ludwig Dehio, "Ranke and German Imperialism" (1950), in *Germany and World Politics in the Twentieth Century*, trans. Dieter Pevsner (1959). A brave attempt, from within the German historical establishment, to reevaluate Ranke's historical work.

Pieter Geyl, "Ranke in the Light of the Catastrophe," in Geyl, *Debates with Historians* (1955), pp. 1–18. A severe and not wholly satisfactory, but much needed, critique.

G. P. Gooch, "Ranke's Interpretation of German History," in Gooch, *Studies in German History* (1948), pp. 210–266. A second visit to territory Gooch had explored much earlier, in *History and Historians in the Nineteenth Century*. (See above, p. 221.)

Eugen Guglia, *Rankes Leben und Werke* (1893). A biography that has been superseded by numerous publications of documents.

Hanno Helbling, *Leopold von Ranke und der historische Stil* (1953). Studies on Ranke's stylistic procedures.

H. F. Helmolt, *Leopold von Rankes Leben und Wirkung* (1921). The most recent biography; too uncritical.

Carl Hinrichs, *Ranke und die Geschichtstheologie der Goethezeit* (1954). A suggestive work on Ranke's world of ideas.

Georg G. Iggers, "The Image of Ranke in American and German Historical Thought," *History and Theory*, 2 (1962), 17–40. A most useful article. (See also Iggers title, p. 227.)

Theodore von Laue, *Leopold Ranke: The Formative Years* (1950). Compact essay on the development of his historical ideas. Makes accessible, in good translations, two important Ranke essays, "A Dialogue on Politics," and "The Great Powers."

Gerhard Masur, *Rankes Begriff der Weltgeschichte* (1926). Very useful on Ranke's ideas on universal history.

Friedrich Meinecke, *Cosmopolitanism and the National State* (1963 ed.; trans. Robert B. Kimber, 1970).

———, *Machiavellianism* (1924; trans. Douglas Scott, 1957).

——, *Historism*, 2 vols. (1936; trans. J. E. Anderson, 1972.) In these three major works, and in many minor ones, Meinecke studied Ranke with affectionate admiration; both affection and admiration seem, at least to me, excessive, though we can learn much about the subtlety of Ranke's mind and (indirectly) the power of Ranke's way of thinking over German historiography. (See Krill title, p. 227.)

——, "Deutung eines Rankewortes," in *Aphorismen und Skizzen zur Geschichte*, 2nd edn. (n.d.), pp. 100–129. Variations on Ranke's saying that all epochs are equally near to God.

——, "Ranke und Burckhardt," in *Aphorismen und Skizzen*, pp. 143–180. An old man's reappraisal; with new reservations and new insights.

Wilhelm Mommsen, *Stein, Ranke, Bismarck: Ein Beitrag zur politischen und sozialen Bewegung des 19. Jahrhunderts* (1954). Interesting essay on Ranke's politics.

Moriz Ritter, *Die Entwicklung der Geschichtswissenschaft, an den führenden Werken betrachtet* (1919), pp. 362–421. A long chapter in a general history of history.

Ernst Simon, *Ranke und Hegel* (1928). An examination of the claim that Ranke was indebted to Hegel's philosophy.

Rudolf Vierhaus, *Ranke und die soziale Welt* (1957). Already referred to (p. 225) for its valuable bibliography, this thoughtful essay seeks to establish Ranke's concern with society and social history; it contains some hitherto unpublished excerpts from Ranke's *Nachlass*.

Ranke's World and Impact

Maarten Cornelis Brands, *Historisme als Ideologie. Het 'Onpolitieke' en 'Anti-Normatieve' Element in de duitse Geschiedwetenschap* (1965). An inquiry into the profession and the practices of the German historicists.

Walter Bussmann, *Treitschke: Sein Welt- und Geschichtsbild* (1962). A good biography of Ranke's great rival.

Ludwig Dehio, "Thoughts on Germany's Mission, 1900–1918" (1952), in Dehio, *Germany and World Politics in the Twentieth Century*, trans. Dieter Pevsner (1959), pp. 72–108. Courageous thoughts on the imperialist world Ranke helped to build. (See also Dehio's essay on Ranke, cited above, p. 225.)

Andreas Dorpalen, *Heinrich von Treitschke* (1957). A critical and fair-minded biography.

Felix Gilbert, *Johann Gustav Droysen und die preussisch-deutsche*

Bibliography

Frage, Beiheft 20, *Historische Zeitschrift* (1931). An illuminating esasy.

Walter Goetz, *Historiker in Meiner Zeit: Gesammelte Aufsätze* (1957). Autobiographical, biographical, and historiographical essays by a liberal German historian; Ranke and his influence mark almost every page. Too respectful but informative.

Wolfgang Hock, *Liberales Denken im Zeitalter der Paulskirche: Droysen und die Frankfurter Mitte* (1957). National liberal historians at a critical time—1848—in the life of German history, and German historians.

Walther Hofer, *Geschichtsschreibung und Weltanschauung* (1950). A searching inquiry into Meinecke's historical work and thought. Highly recommended.

Georg G. Iggers, *The German Conception of History: The National Tradition of Historical Thought from Herder to the Present* (1968). A comprehensive survey, with a chapter on Ranke, but surrounding it with his precursors, his few critics, and many followers. Useful.

Hans-Heinz Krill, *Die Ranke Renaissance: Max Lenz und Erich Marcks* (1962). A scholarly examination of two highly regarded German followers of Ranke. Devastating and important.

Friedrich Meinecke, *Erlebtes, 1862–1919* (1964). A volume of autobiography that chronicles the growth of a Rankean in a highly favorable atmosphere.

W. M. Simon, "Power and Responsibility: Otto Hintze's Place in German Historiography," in *The Responsibility of Power: Historical Essays in Honor of Hajo Holborn*, ed. Leonard Krieger and Fritz Stern (1967), pp. 199–219. Fine essay on a historian marked by Ranke's view of history.

Richard W. Sterling, *Ethics in a World of Power: The Political Ideas of Friedrich Meinecke* (1958). Can be read in conjunction with Hofer, above.

Ernst Weymar, *Das Selbstverständnis der Deutschen* (1961). A report on history teaching in German schools in the age of Ranke; valuable for its concentration on relatively little known writers of textbooks.

3: Macaulay: *Intellectual Voluptuary*

By Macaulay

The Works of Lord Macaulay, 2nd edn., ed. Lady Trevelyan, 8 vols. (1871). A very full but not wholly complete or critical edition. Usable for almost all purposes.

Selected Writings, ed. John Clive and Thomas Pinney (1972). Judicious selections, with excellent bibliography and introduction.

On Macaulay

Walter Bagehot, "Thomas Babington Macaulay," *Literary Studies*, 2 (1879), 221–260. Witty and critical.

Richmond C. Beatty, *Lord Macaulay, Victorian Liberal* (1938). Unimpressive; for the early years wholly superseded by Clive, below.

John Clive, *Macaulay: The Shaping of the Historian* (1973). An impressive study of the growth of the historian's mind, down to his return from India; an important book.

———, "Macaulay's Historical Imagination," *Review of English Literature*, 1 (October 1960), 20–28. A fine essay.

Sir Charles Firth, *A Commentary on Macaulay's History of England* (1938). Posthumous lectures; an immensely valuable survey of style, scholarship, achievements, and prejudices.

G. S. Fraser, "Macaulay's Style as Essayist," *Review of English Literature*, 1 (October 1960), 9–19. A brief helpful survey.

Pieter Geyl, "Macaulay in his Essays," in Geyl, *Debates with Historians* (1955), pp. 19–34. Excessively hostile but deserves attention.

W. E. Gladstone, "Macaulay," in *Gleanings of Past Years*, vol. 2 (1879). An important contemporary assessment.

George Levine, "Macaulay: Progress and Retreat," in Levine, *The Boundaries of Fiction: Carlyle, Macaulay, Newman* (1968). Sensitive analysis; perhaps too emphatic on Macaulay's retreat from reality.

William A. Madden, "Macaulay's Style," in George Levine and William Madden, eds., *The Art of Victorian Prose* (1968), pp. 127–153. Helpful.

John Morley, "Macaulay," *Critical Miscellanies*, vol. 1 (1888). By a late Victorian.

J. H. Plumb, "Thomas Babington Macaulay," *University of Toronto Quarterly*, 26 (1956–1957), 17–31. Traces Macaulay's style (mistakenly, I think) to lack of sexual passion.

Leslie Stephen, "Macaulay," in *Hours in a Library*, 3 vols. (1892), 2: 343–376. Like Morley's appraisal, vigorous and valuable.

———, "Macaulay, Thomas Babington," *Dictionary of National Biography* (1949), 12:410–418. Judicious and summary.

Mark A. Thomson, *Macaulay* (1959). A lucid pamphlet, stressing Macaulay's commitment to politics.

Bibliography

G. M. Trevelyan, "Macaulay and the Sense of Optimism," in *Ideas and Beliefs of the Victorians*, foreword by Harman Grisewood (1949; 1966), pp. 46–52. A brief appreciative appraisal.

G. O. Trevelyan, *The Life and Letters of Lord Macaulay*, 2 vols. (1876; enlarged one-volume edn., 1908). A splendid Victorian machine, filled with judicious views and complete letters; until Thomas Pinney's edition of the Macaulay's letters appears, this (and Clive's) work remains an indispensable source.

Ronald Weber, "Singer and Seer: Macaulay on the Historian as Poet," *Papers on Language and Literature*, 3 (Summer 1967), 210–219. Good study of the part that literary art played in Macaulay's historical work.

G. M. Young, "Macaulay" (1937), in *Victorian Essays*, selected by W. D. Handcock (1962), pp. 35–45. Elegant and discriminating.

Macaulay's World

Noel Annan, *Leslie Stephen: His Thought and Character in Relation to His Time* (1952). A brilliant study of Evangelicalism and its aftermath in Victorian England.

———, "The Intellectual Aristocracy," in *Studies in Social History: A Tribute to G. M. Trevelyan*, ed. J. H. Plumb (1955), pp. 241–287. Important.

Sir Herbert Butterfield, *The Whig Interpretation of History* (1932). A minor classic in the modern critique of liberal historiography.

J. W. Burrow, *Evolution and Society: A Study in Victorian Social Theory* (1970). Foundations of evolutionary views in Spencer, Tylor, and others; highly relevant to Macaulay's perception of the past.

E. M. Forster, *Marianne Thornton: A Domestic Biography*, 1797–1887 (1956). A loving account of Clapham, by a famous descendant.

William Minto, *A Manual of English Prose Literature* (edn. 1891). A general, thoroughgoing survey that pays close attention to Macaulay.

John Morley, *Recollections*, 2 vols. (1917). Reminiscences and scattered diary entries by a cultivated late Victorian.

Mario Praz, *The Hero in Eclipse in Victorian Fiction*, trans. Angus Davidson (1956). Places Macaulay into a general bourgeois, anti-heroic framework (see especially pages 102–117, which are specifically devoted to Macaulay); too mechanical in pursuit of a thesis, but worth reading.

Eric Stokes, *The English Utilitarians and India* (1959). Excellent; should be read in conjunction with Clive.

Hippolyte Taine, *History of English Literature*, trans. H. van Laun (1873). Contains a long and remarkable chapter on Macaulay (Book V, chap. 3).

R. K. Webb, *Harriet Martineau: A Radical Victorian* (1960). A fine biography of one of Macaulay's most significant contemporaries.

G. M. Young, *Victorian England: Portrait of an Age*, 2nd edn. (1953). Amidst a large literature, still an outstanding general essay.

4: Burckhardt: *The Poet of Truth*

By Burckhardt

Jacob Burckhardt-Gesamtausgabe, ed. Albert Oeri, Heinrich Wölfflin, and others, 14 vols. (1929–1933). The standard edition.

Briefe, ed. Max Burckhardt, 7 vols. to date (1949–1969). This will be definitive, when complete. Meanwhile the following selections, all rather different, are most helpful:

Briefe, selected by Max Burckhardt (1965).

Briefe, ed. Walther Rehm (1946).

Briefe zur Erkenntnis seiner geistigen Gestalt, ed. Fritz Kaphan (1935). A pioneering selection.

Letters, ed. and trans. Alexander Dru (1955). The first English collection.

The Age of Constantine the Great, trans. Moses Hadas (1949). Good English version of Burckhardt's *Zeit Constantins des Grossen* (1853; 2nd edn., 1880).

The Cicerone: An Art Guide to Painting in Italy for the Use of Travelers and Students (1908). Partial translation of *Der Cicerone* (1855).

The Civilization of the Renaissance in Italy: An Essay, trans. S. G. C. Middlemore (1878). There is a good and accessible illustrated edition, introduction by L. Goldscheider (2nd. edn., 1945). Among German editions of *Die Kultur der Renaissance in Italien: Ein Versuch* (1860), the Kröner Verlag edition is handy and kept in print.

Force and Freedom: Reflections on History (trans. Anonymous, 1943). The important posthumous *Weltgeschichtliche Betrachtungen* (1905) in English.

Recollections of Rubens, trans. Mary Hottinger (1950). A revealing late essay, published posthumously in 1898.

[230]

Bibliography

On Burckhardt

Wallace K. Ferguson, *The Renaissance in Historical Thought: Five Centuries of Interpretation* (1948). Though much more inclusive than Burckhardt, gives him pride of place and puts him into the historiographical context.

Alfred Lukas Gass, *Die Dichtung im Leben und Werk Jacob Burckhardts* (1967). On the place of poetry and literature in Burckhardt; very suggestive and informative.

Peter Gay, "Burckhardt's *Renaissance*: Between Responsibility and Power," in *The Responsibility of Power: Historical Essays in Honor of Hajo Holborn*, ed. Leonard Krieger and Fritz Stern (1967), pp. 183–198. An essay on which I have drawn.

Hajo Holborn, "Introduction" to Burckhardt, *Civilization of the Renaissance in Italy* (Modern Library edition, 1954). Short but excellent.

Karl Joel, *Jacob Burckhardt als Geschichtsphilosoph* (1918). Useful essay.

Werner Kaegi, *Jacob Burckhardt: Eine Biographie*, 4 vols. to date (1947–   ). Definitive. Most useful for this book were vol. 2, *Das Erlebnis der geschichtlichen Welt* (1950), and vol. 3, *Die Zeit der klassischen Werke* (1956).

Karl Löwith, *Jacob Burckhardt: Der Mensch inmitten der Geschichte* (1936). Essays, including one on Burckhardt's "relation to language."

Burckhardt's Renaissance

Hans Baron, *The Crisis of the Early Italian Renaissance: Civic Humanism and Republican Liberty in an Age of Classicism and Tyranny*, rev. edn. (1966). The classic account of civic humanism.

Ernst Cassirer, *The Individual and the Cosmos in Renaissance Philosophy*, trans. Mario Domandi (1963). A profound study.

Federico Chabod, "The Concept of the Renaissance," in Chabod, *Machiavelli and the Renaissance*, trans. David Moore (1958), pp. 149–200. A lucid orienting essay.

——— , "Cultural History and its Problems," *Rapports*, Eleventh International Congress of Historical Sciences (1960), 1:40–58. A valuable report.

Eugenio Garin, *Italian Humanism*, trans. P. Munz (1966). A splendidly balanced survey.

Felix Gilbert, *Machiavelli and Guicciardini: Politics and History in*

Sixteenth-Century Florence (1965). An excellent double essay in intellectual-cultural-political history.

E. H. Gombrich, *In Search of Cultural History* (1969). An expanded lecture; a vigorous attack, from a position close to Sir Karl Popper's, on Hegelian holism, including Burckhardt's. If too severe, worth pondering.

——, *Norm and Form* (1966). Interesting essays on Renaissance art.

Denys Hay, *The Italian Renaissance in Its Historical Background* (1961). A very good short account, independent of, but openly indebted to, Burckhardt.

Paul Oskar Kristeller, *Renaissance Thought: The Classic, Scholastic, and Humanist Strains* (1961).

——, *Renaissance Thought II: Papers on Humanism and the Arts* (1965). Two learned and lucid collections of Renaissance thought and culture. Very valuable.

Erwin Panofsky, *Renaissance and Renascences in Western Art* (1960). A modern vindication of Burckhardt's view that there was a distinct Renaissance, by one of the great art historians of our century.

On Intuition and Knowledge

Claude Bernard, *Introduction à l'étude de la médecine expérimentale* (1865). A great work by a distinguished biologist on how scientists actually proceed.

P. B. Medawar, *The Art of the Soluble: Creativity and Originality in Science* (edn. 1969). A series of essays and reviews in scientific philosophy and procedures; lucid expositions of the anti-inductivist position.

——, *Induction and Intuition in Scientific Thought* (1969). Lectures on scientific method; carries forward the nineteenth-century arguments of Bernard and Whewell.

Karl R. Popper, *Conjectures and Refutations: The Growth of Scientific Knowledge*, 2nd edn. (1965). A series of related essays setting forth Popper's anti-inductivist theory of knowledge.

——, *The Logic of Scientific Discovery* (trans. 1959). The English version of an important treatise in epistemology first published in 1934.

William Whewell, *The Philosophy of Discovery* (1860).

——, *The Philosophy of the Inductive Sciences*, 2nd edn., 2 vols. (1847). Highly significant challenges to the empiricist epistemology of John Stuart Mill.

Bibliography

Conclusion: *On Style in History*

(Many of the titles listed in the Introduction are applicable here.)

History: Art or Science?

Charles Beard, "Written History as an Act of Faith," *American Historical Review*, 39, no. 2 (January 1934), 219–229; conveniently reprinted in Hans Meyerhoff, ed., *The Philosophy of History in our Time: An Anthology* (1959), pp. 140–151. The famous presidential address bringing Idealism to the American historical profession.

Carl Becker, "What are Historical Facts?" *The Western Political Quarterly*, 8, no. 3 (September 1955), 327–340; available in Meyerhoff, *Philosophy of History*, pp. 120–137. A characteristically witty relativist statement, first written in 1926.

Marc Bloch, *The Historian's Craft*, trans. Peter Putnam (1953). Fragmentary but immensely illuminating thoughts by a great and heroic historian.

L. P. Curtis, Jr., ed., *The Historian's Workshop* (1971). A pioneering, not always successful, set of sixteen essays by contemporary historians linking their backgrounds and motives to their work. A genre that deserves further exploration. (See Namier title below.)

Arthur C. Danto, *Analytical Philosophy of History* (1965). An influential view, from the standpoint of analytical philosophy, holding that history had its own, storytelling logic.

John Dewey, *Logic: The Theory of Inquiry* (1938), especially chap. 12. The *locus classicus* of the pragmatist argument that history is essentially responsive to the historian's need. (See Lovejoy title below.)

William H. Dray, *Philosophy of History* (1964). A clear and fairminded introduction.

G. R. Elton, *The Practice of History* (1967).

———, *Political History: Principles and Practices* (1970). Vigorous, in fact combative, assessments of the craft by a practicing craftsman. Good common sense mixed in generous proportions with elementary philosophical confusions.

David Hackett Fischer, *Historians' Fallacies: Toward a Logic of Historical Thought* (1970). Pert, often impertinent attack on other historians; sometimes amusing, but filled with its own fallacies.

[233]

V. H. Galbraith, *An Introduction to the Study of History* (1964). Clearheaded defense of history as truth-seeking.

W. B. Gallie, *Philosophy and the Historical Understanding* (1964). Defense of the view of history as storytelling. Impressive but (to my mind) unconvincing.

Patrick Gardiner, *The Nature of Historical Explanation* (1955). Part of philosophers' debate over the place of causal analysis in history.

Felix Gilbert, *Machiavelli and Guicciardini: Politics and History in Sixteenth-Century Florence* (1965). Again: a splendid study.

Hanna H. Gray, "Renaissance Humanism: The Pursuit of Eloquence," *Journal of the History of Ideas*, 24, no. 4 (October–December 1963), 497–514. A pioneering essay.

J. H. Hexter, "The Historian and His Day," in Hexter, *Reappraisals in History* (1961). pp. 1–13. A typically energetic account of the way in which historians really work.

———, "The Rhetoric of History," in *International Encyclopedia of the Social Sciences*, ed. David L. Sills, 17 vols. (1968) 6:368–394. A deservedly familiar essay, seeking to establish an independent place for history through its rhetoric. Amusing, vigorous but, I think, unpersuasive.

———, *The History Primer* (1971). Expansion of the view expressed in "The Rhetoric of History."

Richard Hofstadter, "History and the Social Sciences," in *The Varieties of History*, ed. Fritz Stern (1956), pp. 359–370. Short, informal, humane.

H. Stuart Hughes, *History as Art and as Science* (1964). Subtitled "Twin Vistas on the Past," this interesting collection of essays examines the relation of history to literature, psychoanalysis, anthropology, and other neighbors.

Donald R. Kelley, *Foundations of Modern Historical Scholarship: Language, Law, and History in the French Renaissance* (1970). An excellent analysis.

David S. Landes and Charles Tilly, eds., *History as Social Science* (1971). Brief report on interdisciplinary work being done or needing doing; sketchy but rather helpful.

Gordon Leff, *History and Social Theory* (1969). A strong critique of the Marxist view of history and an examination of the place of history among the sciences of man.

Arthur O. Lovejoy, "Present Standpoints and Past History" (1939), conveniently reprinted in slightly abridged form in Hans Meyerhoff, ed., *The Philosophy of History in Our Time: An Anthology* (1959), pp. 173–187. A powerful refutation of Dewey's attack on objectivity; develops the idea of "interestingness" as a cause for inquiry.

Maurice Mandelbaum, *The Problem of Historical Knowledge: An Answer to Relativism* (1967). A philosophically sophisticated reply to Dilthey, Mannheim, and others; a valuable analysis.

H.-I. Marrou, *De la connaissance historique,* 4th edn. (1959). Reflectons by a distinguished ancient historian.

Hans Meyerhoff, *The Philosophy of History in Our Time: An Anthology* (1959). Well-chosen series of excerpts from a variety of philosophical positions.

Julia Namier, *Lewis Namier: A Biography* (1971). A rare thing: a candid biography of a controversial historian; while it does not assess Namier's histories, it clarifies his psychological makeup.

Lewis Namier, "History," in Namier, *Avenues of History* (1952), pp. 1–10. Witty, brief observations.

Emery Neff, *The Poetry of History: The Contribution of Literature and Literary Scholarship to the Writing of History Since Voltaire* (1947). An elegant, rather neglected essay on the subject of my Conclusion: the definition of history.

J. H. Plumb, *The Death of the Past* (1970). A wide-ranging survey of the way cultures have used their past; stimulating and informative.

David M. Potter, *History and American Society,* ed. Don E. Fehrenbacher (1973). A beautiful collection of essays that illuminate the debts the historian owes to culture, and culture to the historian.

Social Science Research Council, Bulletin 54, *Theory and Practice in Historical Study* (1946).

————, Bulletin 64, *The Social Sciences in Historical Study* (1954). Instructive; should be read together as illustrations of development of thought in the American profession. Chronicles a certain decline in relativism.

Fritz Stern, ed., *The Varieties of History, From Voltaire to the Present* (1956). A useful, varied anthology.

G. M. Trevelyan, "Clio: A Muse" (1903). Conveniently reprinted in somewhat abridged form in Stern, *Varieties of History,* pp. 227–245. Important defense of history as literature.

H. R. Trevor-Roper, *History: Professional and Lay* (1957). A spirited plea for history as a literary pursuit.

Stephen Usher, *The Historians of Greece and Rome* (1969). An intelligent survey.

W. H. Walsh, *Philosophy of History: An Introduction,* rev. edn. (1958). Introductory, but clear and intelligent.

George Watson, *The Study of Literature: A New Rationale of Literary History* (1969). A clear-headed essay.

Morton White, *Foundations of Historical Knowledge* (1965). A philosopher's technical analysis.

Peter Winch, *The Idea of a Social Science and Its Relation to Philosophy* (1958). Among the best known of the writings on "philosophical psychology" identified with Wittgenstein's argument that the science of man and the sciences of nature are wholly distinct. Other well-known titles in this school include A. I. Melden, *Free Action* (1961), and R. S. Peters, *The Concept of Motivation* (1960). But see, for a defense of determinism as being quite compatible with free action, Alasdair MacIntyre, "The Antecedents of Action" and "The Idea of a Social Science," in MacIntyre, *Against the Self-Images of the Age: Essays on Ideology and Philosophy* (1971), pp. 191–210, 211–229.

C. Vann Woodward, *The Age of Reinterpretation*, Publication No. 35, Service Center For Teachers of History (1961). A persuasive essay.

On the Definition of Science

R. B. Braithwaite, *Scientific Explanation: A Study of the Function of Theory, Probability and Law in Science* (1953). Technical but lucid.

Arthur Danto and Sidney Morgenbesser, eds., *Philosophy of Science* (1960). One of the most useful of several anthologies.

George Devereux, *From Anxiety to Method in the Behavioral Sciences* (1967). A very important essay by an imaginative scholar, both psychoanalyst and anthropologist, on the psychological charges the researcher puts into his research, and how to neutralize them. (See also Myrdal, below.)

Herbert Feigl and Wilfrid Sellars, eds., *Readings in Philosophical Analysis* (1949). Though no longer new, this anthology contains a number of now classic articles illuminating the nature of modern scientific thinking.

Charles Coulston Gillispie, *The Edge of Objectivity: An Essay in the History of Scientific Ideas* (1960). A valuable contribution to the definition of science.

Carl G. Hempel, *Aspects of Scientific Explanation and Other Essays in the Philosophy of Science* (1965). A collection of seminal essays, including the classic "The Function of General Laws in History," by a philosopher persuasively arguing that the logic of history and that of the natural sciences are the same. Indispensable. (See also Nagel, below.)

————, *Philosophy of Natural Science* (1966). Beautifully clear and remarkably brief.

Gunnar Myrdal, *Objectivity in Social Research* (1969). A vigorous plea that social scientists recognize the peculiar nature of their science and acknowledge (in order to overcome) their biases. Fits equally well into the next category.

Ernest Nagel, *The Structure of Science: Problems in the Logic of Scientific Explanation* (1961). A splendidly clear exposition of the positivist position, assimilating history to science and incidentally refuting, with great dash, opposing points of view. An important book.

On Perception

J. L. Austin, *Philosophical Papers*, ed. J. O. Urmson and G. J. Warnock (1961).

————, *How To Do Things With Words*, ed. J. O. Urmson (1962).

————, *Sense and Sensibilia*, reconstructed from notes by G. J. Warnock (1962). Witty lectures and articles constituting a brilliant assault on the sense-data theory and an amusing and profound restatement of Realism.

Egon Brunswik, "The Conceptual Framework of Psychology," *International Encyclopedia of Unified Science*, 1, No. 10 (1952). A fine short essay on what kind of science psychology in fact is.

Sigmund Freud, "Formulations on the Two Principles of Mental Functioning" (1911), in *The Standard Edition of the Complete Psychological Works of Sigmund Freud*, ed. James Strachey et al., 23 vols. to date (1953–   ), 12:213–226. The first compressed statement on the pleasure and the reality principles. In an important sense, of course, all of Freud's work is relevant to the study of the way in which the perceiver grasps, masters, and distorts reality.

James J. Gibson, *The Perception of the Visual World* (1950).

————, *The Senses Considered as Perceptual Systems* (1966). Two masterly statements of the view that perception is in general strikingly adequate, and can be improved. Highly pertinent to my Conclusion.

Nelson Goodman, "The Way The World Is," *The Review of Metaphysics*, 14, no. 1 (September 1960), pp. 48–56.

Heinz Hartmann, *Ego Psychology and the Problem of Adaptation*

(1939; trans. David Rapaport, 1958). A classic essay on the "conflict-free sphere of the ego" by Freud's distinguished disciple.

————, *Essays on Ego Psychology: Selected Problems in Psychoanalytic Theory* (1964). Several essays contained in this volume directly relate to man's perception of his world; an authoritative statement of ego psychology, further advancing Freud's effort to make psychoanalysis into a general psychology.

George S. Klein, *Perception, Motives, and Personality* (1970). A brilliant series of studies by a psychologist of perception wholly at home in psychoanalytic theory; an impressive attempt to mediate between the objectivism of Gibson and the subjectivism of other psychologists. Its formulations were important to my Conclusion.

Ivo Kohler, *The Formation and Transformation of the Perceptual World* (1951; trans. H. Fiss, 1964). A seminal essay, from which American psychologists of perception have learned much.

Robert J. Swartz, ed., *Perceiving, Sensing, and Knowing* (1965). A sound selection of articles on the philosophy of perception.

On Mommsen

Ludo Moritz Hartmann, *Theodor Mommsen, Eine Biographische Skizze* (1908). A very useful first sketch; with much unpublished correspondence.

Alfred Heuss, *Theodor Mommsen und das 19. Jahrhundert* (1956). Excellent appraisal.

David Knowles, "The *Monumenta Germaniae Historica*," in *Great Historical Enterprises; Problems in Monastic History* (1963), pp. 63–97. Includes a discussion of Mommsen's scholarly activities.

Theodor Mommsen, *Reden und Aufsätze*, 3rd printing (1912). A spirited collection of essays and addresses.

————, *Römische Geschichte*, 3rd edn., 3 vols. (1861). The Republic down to—or up to—Julius Caesar.

Lily Ross Taylor, *Party Politics in the Age of Caesar* (1949). A scholarly examination of the age to which Mommsen gave his historical passion; a fine summary of the historiographical work of Gelzer and Premerstein.

Lothar Wickert, *Theodor Mommsen: Eine Biographie*, 3 vols. to date (1959–   ). Stodgy but authoritative.

Albert Wucher, *Theodor Mommsen: Geschichtsschreibung und Politik* (1956). A fine, thorough essay; very favorable to Mommsen, but justifies its point of view.

INDEX

[239]